THE
EVERYTHING®
RESUME
BOOK
4TH EDITION

Dear Reader,

To the inexperienced eye, the difference between an *average* resume and a *great* one is minimal, but to the sophisticated eye of the corporate recruiter or prospective employer, the difference is enormous. It translates into getting the interview or simply being dismissed, even if your credentials and work experience are strong.

This book is meant for all readers—the ones who are writing their resumes from scratch and the ones who are eager to improve them. You always want to present your best version of yourself so that hiring authorities are eager to meet you. The Everything® book format makes creating a *great* easy for all levels of job candidates. It also will help you navigate the technology and resume the methods that today's job seeker uses to get noticed.

Use your resume as your access to a world of job opportunities. Good luck with your career.

Lin Grensing-Pophal, SPHR

Welcome to the EVERYTHING Series!

These handy, accessible books give you all you need to tackle a difficult project, gain a new hobby, comprehend a fascinating topic, prepare for an exam, or even brush up on something you learned back in school but have since forgotten.

You can choose to read an Everything® book from cover to cover or just pick out the information you want from our four useful boxes: e-questions, e-facts, e-alerts, and e-ssentials.

We give you everything you need to know on the subject, but throw in a lot of fun stuff along the way, too.

We now have more than 400 Everything® books in print, spanning such wide-ranging categories as weddings, pregnancy, cooking, music instruction, foreign language, crafts, pets, New Age, and so much more. When you're done reading them all, you can finally say you know Everything®!

QUESTION

Answers to common questions

FACT

Important snippets of information

ALERT

Urgent warnings

ESSENTIAL

Quick handy tips

PUBLISHER Karen Cooper

MANAGING EDITOR, EVERYTHING® SERIES Lisa Laing

COPY CHIEF Casey Ebert

ASSISTANT PRODUCTION EDITOR Mary Beth Dolan

ASSOCIATE ACQUISITIONS EDITOR Kate Powers

DEVELOPMENT EDITOR Katie Corcoran Lytle

EVERYTHING® SERIES COVER DESIGNER Erin Alexander

Visit the entire Everything® series at *www.everything.com*

THE
EVERYTHING®
RESUME
BOOK
4TH EDITION

From using social media to choosing
the right keywords, all you need to have
a resume that stands out from the crowd!

Lin Grensing-Pophal, SPHR

Aadamsmedia
Avon, Massachusetts

I'd like to dedicate this book to my son, Justin Grensing, who is in the throes of his first professional job hunt after graduating with a JD/MBA from the University of Minnesota. Here's hoping that first job will launch a very successful career!

An Everything® Series Book.
Everything® and everything.com® are registered trademarks of F+W Media, Inc.

Published by Adams Media, a division of F+W Media, Inc.
57 Littlefield Street, Avon, MA 02322 U.S.A.
www.adamsmedia.com

ISBN 10: 1-4405-5056-5
ISBN 13: 978-1-4405-5056-0
eISBN 10: 1-4405-5057-3
eISBN 13: 978-1-4405-5057-7

Printed in the United States of America.

10 9 8 7 6 5 4 3 2

Library of Congress Cataloging-in-Publication Data
Grensing-Pophal, Lin
  The everything resume book / Lin Grensing-Pophal. – 4th ed.
     p. cm.
  Rev. ed. of: The everything resume book : create a winning resume that stands out from the crowd / Nancy Schuman. 3rd ed.
  Includes index.
  ISBN 978-1-4405-5056-0 (pbk.) – ISBN 1-4405-5056-5 (pbk.) – ISBN 978-1-4405-5057-7 (ebook) – ISBN 1-4405-5057-3 (ebook)
  1. Resumes (Employment) I. Schuman, Nancy. Everything resume book. II. Title.
  HF5383.G637 2012
  650.14'2–dc23
                    2012030648

This publication is designed to provide accurate and authoritative information with regard to the subject matter covered. It is sold with the understanding that the publisher is not engaged in rendering legal, accounting, or other professional advice. If legal advice or other expert assistance is required, the services of a competent professional person should be sought.
                    —From a *Declaration of Principles* jointly adopted by a Committee of the American Bar Association and a Committee of Publishers and Associations

Many of the designations used by manufacturers and sellers to distinguish their products are claimed as trademarks. Where those designations appear in this book and Adams Media was aware of a trademark claim, the designations have been printed with initial capital letters.

This book is available at quantity discounts for bulk purchases.
For information, please call 1-800-289-0963.

Contents

Part 1: **Resume Writing / 13**

01 Resume Writing and the Job Search / 15

02 Writing Your Resume / 33

03 Seven Steps to Resume Writing Success / 53

09 **What They Say about**
Your Resume / 163

Part 2: Sample Resumes/ 177

10 **Sample Designs / 179**

11 **Sample Resumes / 187**

Acknowledgments

I'd like to thank Kate Powers, my project manager, for keeping me on track. I'd also like to thank Bob Diforio, my agent, for recommending me for this project. And, my son, for his help with background research, which aided immensely in helping me meet my deadlines!

Top Ten Reasons to Update Your Resume

1. You've been promoted!

2. Economic ups and downs in your industry mean you might be subject to downsizing or a layoff.

3. You can do the job better than your boss.

4. Your contact information has changed, such as new cell number, married name, new address, or different e-mail provider.

5. You are thinking about moving to a new city, state, or industry!

6. You have new career goals, aspire to a better position, or want to transition to a different field.

7. Your education has changed . . . you've just gotten a new degree, taken new classes, or have gotten trained in a new skill.

8. It's been more than two years since your last update.

9. You've been asked for your credentials for an award, board position, membership, or networking opportunity.

10. You might be recruited when you least expect it.

Introduction

THE PHRASE, "IT'S TIME to get your resume together," sends shivers down many a spine, causing headaches as well as heartaches. Graduating from college; hunting for a new, more responsible position; and losing a job can all cause nervous palpitations. It is possible, however, to be invigorated by a review of your achievements and to look forward to a challenging and rewarding future.

There is something very positive about seeing your education, experience, and achievements presented in a visually appealing document. Creating this document need not make you anxious or uncomfortable. Resume writing is not as difficult as you might think, and by following the rules and advice outlined in this book, you will be on your way to getting the job you want. The first step in this process is a well-written resume that calls attention to your strengths and skills and makes the prospective employer want to interview you. That's really the main purpose of a resume—to get your foot in the door.

To do this, you need a great resume, one that sets you apart from your competition. Of course, times have also changed, so you need to make sure that you pay attention to keywords, consider today's technology, and follow new methods for job seeking and personal networking. *The Everything®* *Resume Book, 4th Edition* is designed to help you conduct an effective job search using both traditional techniques and those associated with the web. Read and act upon the powerful ideas presented in this book to create a dynamic resume, which will inspire and facilitate an effective job search.

For centuries, we have used documents to confirm our identities, make introductions, and inspire others to see us as useful, valuable, and capable. Regardless of its origins or the new formats and methods used to present the modern resume, it still is one of the most important tools necessary to getting or changing jobs and advancing your career.

PART 1

Resume Writing

CHAPTER 1

Resume Writing and the Job Search

A resume is an important tool in your search for employment. Internet advances and social media have vastly altered the realm of job searching in a few short years. Technology has also changed the way job seekers write and transmit their resumes. Job seekers need to keep pace with the technology and hiring methods of today's employers, and their resumes must reflect the new recruiting practices and the ways employers identify and consider talent. The right resume will help you get the job, while the wrong resume will completely eliminate you from the competition.

Resume Writing for Today's Job World

The vast number of books written on the subject of resume writing is mind boggling. Over the years, there have been almost as many suggestions for format, content, and approaches as there are resume books in print.

Books published only a few years ago are already out of date. As technology changes, so do the concepts that have always applied to resume writing. While books once detailed how to prepare a resume suitable for a quick scan by a potential employer, today's resumes are typically transmitted by e-mail or posted on the web. That means that you need to put a greater focus on developing strong content, paying increased attention to keywords for online searches, and creating a resume that is easily viewed by the reader, regardless of platform or application. Many employers now target the *passive job seeker*—someone who isn't currently seeking employment, but whose work experience makes him or her desirable for hire, and who can be found via the web.

This book addresses traditional resumes as well as e-resumes. Samples like those included in the appendices should inspire you. Keep in mind that resume illustrations can often appear intimidating, as presentations of perfect job candidates. Don't worry! You aren't competing with these mythical people for jobs, but you can use their examples to make your resume as dynamic as theirs.

Seeking Inspiration

One search of an online book retailer's inventory returned more than 12,000 results on the keyword search "resume." You, too, have probably encountered the confusion of shelf after shelf of titles in the career section of your local bookstore, but no matter how, where, or why you purchased this edition of *The Everything® Resume Book*, you have taken a solid first step toward new employment. You are now ready for education as well as motivation. Knowing the latest trends in resume design and delivery tells your prospective employer that you are aware of contemporary practices that enhance communication between the generations of Gen X, Gen Y, and baby boomers, regardless of which one is the candidate or hiring manager.

The Old Approach: "Resumes Any Way"

For years, resume books have established and reinforced a "resumes any way" attitude. No matter the title, these books all espoused the same belief: "There is no one perfect resume." Most, if not all, of those books focused on creating the resume that potential employers, human resources professionals, managers, recruiters, and executives (the infamous "they") would want to see.

Readers were encouraged to assume the thoughts and preferences of their prospective employers while creating their resumes. Energies and attitudes were focused on what "they" wanted to see in job search documents like resumes, cover letters, and other supporting material. The "resumes any way" approach covered too many bases and included long, often contradictory, laundry lists of what "they" wanted.

Such an approach has an obvious disadvantage. There's no way that you, the job hunter, can possibly know what "they" want to see in your resume. A far more sensible—and effective—approach is to focus on what you do know: *yourself.* A successful, effective resume presents you as a person who knows the job and has the skills and abilities to do that job better than anyone else. It's that simple!

The New Way: Web 2.0

Web 2.0 is generally understood to be the second generation of how computer users relate to and utilize the Internet. This matters to job seekers because the venues associated with Web 2.0 impact how you conduct your job search in this age of technology. New tools, including blogs, videos, podcasts, social networking sites, and more, allow personal opinion and general information to be shared by various web users in ways that were formerly not possible.

Do you really need to know this techie stuff?

Absolutely. This know-how will give you greater opportunity to direct your resume to the employers of your choice and will demonstrate that you are Internet savvy and familiar with sources and methods used by organizations to locate candidate talent.

For example, social media tools like LinkedIn can help you identify names of people who work at your target company and provide you with insights on what they think about the organization's corporate culture. You will learn more about these new opportunities in Chapter 5.

Focus on Yourself

With the proper attitude, guidance, and communication tools, anyone can successfully look for a job. You don't have to be a hotshot Ivy League graduate. Whoever you are, and whatever you have done to date, you can develop a powerful resume that will help you achieve your career goals. As your resume will reveal, you are the best candidate for the job.

Your Personal Brand

Some resume professionals currently advocate creating a *Personal Brand* for yourself and using your resume to convey this strategy. Your brand is what differentiates you from the next candidate, the same way one product is set apart from another. Why do some people spend $4 on a cup of coffee? It is because of the perceived value of that particular brand of coffee and what it says about image, taste, and quality. You can make the same principles apply to yourself. You can probably think of real people who have their own personal brand. A few good examples include Madonna, Tiger Woods, Oprah and Bill Gates.

ALERT

To have a clear brand, all of your job search materials must be consistent. This starts with simple design. Your resume and all correspondence should all be created with the same look and feel, using the same letterhead, as appropriate, and the same font. The language you use and the key points you emphasize also create an image that should be consistent throughout all of your communications.

Your resume brand must showcase your unique skills and the value you can bring to the employer. This is called your *unique value proposition*. You need to think about what makes you different than the next candidate and be able to articulate your unique value proposition by detailing your distinctive talents, skills, and abilities. This will come across in your resume and during your interview. You want your prospective employer to invest in you, the same way the coffee company wants you to invest in their high priced beverage. Additionally, the design, format, and content of your resume, cover letter, and any other correspondence must be consistent and appealing. They create an image for you the moment the employer sees them and, in essence, presell you before you walk through their door.

Simplified Steps to Job Search Success

Great resumes are the beginning of job search success! Through the process of resume writing, you will also be empowered to do the following:

1. Set and articulate professional goals.
2. Create or update a goal-directed resume.
3. Develop a "target list" of potential employers, and a "network" of advocates both through one-to-one contact and through the web.
4. Respond to job postings in all mediums, as well as apply directly to desirable employers.
5. Submit your resume, cover letter, and any appropriate supporting materials by the employer's preferred method (web posting, e-mail, fax, or snail mail).
6. Follow up, assess strategies, follow up, enhance competencies, then follow up again and again.
7. Interview using your resume for guidance.
8. Receive offers, and accept one.

An important first step that you will need to take is to consider your specific professional goals. As you approach potential employers or respond to job openings you will want to ensure that you focus specifically on what you have to offer based on your goals and how you can align those goals with an employer's specific needs.

Set and Articulate Professional Goals

Your resume does not have to set and state your lifelong goals. But it should express the aim of your immediate job search, and you should understand how these aims fit in to your long-term career plan. Pre-research (that is, research before job search) is the key to goal setting, and that includes an inventory of your achievements and qualifications. A successful, goal-oriented resume projects focus and mirrors self-knowledge. The most powerful resumes make clear statements of the job hunter's objectives.

ESSENTIAL

Pre-research, the time before putting your resume together, when you investigate your chosen job field, is conducted using four techniques:

1. Paper and pencil or eyes to screen (using printed and web resources)
2. Person-to-person (conducting information conversations)
3. Exploration by academics (taking courses or seminars)
4. Exploration by experience (including internships or special projects)

An objective like, "I'm looking for anything, anywhere," is not focused enough to be effective. As you create and update your resume, focus will become easier, and it will be easier to project the confidence you gain from self-assessment. Goal setting often begins by assessing yourself (identifying your values, interests, and skills). Next comes research into careers, job functions, and academic options. When you write your resume and other job search documents, you project the knowledge you've gained about yourself and your chosen field, creating a powerful self-presentation. The interview, at that point, is your opportunity to flesh out in person the image you've already created on paper or on screen.

The list found earlier in this section spells out eight steps to a successful job search. You must be able to articulate your goals and qualifications in order to complete all eight (in other words, to get the job you want). Career counseling is available from a variety of sources that can help you with your self-assessment. If you are a college student or graduate, your college career center may provide services to address your needs. There are also private counselors or career coaches who can work with you one-on-one to help you personally manage your job search. Many career guidance books include do-it-yourself assessment exercises designed to help you find your chosen career. Some websites also provide assessment exercises. Appendix

B lists valuable resources for undertaking this first critical step to job search success.

One of the best and simplest ways of focusing your career goals is to read the trade magazines and other publications of a few industries. In as little as a few hours of reading, you can learn enough about job requirements and how your own skill set can contribute to a powerful and clear statement of professional objectives.

ESSENTIAL

Looking in the mirror is self-reflection for some, but it's not the kind of assessment you need for job search success. Don't confuse introspection with assessment or active exploration. Meditation rarely yields goal articulation, but reading a book or two might help. Printed and online resources also help. Reference librarians and online search engines like Monster.com and LinkedIn are excellent and often underused resources.

Not coincidently, the steps for creating or updating your resume run parallel to the steps you take toward identifying and articulating your professional goals. In turn, a strong resume inspires you to write dynamic cover letters and follow-ups. This chapter prepares you to complete a fast, effective resume. (Chapter 7 provides more guidance and inspiration for painless resume writing.)

Develop a "Target List" of Potential Employers

Just as important as your resume is your target list of people, places, and organizations that might be potential employers. You develop this list starting with professional directories and other printed and online resources. (Online resources can provide a wealth of contact information, as detailed in Appendix B.) Your colleagues, friends, family, faculty, and fellow graduates can also help with pre-research, networking, and actual job search efforts. When you ask around for assistance and job referrals, always include a copy of your resume with your request. This is a good way of projecting your potential and of inspiring continued support from your advocates. Go online. Read a prospective company's home page. Explore opportunities that are often listed under "Employment" or "Careers" on their web pages. If there is a Media section, review current and archived press releases, particularly those that reference department heads or corporate leadership. Once you've collected some names and numbers, it's time to do some detective work online. Use a search engine like Google to see if your contact's name appears along with any other helpful information. You should also see if the individual is active on social networking sites like LinkedIn, Twitter, or Facebook. (More on this topic later on.) An Internet search or visit to the web site of the company where you're applying are your best ways to confirm the proper contact people and, if possible, to clarify the nature of any jobs available. Keep updating your list, and maintain clear records of your contacts. Know who you've talked to, when you talked, and what you talked about. Follow-up is critical, so you must always know the status of your interactions with those on your target list.

QUESTION

What is a job search advocate?
Job search advocates are those people who actively support your efforts to find your ideal job. They offer ongoing advice and regularly refer you to postings and, when possible, to prospective employers. Advocates are most often nurtured, not just found. Some people call them career mentors. Often, they are simply regular people in your life who are well connected to the career, industry, or company you seek to be employed in. Tap into your resources!

Talking to people is the best way to gather, analyze, and prioritize information regarding employment options and referrals. Initiate the networking process with a call or an e-mail. When you e-mail, introduce yourself and state that you will soon follow up with a call. Always be courteous and clear about why you're getting in touch and feel free to ask for specific referrals or informal "informational interviews." Conversations like these are a good way to learn about the careers of people in your chosen industry and to solicit their help in your job search. These contacts can act as advocates within their organizations, offering direct referrals and providing recommendations. They can also introduce you to associates in other companies, thus increasing the scope and power of your network.

Building Your Network

The purpose of networking is twofold. First, you want to know as much about your chosen field as possible. Network with as many people as you can in that field to get all of their input and points of view. Second, you want to become known in your chosen field. The more people you meet, the more your name and your qualifications become known. Networking is a powerful component of any successful job search.

Professional groups and online resources like field-focused websites or mailing lists are good ways to begin networking. Go slowly. Instead of introducing yourself right away as a job seeker, ask for a business card or contact information. Then, in follow-up communications, you can identify your career goals and ask for guidance. Once the person has responded to your request, share your resume as an effective way of presenting your goals and qualifications.

Successful job seekers often cite networking as one of the most important factors in their success. Most polls of experienced job candidates rank networking as a top tool. Even in this Internet age, person-to-person networking is still important, yet few do it well.

Today's job seeker should also explore social networking websites. Some popular ones of the moment include LinkedIn, Facebook and Twitter, particularly with Gen X and Gen Y candidates. These sites allow you to create personal profiles and to opt in to one or more of the many networking groups on their sites, some relating to shared pursuits such as schools attended, employment/industry, or personal interests. By joining these sites, you are able to communicate with members, read public profiles (or blogs), view photos and, in short, bring newcomers who you might never have met previously into your world. Any one of whom might be able to assist you in your quest for your ideal employment. Additional information about social networking sites will be discussed in Chapter 5.

End each networking conversation by getting guidance on what you should do next, who you should contact, and, of course, with a resounding, "Thank you!" Keep communications current by getting in touch with your contacts every now and then to keep them informed of your progress.

Finding Job Postings and Advertisements

Many people fool themselves into thinking they are conducting a comprehensive job search just because their resumes are uploaded onto a few of the big name job boards. It's true that web-based job postings are part of an effective job search strategy. But answering these ads is a reactive effort—that is, a reaction, rather than an action—and that's just part of a comprehensive campaign. An effective job search must also include proactive strategies, including networking. In later chapters you will learn some effective proactive strategies and will be directed toward some excellent web and other resources.

ESSENTIAL

Comprehensive job search campaigns include proactive as well as reactive strategies and resources. No matter how proactive you are, you should still be prepared to maximize your reactive efforts. Old-fashioned newspaper want ads can't be discounted as a good source of information about potential jobs. Don't forget about postings printed in general and subject-specific periodicals or niche websites. Professional newsletters and journals are too often ignored.

Get Your Resume into the Marketplace

Your goal is to inform as many people as possible about your goals. To do this successfully, keep the flow of communications persistent, but make sure your communications are appropriate, too. Here are some communication tips for strengthening your network and approaching others effectively:

- Don't ever wait to communicate! First, call to confirm your contact person. When possible, request detailed information regarding available positions and posting methods.

- If you are told not to contact someone directly, respect this request.
- Submit documentation as instructed, confident that it will be processed and forwarded appropriately.
- After making the initial call, submit your resume. Attach a resume to your initial correspondence as well as any future follow-up e-mails, faxed notes, or printed correspondence.

Don't worry about how your initial inquiries are interpreted. It's okay to ask for basic information. In fact, if you fail to take those courageous first steps, you will be unlikely to succeed at all. Typical first contacts might sound like the following.

"Hello. I would like to speak with the person in charge of hiring for your firm. Could you provide me with his/her name and title, then forward me to him/her? Thank you."

"Hello. My name is Chris Smith. I am interested in a position with your firm. I would like to submit my resume. What is the most convenient method, and to whom should I address my inquiry?"

Be prepared for the employer to tell you to apply online or to review the firm's current openings on their website. If you have seen a posting that interests you, you might ask if it has been filled or if you can submit your resume to a manager directly, rather than generically applying online or to an anonymous e-mail address.

ESSENTIAL

Use the web as a navigational tool to identify employment opportunities. According to the National Association of Colleges and Employers (NACE), 90 percent of employers prefer to receive electronic resumes via e-mail or on their company home page instead of print versions through the U.S. mail.

The best way to view your job search is to think of it as a communication process. You initiate the communication reactively when you answer postings; you are proactive when you contact the people on your target list. Don't hesitate to communicate, and be polite and respectful when doing so.

Follow Up, Follow Up, Follow Up

There is always an appropriate way to follow up and e-mail has become the most widely acceptable format. It's usually easier to be clear in writing, and you can send your message after hours, when you have time to clearly pose questions or convey your appreciation. You can also e-mail a thank-you note; however, a handwritten mailed note shows a personal touch and attention to detail. Continue to build your relationships with prospective employers, and reinforce your existing networking relationships via a well-crafted series of e-mails or phone calls.

Enthusiastic and upbeat questions and comments are obviously much more effective than impatient and demanding inquiries. Be sensitive and creative in your follow-up communications. Be persistent, but don't pester.

It's sometimes difficult to pick up the phone or compose yet another friendly follow-up e-mail. But remember that each follow-up effort increases your chances of reaching your goal and getting that job. Regularly assess the effectiveness of your follow-up efforts (did your follow-up lead to another conversation? a return letter? an interview?) and refocus if you need to.

Be polite and persistent. Always call to confirm whether materials were received. This gives you a chance to ask your contact what will happen next and when you should take your next step. You can ask whether you should communicate again within a designated time period. If the answer is, "Be patient," don't make a pest of yourself by calling back anyway.

ALERT

"Phone-a-phobia" can be fatal. E-mail may be state of the art, but the telephone is still a powerful communication tool. In fact, it's essential to your job search. Decide what you will say before you call. Be sure to confirm receipt of previous letters, identify next steps, and politely request an interview. Your call can offer you a distinct advantage over your competition since many job seekers never think to go beyond hitting the e-mail "send" button.

It is your responsibility to communicate effectively during your job search. Don't expect prospective employers to follow up with you, and don't expect your resume to get you in the door all on its own. Your resume is a crucial part of your job search, but it is the personal follow-up that will fuel your success.

The Interview

Chapter 7 provides detailed preparation for interviews, with specific questions and answers. The first and most basic thing to remember about interviewing is to project confidence, whether the interview is in person or over the phone. To be confident, you need to be prepared.

Your resume is the focal point and foundation for interview preparation. Be confident in the abilities you describe in your resume and in your qualifications to perform the job. In addition, it is best to know as much as possible about the interview situation. Ask beforehand about how many people will be interviewing you and how long the interview is scheduled to take. Are there any materials your interviewers recommend you read before they talk to you? Inquire about proper attire. "Business casual" means pressed slacks, an ironed shirt, and a tie (with sport coat optional) for men, and slacks or skirt, ironed shirt, or sweater appropriate for women. Others are "business formal," with suits required for men and women.

ALERT

When preparing for your interview, don't memorize answers to typical questions, and don't practice too much or else your responses might sound false or canned. Role-play is a good way to become familiar with topics and build confidence, while still improvising as you go. Use your resume as a checklist, but be prepared to talk about other topics and concepts as well.

There are different types of interviews, and it is best to be prepared for any of them. In the "conversational" type of interview, interviewers chat with candidates and ask fairly typical interview questions. Another type is the "behavioral" interview, in which you are asked about past achievements and about details regarding behaviors (and skills) that contributed to these undertakings. Behavioral interviewers typically ask, "What have you done in this situation?" Occasionally, particularly for consulting firms, interviews are "case studies," in which interviewers ask you to analyze specific situations so they can see how you "think on your feet." You might also be given a specific project and be asked to come back with a solution or presentation. This trend has emerged as a result of television shows where candidates "audition" for positions. Practice may not make perfect, but practicing your responses to these types of scenarios before the interview will build confidence.

Offers and Acceptance

You are going to get a job offer, and you will need the skills to analyze and appropriately respond to it. Remain focused. Comparative salary data is available online (see resources in Appendix B) and in books. Here's where your network comes in really handy; ask around to see what kind of offer you should expect and how to negotiate, if necessary. Try to get a sense of salary range for the position you seek and determine if your target number falls within that range. Once you accept an offer, stop your job search. Period. Do not take another offer and renege on the first one. If you need to know about an offer, conduct your research before you accept. With an offer in hand, it is much easier to call other prospective employers and talk about your chances of their offering you a position. Don't hesitate to make those calls if you think their input might help you make a good decision.

Psychological Barriers

For some, the idea of updating or creating a resume generates a counterproductive attitude. They know it's important to keep their resume up-to-date, but the prospect of going through the process again can be daunting. Why? Because these negative beliefs include the following:

- I can't create a resume if I don't have anything to offer.
- Even the sample resumes look better than mine.
- I haven't done much, so I shouldn't update my resume.
- If I don't have an ideal job in mind, I can't create or update my resume.
- I don't know what employers want to see, so I can't start or finish my resume.

- I've heard they don't really read resumes, so why bother.
- It's not really the right time to look for a job, so I don't have to create or update my resume.

It is important to approach the job search from the standpoint of the potential employer, carefully considering what you have to offer and outlining that in your updated resume. Try to maintain a positive attitude as you do this; even if it's only been a few months since you last updated your resume, chances are you have some new experiences, skills or interests to show.

Resumes Created in a Day

The search for the perfect resume and the ideal time to create or update one may last forever for those suffering from self-doubt and lack of focus. You know you need a resume to start and complete your job search. In fact, you should have a current resume whether or not you are currently seeking new employment because you never know when you might be approached or recruited by an employer who desires your skills and experience. Ironically, if you delay your resume writing and subsequent job search, you also delay the ultimate positive reinforcement that comes with interviews and, yes, offers.

Some Excuses

The reasons and excuses for avoiding creating and updating a resume are too numerous to name. The following examples show how futile and pointless these excuses are in the face of such an important need, the need for a powerful resume.

- I can't find my old version, and I don't have time to create a new one.
- I don't have enough money to pay for one of those professional resume developers, so I'll wait.
- I can't seem to get it to one page, so it's hopeless.
- I missed the deadline for that job posting, so I have some time before I need to finish my resume.
- I don't know what employers want to see, so I can't start or finish my resume.

The bottom line. It is worth your time, effort and energy to make sure your resume presents the most up-to-date view of you and your skills as possible. Just do it!

Easy Steps to Get You Started

Even people who think of the job search as difficult and fraught with anxiety must agree that it ends with success! You will attain your goals! It all begins with a few easy steps. Chapter 2 describes the seven steps to a successful resume, which are illustrated throughout this book (especially in the sample resumes), but here's how you get your start:

1. Review some samples, including your old resumes and the examples in this book. Pay particular attention to those related to your goals.
2. Pick the approach that you want to model. Imitation is more than flattery. It is the best strategy in writing your resume.
3. Determine the format, content, and order of your resume. Will you use headlines? What entries will be presented within these categories? In what order will these sections appear?

FACT

Most experts agree that a job search takes at least three months. Be surprised if it takes only a few weeks, and remain determined and upbeat if it takes longer than the estimated three months. Everything starts with the proper attitude. Eventually, all true job searches end with success.

Next, if you have not already done so, identify your objectives and target audiences. What is your job search target? (This is not necessarily your career goal.) Can you clearly and concisely articulate your goals? If not, don't fret. Chapter 4 will take you through this step with minimal pain.

Once you've defined your goals, you really can create a resume in just one day. Put your goals on paper, then list your relevant qualifications and achievements. Examine your general qualifications, and present your specific competencies and capabilities in terms of their importance. Once you have a draft together, read it over with an eye to the person (you) it represents. Your aim is to present yourself as qualified, knowledgeable, and self-confident. By following these steps, you can create a resume in just one day. Why not make it today?

Your Job Search Foundation

Resume writing happens through a series of cognitive and behavioral steps. These steps also form a foundation for your effective job search campaign. Each of the eight steps toward job search success (the steps outlined earlier in this chapter) depends on a powerful, goal-oriented resume. The only way to write a focused, targeted resume is to set and articulate your goals—Step One. For many people, goal articulation is the missing link to resume writing and job search. Those seeking "anything, anywhere," often find "nothing, nowhere."

With focus, you will create or update goal-directed resumes and you can have more than one targeted resume, each reflecting a different goal. These are your tools for initial contact, follow-up, interview prep, and interviews themselves.

ESSENTIAL

Here's a confidence-building exercise. Take out a piece of paper, or open a new file on your computer. At the top of the page, write your name, address, telephone number, and e-mail address. You've just started your resume.

When you call first, then e-mail, and, finally, mail your resumes to potential employers, you begin a communication process that includes your resume at every step. As you stop to follow up and assess your strategy, you refocus your job search efforts. This includes updating your resume. Ultimately, when your efforts yield an interview, your resume will be your preparation tool. Throughout the process, your resume is your key communication device. It presents your past performance and your future potential. It is the reference point for potential employers to use in selecting you as a worthy job candidate.

After you ace the interview—using your resume as a powerful tool—and accept an offer, you might want to update your resume right away. Now, you don't have to begin your next job search so soon. But entering your new position on your resume makes a bold, confident psychological statement. Your new resume will honestly and accurately reflect that you started that very day.

CHAPTER 2

Writing Your Resume

During the years that the "resumes any way" attitude prevailed, authors echoed the belief that "there is no one perfect resume." This mentality made it difficult for resume writers to find the focus necessary to present themselves successfully on paper. This chapter focuses on creating resumes "your way"—whether you're a recent grad or someone looking to advance your career—by following a methodical approach to creating successful resumes.

The Seven Key Steps to Writing a Resume

Gaining focus and creating a strong, content-rich resume is easy when you follow these seven simple steps:

1. **Review as many resume samples as you can.** Look over old versions of your own resume, and ask friends, family members and trusted associates if they'd mind letting you take a look at theirs. This book includes many samples of many different resumes, designed for many different fields. You can also find a wide range of resume samples on the web.

2. **Analyze those resumes.** Think about what makes them work (or not work). Effective elements might include things like format, content, typeface, and the order of information.

3. **Identify your job objectives and your target audience.** This doesn't mean you need to include a "Career Objective" on your resume. It does mean that you need an understanding of the field you plan to pursue. Be sure you know the proper terminology, the job functions that will make you valuable, and how to present yourself as a viable candidate.

4. **Perform an inventory of your qualifications and achievements.** Knowing yourself and being confident in your abilities is key to creating a powerful resume.

5. **Analyze your competencies and capabilities as they relate to your job goals and your chosen field.** This is another aspect of the "know yourself" mantra. How do you see yourself contributing to this field? Remember your unique value proposition, (discussed in Chapter 1) and identify what makes you the most desirable candidate for the job you seek.

6. **Draft your resume, and critique it.** Compare your draft to the samples that you've analyzed and admired. How does it compare in terms of format, content, and order of information you've presented? Fix those elements you see can be stronger. Proofread it carefully, and after you're sure it's perfect, ask a friend to look it over.

7. **Make plenty of copies, and distribute your resume whenever appropriate.** Try sending it by e-mail to several friends. See if any of them have trouble opening up the document or if your layout or fonts become altered.

Taking the time to carefully review your resume and to attain input from others is a great way to ensure that you are putting your best foot forward. Your efforts now will pay off in the long run.

The Resume Your Way

If there is no perfect resume, how can you hope to create a document that all employers would want to see? The answer comes from a change in emphasis. Stop thinking about "resumes any way," designed to present yourself as you think "they" want to see you. Start writing resumes *your* way.

A good resume presents your past achievements as well as the assets and capabilities that qualify you for this new job. As you get better at communicating your qualifications, you will approach the job of writing your resume with confidence. The seven steps to success are good guidelines, and they should inspire confidence. But before you start writing, it is also a good idea to understand the different types of resumes and the purposes they serve. The following sections describe some traditional types and formats of resumes.

Chronological, Functional, and Combined Resumes

Chronological resumes present information in reverse chronological order, starting with the present and working backward. They traditionally use one-word "headers" to identify content sections. As you've read and heard again and again, they are usually no longer than one or two pages in length.

Functional resumes present candidate skill sets independent from job descriptions, if those descriptions are included at all. Most resume guides recommend functional formats for "career changers" or for those who are "keeping their options open," while the chronological format is usually recommended for all others.

Combined resumes include a skill profile and present work history, educational background, and other content under typical headers and usually appear in reverse chronological order.

Targeted and Customized Resumes

Recent resume guides use phrases like "targeted" and "customized." Targeted resumes include either a branding statement, or a clear objective and/or description of professional goals. Like targeted resumes, customized resumes are often created for a specific job title or employer, particularly when you know the desired skills and hiring criteria. A targeted approach will help your resume appear in keyword searches done by recruiters or the services they employ to comb job boards seeking out talent.

Combinations, Permutations, and Confusion

If you recall some basic math, we see that these various types of resumes give us multiple permutations, or variations, in the resume equation. Knowing that your resume is in "a targeted and chronological format" doesn't make it a better job search tool, nor you a better job seeker, but at least you know what to call it.

Some guides advise you to include all the schools you attended. Some suggest that you include only those schools where you were conferred a degree. Many books and articles emphatically suggest that you list courses, while as many others strongly urge you not to because "interviewers will know what someone with your major took." Some suggest that you present all scholarships and honors, no matter how small, because the longer the list, the more "they" will be impressed. Still others encourage you not to present all scholarships and honors. But when it comes to grades, everyone agrees: Only include good grades and averages!

ALERT

Amazingly, authors, resume counselors, and others continue to encourage functional resumes when almost all inquiries to prospective employers reveal that this format is ineffective and difficult to review. According to studies and polls, the pure functional resume format is the least preferred.

Advice regarding experience is equally conflicted. Some say that your resume should describe all jobs, no matter how small, in active terms, in hopes that some of those verbs will catch a prospective employer's eye. Others state with conviction that you should only include impressive jobs. Should you list volunteer and community service experience? Some say yes, but some say no; the same goes for personal interests. In years past, the phrase "References available upon request" indicated the standard close of the resume. Most resume professionals now omit this phrase and see it as unnecessary.

The Modern Resume Your Way

As you focus on your chosen career field and articulate your abilities, your resume writing and your job search will be inspired. A resume that projects "me and my goals" will strengthen the rest of your job search and it will also have an impact on the outcome. Keep your goals firmly in mind. Enhance the power and purpose of your resume. Plan and implement strategic actions.

Goal setting is critical to all resume writing and job search efforts. While useful multipurpose documents abound, targeted resumes are the most powerful. Overall, goal development and articulation are the most crucial components of resume writing and your comprehensive job search.

State-of-the-Art Documents Focused on You

A resume that focuses upon you makes you the central figure in the resume writing and job search process. You must clarify and articulate your goals, on paper but also in person. If anyone asks how you created such an effective resume, you can tell them that you place a high value on your career goals and have a good understanding of what will mutually benefit you and your employer.

The first sample resume that follows is an adaptation of the "Harvard Business School Resume." For generations, this was the required format for graduates of this prestigious school of business, and it illustrates a frequently copied and generally effective resume.

The Harvard Business School format was generally considered appropriate for investment banking and consulting positions. However, no single resume format is specifically required by any particular field. The samples presented in this book are aimed for many popular fields. It's up to you, the job seeker, to establish your targets and create or update the formats you deem appropriate.

Sample Resume: Harvard Business School Format

CHRIS SMITH

100 Main Street, Apartment 1 • Hometown, NY 00000
csmith@company.com • H (555) 555-1234 C (555) 555-5678

education

2010–2012 HARVARD GRADUATE SCHOOL OF BUSINESS   BOSTON, MA
Candidate for Master in Business Administration degree, June 2012.
Vice President of Marketing Club. Codirector of Marketing Project. Outreach 2006 Volunteer Program. Tutor first-year students.

2001–2005 CORNELL UNIVERSITY   ITHACA, NY
Bachelor of Arts degree, double major in American Civilization and French, May 2005. Studied international relations and political science in Paris at L'Institut d'Études Politiques. Freshman Advisor. Chair, Visiting Prospective Students Program and Student/Alumni Network.

experience

Summer 2011 UNIVERSAL STUDIOS   LOS ANGELES, CA
Summer Assistant Marketing Manager, Consumer Products/Interactive Division: Worked with Vice President of Sales and Marketing to create business vision and branding strategy for introduction of new brand in educational interactive products industry.
- Developed brand elements and positioning statements and contributed to brand-name generation.
- Created preliminary marketing and communications programs for brand launch and national product rollout, targeting both home and academic markets.
- Analyzed economic and consumer trends and conducted competitor analysis, resulting in entry strategy recommendation.

2007–2010 THE MAXIMUM MARKETING GROUP   NEW YORK, NY
Associate Supervisor: Directed marketing communications activities for Nikon, agency's largest account, representing 65% of annual billings at start-up firm specializing in consumer products.
- Created strategic plan to increase brand awareness and loyalty in consumer and professional photography markets. Addressed shrinking market share and increased competition.
- Managed new product launches from concept development to market for existing and new products. Led multifunctional team responsible for product positioning, competitor analysis, media coverage, and dealer/sales education.

2005–2007 PUBLIC RELATIONS ASSOCIATES   NEW YORK, NY
Account Coordinator: Developed and implemented national media campaigns in support of new product launches for Nikon Lite-Touch, Reebok Pump, and Step Reebok aerobic workout program.

personal

Fluent in French. Active Cornell alumni interviewer and volunteer for youth hockey program.

This format is a "multipurpose chronological resume." Note the use of one-word headers and the condensed presentation of educational information. Work experience is first described in general terms, and specific achievements are then highlighted using bullets. The format efficiently uses space and highlighting techniques, including capitalization, bold, and italics. In some ways, this resume is still "they" oriented, presented to meet the (unknown) expectations of the potential employer. This is a solid example of this type of resume, but one that is not quite evolved to the approach suggested in this book. Samples shown later in this book illustrate techniques for building a stronger resume, including the following:

- Headlines or objective statements that clearly project focus. Well-crafted headlines advertise the nature of your content and reinforce your stated job goal or career focus.
- A comprehensive "summary of qualifications" section, including appropriate terminology and field-focused verbs and nouns, which projects a knowledge of self as well as a knowledge of the field (and is critical for keyword searches).
- Rather than chronologically, information is presented to highlight the most important information first.
- Relevant courses, academic accomplishments, and other pertinent activities are listed briefly.
- Descriptions of work experience appear under headlines in order of significance. They project your capabilities and industry knowledge, as well as your accomplishments.
- Left-justified and text block formats are easy to e-mail and to upload into PDF-based resume banks and job board sites.

ESSENTIAL

The best resumes have common components. They use headlines rather than headers. They include qualification summaries, lists of courses and projects, and highlights of specific accomplishments. The best resumes use field-focused terminology and present information in order of importance.

When you're reviewing these resume samples, examine those that match your field(s) of interest, but don't limit yourself. Review all the samples, and pick out the formats and contents you'd like to model. Be analytical and curious. Your background may be different from the fictional Chris Smith whose qualifications are presented over and over, but you and Chris are not in competition. Avoid focusing your resume on the "they" who will be reading it. Project your knowledge of the field and functional goals. Focus on *you* because when you do get the interview, the hiring manager will use your resume to establish a dialogue. Your resume must say everything important to helping you get the offer.

The sample in this chapter shows an effective resume for a soon-to-be business school graduate. If it inspired you to think about what your resume should look like, this book has already been effective. Remember that the first two steps in resume writing involve review and analysis of samples.

The College Graduation Benchmark

The people who most need resume guidance are those who have no, or very little, experience preparing one. Many who find themselves in the market for their first "real" jobs belong in the "college grad" category, which includes the following:

- First- and second-semester college seniors
- Those who have just graduated
- Those whose job search continues at least three to six months beyond commencement
- Juniors, seniors, and others seeking internships

Campus career centers offer counseling and job search coaching, with seniors being the most likely to take advantage of these services. First-semester seniors spend a lot of time on resumes for on-campus recruiting, career fairs, and other job-placement offerings. On-campus counseling usually produces resumes focused on what the recruiter expects, rather than the candidate's qualifications and focus. In their urgency to create and update their resumes, first-semester seniors often overlook the assessment and research steps that lead to goal setting. Fear of focus often motivates them to avoid these critical steps to college resume writing success.

New job candidates usually hope that a large quantity of data will overcome any issues of quality. Anxious about "what recruiters want to see," and hoping that *something* in their arsenal will get them on-campus interviews, they include everything. Myths about recruiters seeking "well-rounded" individuals inspire this kind of unfocused volume. Ironically, candidates are actually screened with narrow, rather than diverse criteria. Reviewers of college resumes are most on the lookout for field-focused majors, high grade point averages, and pertinent internships.

An Internet poll of more than 500 top entry level employers revealed that hiring employers ranked a student's major as most important at 42.8 percent followed by interviewing skills at 25 percent and internship experience at 15.9 percent.

Second-semester seniors are either inspired by reactions of recruiters gained during the fall, or they become anxious and pessimistic because few responded favorably to their resumes. Those with goals matching the fields and functions that recruiters are looking for often use the same resume and reactive strategies through the spring semester and beyond. Those whose goals do not match recruiters' needs, and those who cannot express their goals, get very anxious around commencement time. This anxiety often inspires unfocused, multipurpose resumes, or leads to procrastination that lingers well past commencement day.

College graduates are commonly confused by misunderstood job-related data and statistics. Many feel that the top students take all the good jobs, with nothing left by commencement. In reality, recruiting seasons are on-campus anomalies. In the real world, the job search goes on well after June. Many, many candidates get their jobs three to six months after they graduate.

Regardless of the school of type of school they attended, placement statistics indicated that approximately 30–50 percent of college graduates keep looking for a job after commencement. About 15–25 percent failed to set goals or start their job search before graduation. For these candidates, like anyone else looking for a new job, it's important to work through the seven steps to resume success. The assessment and research steps are particularly effective for gaining and projecting focus. This is critical, as a complete, effective job search mirrors the candidate's knowledge of qualifications and field-specific competencies.

Here are a few questions that are common among recent or soon-to-be graduates:

- **How do I make my resume stand out?** Flawless spelling, punctuation, and sentence structure. Use an appealing visual format. Emphasize professionalism. Write strong content that plays up work experience while in school, internships, coursework, and extracurricular activities, as well as any honors.
- **What if I don't have related experience or education?** Emphasize the contributions and skills that you possess that are universal to all employers, and focus on transferable skills such as coordinating events, customer service, computer skills, or budget planning. Find the common thread between what you've done and what you want to do. Talk to a professor or mentor to see if they can help you bridge any relevancy gaps based on their knowledge of the workplace.
- **Should I include education or experiences from high school?** If you are an entry level grad, it is permissible to do so if you were a stellar student who received awards or scholarships or held officer titles in school clubs or community groups. Otherwise, focus on college experiences.
- **When and how do I present my most significant work experience?** Lead it off directly under the "Employment" heading, but recent grads need to list education first. Use descriptive keywords that illustrate actions taken and any important on-the-job achievements.
- **If I had one very relevant course and project, how do I highlight both, or either?** The project can be set off under "Education" as "Thesis" or "Case Study." Treat it like a work experience.

- **If I haven't been successful getting an interview, should I change my resume?** Probably—or maybe your methodology. Ask for some critical feedback from any senior-level business professionals you know. See if anything strikes them as problematic. Compare your resume to others you can view on the web. Assess whether you are being proactive enough in your approach or are just being a passive job seeker, waiting to be called.
- **My GPA in my major is higher than my cumulative average. Should I include it?** Include a GPA in your major or overall GPA only if it is 3.5 or above. Otherwise, leave it for discussion at the interview should it come up.

More than any other kind of job candidate, if you are a soon-to-be or recent graduate, you must work hard on identifying and articulating your goals. Identify and analyze what you learned in the classroom and beyond. Pick out your most significant courses, labs, and projects, and present those in terms of their potential for making you valuable and effective on the job. Focus your resume and your search for a job or internship on your academic achievements, but don't forget to analyze what you've learned in terms of your personal exploration and your choice of a career field.

Intern Candidates

About 75 percent of college students use resumes in their search for an internship. Internships are difficult to define. In general, an internship is more sophisticated than a summer job. There are both paid and unpaid positions. Some internships offer academic credit, while others are more project-focused, offering the opportunity to build skills and explore a field of interest. Some internships are promoted through large, well-publicized, and structured programs, and others are identified through networking and self-initiated efforts.

Internships are growing in importance. Students in search of an internship should use their resumes to project their curiosity, competency, and their awareness of the field.

Just like any other job candidate, those seeking internships must project focus since competition is high. You're probably looking for an internship to get a deeper knowledge of your field of interest, but—in an ironic twist—you need to project focus and some familiarity with the field before you can get that internship. Do that on your resume!

ESSENTIAL

As college students become more sophisticated about their career aspirations, internships have grown in importance and popularity. A 2010 study by Intern Bridge showed that 75 percent of college students complete one more internships before graduation, compared with just 3 percent in the early 1980s.

First Jobs

This category includes people who have worked two years or less in a volunteer or other nonprofessional position. It also includes people with up to three years of on-the-job experience.

Many college grads do not get their dream jobs right away, nor do they usually start out on a clearly defined career path. Often these young men and women lack the focus to begin their true career development or to implement a goal-directed job search. So, naturally, they find "transition positions."

These positions include a variety of experience. Some people plan to enter graduate school, so they seek "something meaningful to do." The jobs can be "for experience" or "adventures," such as the Peace Corps, AmeriCorps, Teach for America, or maybe a job teaching English in another country. The job might also be something practical, such as a retail sales job, just for a paycheck. Still other jobs might be unrelated to a grad's major, but are with a well-known employer and offer name recognition and prestige.

No matter what the position is, the resume must support and inspire a first step onto a true career path. In these cases it is best to avoid the reverse-chronological format, as experience is still limited and the format will make it difficult to project any sense of goal or focus. It's most important to present your potential and identify your goals for the future.

Here are some common questions that new job seekers generally ask:

- **If what I am doing now has nothing to do with my goals, how and where do I present my experience?** Spend some time on self-assessment. Find some commonality between your goals and current or past experience. If there is no connection, employers will not view you as qualified for their opening. Consider taking additional coursework with your goals in mind. Or, take a step back and go for a lower-level job in the area of your goal to gain some credible work history.
- **What about education; specifically, my major?** Build this up as it applies to your job target. Show how your education and recent training will be advantageous to the new employer.
- **Do I highlight what I have been doing for the past few years?** Yes—but focus on specific responsibilities that are similar in scope or typical of what you will be doing in your new job. What can you bring to this position that others cannot?
- **Where and how do I present my most recent experiences?** Any job candidate except a recent college graduate should place work experience above education, near the top of the resume and/or a qualification summary. Follow the examples in this book on formatting and presentation.
- **If I wasn't given enough responsibilities to yield achievements, how do I leverage my current job?** Surely, something you did makes you proud—what is it? Did you streamline a process? Did you generate more reports than your predecessor? Did you volunteer for any committees? If you think you haven't had any notable achievements, you need to re-examine your work and the challenges you've faced. Almost all employment experiences can be positioned to showcase the job seeker in some way. Additionally, consider your present employer's reputation. A position with negligible responsibilities at a company that is a household name may generate interest simply because of the kind of environment or leadership interaction you faced on a daily basis.

Candidates seeking their first jobs must focus their resumes, job search correspondence, and interviews on the qualifications they already have and that they will need to succeed in the future. Resumes must target the newly identified goals. Objective must be presented clearly and supported with powerful summaries of your qualifications.

Focus here is critical. You must use the resume writing process to identify and articulate your goals. (Working through the first five of the seven steps will help.) You must abandon the attitude of "leaving your options open" if you're going to focus on future goals.

Beyond Entry Level

Some people take their first steps (or giant leaps) on their career paths right after they graduate. Two or three years later, they're ready for more responsibility. Job advice from a career center is easy to find for college seniors, but sound guidance is much less accessible later on. Entry level workers, those with two to five years of experience, can become confused and anxious. As with anyone, fear of change plus fear of focus yields procrastination and anxiety.

ESSENTIAL

Some recent graduates seek change in a subconscious effort to recapture their college experience. In college we get to choose our courses. Our lives change from semester to semester, always offering something new. As a new member of the work force, either seeking promotion or a new position, you must decide what is driving you. Do you miss cyclical changes of academic life, or are you motivated by ambition and the need to develop your career? Taking stock of your own motivations now can help you be prepared for the questions that will inevitably come from those you will interview with. They will certainly be asking you about what is driving your interest in the position you have applied for.

Steps four and five of the resume writing process encourage you to analyze your accomplishments so far and to assess your capabilities. This proactive approach is positive. It motivates you to present your experience dynamically, in terms of what you've accomplished. As you consider your past achievements, your performance potential for the future becomes clearer.

Resumes for All

Whether you're called an "hourly worker," "nonexempt," or—more traditionally—a "blue-collar laborer," you may be working in an administrative, food service, customer service, or manufacturing position. People in these fields often fail to create or update resumes that reflect their potential for continued success. Too often, when it's time to look for a new job, they depend upon applications, references, or word of mouth. However, everyone needs and deserves a powerful resume. Word of mouth can be translated into words on paper, creating an effective resume that mirrors capabilities and projects a clear future focus.

People at the other end of the professional spectrum are also often guilty of overlooking their resumes. In most cases, those we call "senior management" have old, vague resumes or no resume at all. Though they're responsible for large operations and organizations, and though they generally supervise many others, these people may not be as ready for the job search as they should be. However, with our culture focusing more and more on career advancement and reinvention of self, many senior leadership professionals are taking the time to keep their resumes current in anticipation of being recruited or finding new ways to use their talents and enjoy meaningful job satisfaction.

Anyone, on any rung of the job-success ladder, should use the resume writing process to identify and articulate their goals. No matter how diverse your interests or background, creating a powerful resume will enhance your focus and effectively project your qualifications and commitment for your future performance.

Resumes Between Generations

As baby boomers age and Gen X and Gen Y advance within the workplace, it is important that the generations understand each other's skills and strengths as denoted by their resumes. The younger Millennials tend to like electronic resumes and some do not even possess paper versions. On the other hand, baby boomers may feel more comfortable with printed resumes and might be reluctant to post their resumes online or are unsure how to format their resumes for readability by varying computer users. Each generation must be sure that their resume can be understood and appreciated by the other, even though the mindsets of each group might differ in their personal values.

FACT

According to PewResearchCenter, beginning on Jan.1, 2011, and every day after that for the next nineteen years, 10,000 baby boomers will reach age 65. U.S. Bureau of Labor Statistics indicate that the number of people who are over fifty-five will increase by 73 percent by 2020, while the number of younger workers will grow only by 5 percent. As droves of people begin to retire, this means it will be a "candidate's market" with employers competing hard for talent.

If you're a baby boomer you must be sure that your resume doesn't date you unnecessarily or work to your detriment. You can't keep adding to a resume that was originally written twenty years ago. If you're guilty of this, it's time for a rewrite. Go online and review newer job descriptions, even for some of your old titles. Update your terminology. Industry speak is critical for keyword searches and to demonstrate you have kept pace with your field. Remove the "References on Request" close—that's old school. Have you included jobs that have no bearing on your current position or the one you desire? Go back only as far as your current employment objectives, use the rule of relevancy to determine which jobs to highlight. If you've been with one employer for many years, separate your tenure by positions and changes in responsibility. Remember, one resume doesn't fit all. It may be necessary for you to have two or three different versions, each with a different focus. Maintain several formats to accommodate different users: a standard Microsoft Word formatted resume, a PDF version for downloading, and a plain text version to paste into an e-mail message.

Those in Gen X and Gen Y tend to have many more jobs than baby boomers. You might need to communicate the reason behind your multiple moves to the baby boomer hiring manager who could perceive these "job hops" as restlessness, rather than growth. And if you're a Millennial who uses text messaging and casual e-mails as a way of life, remember to be more formal in your approach to prospective employers by watching your use of abbreviations. Not everyone knows that webspeak such as *PTMM* equals *Please Tell Me More*, or *NRN* equals *No Reply Necessary*.

The Video Resume

A recent trend in the employment marketplace is the video resume. These presentations range from homemade versions from job seekers equipped with web cams and movie-making software, to more professionally produced videos created by videographers, executive search firms, or special video resume services. While the interest in the use of such resumes grows in some sectors, they remain uncharted territory for most job hunters and employers, many of whom are wary of the potential discrimination based on race, age, or other factors that would not be obvious from a more traditional resume. You can view a variety of video resumes online by doing a simple online search, or on YouTube, which also offers some how-to and related videos with helpful tips and advice. Be sure to view several samples before creating your own to give yourself a good idea of what works and what doesn't and whether this format is a good fit for you. Many video resumes can seem a little bit like infomercials, but the individual's comfort level speaking on camera and their overall appearance can give some candidates leverage in their job hunt.

FACT

Eighty-nine percent of employers said they would watch a video resume if it were submitted to them with the primary reason being to better assess a candidate's professional presentation and demeanor. Only 17 percent admitted to actually having viewed this kind of job search technology.

The use of video resumes may continue to grow as technology permeates all facets of our workplaces, but just like the traditional resume, you may want to have several versions depending on your target audience. If you're not comfortable speaking on camera, rethink your need for one. What can you convey in video that would not be possible in print? Are you truly making yourself a more desirable candidate on screen or will your credentials be better represented in a traditional format? Be careful not to get caught up in a trend that may not be advantageous to your personality or skill set. We live in an age where people have high media standards and you don't want your video resume to seem like a bad TV audition. However, if you are comfortable on camera, speak well, and have good "stage presence," a video resume may give you a leg up over the competition.

To prepare an effective video resume:

- Dress as though you were going to the interview
- Talk into the camera; make good eye contact
- Smile, speak clearly without pauses and not too fast
- Introduce yourself by your first and last name
- Outline your skills, experience, education, and what you can contribute
- Eliminate background noises or other distractions
- Keep it short . . . two to three minutes maximum
- Conclude with a thank-you and information on how you can be reached

Some of the major job boards and specialty sites now have sections where you can upload your video. You can also create your own page and link to your video resume. Have others screen it to get their opinion. If the reaction is favorable, include a link for viewing on your e-resume.

Virtual Job Fairs

A variation on the video resume is the virtual job fair. They are becoming increasingly popular and offer both employers and potential employees the benefit of connecting without the expense of travel and with limited time investment. Virtual job fairs, like traditional job fairs, put candidates together with employers who are recruiting for open positions—often a large number of open positions—and are essentially a "live chat" between recruiters and candidates. Virtual job fairs tend to be used by employers that have a large remote work force, as well as employers who may be interested in campus recruitment but concerned about the time and costs involved. For example, companies like the Brazen Careerist, a career management website (*www.brazencareerist.com*) works with clients ranging from Amazon to State Farm and Safeway to host virtual job fairs.

From a resume standpoint, you should be prepared with your "virtual" resume—generally in PDF format—to share with the recruiters you meet at the virtual fair. You should also follow up after the event with an e-mail and another copy of your resume.

The Vitae Alternative

For professors, physicians, and scientists, resumes are not enough to present accomplishments and experiences. Vitae, or "curriculum vitae," are comprehensive documentation of academic and employment performance. Still, it isn't a bad idea for these professionals to prepare a powerful resume that encapsulates their goals and abilities on a single page.

ALERT

Don't be confused or delay your response if someone asks for a "vitae." Unless you are seeking positions outside the United States or within special fields, respond to requests with your resume. If applying overseas, create a vita by adding information including date of birth, sex, height and weight, and marital status; and all educational experiences, including high school.

Even though vitae are usually lengthy documents, listing publication citations, research projects, presentations, affiliations, and educational and training experiences, they don't have to be passive collections of data. The same qualities that make for a powerful resume—self-knowledge, goal focus, and a clear statement of objectives—also apply to a quality vita.

CHAPTER 3

Seven Steps to Resume Writing Success

Just like those popular home repair shows that teach you to follow well-conceived plans to minimize costs, eliminate errors, and maximize outcomes, this chapter provides you with the blueprint for a great resume. It details do-it-yourself steps, identifies quick fixes, and addresses issues for job seekers who might need special tools.

The Process

Resume writing is not as difficult as many believe. Creating your resume is an opportunity to identify the positive things about very important aspects of your life. The process can be simplified to seven easy steps (those outlined in Chapter 2) that you can use to update or create resumes in just a day. Here are the steps again, in brief:

1. Review samples.
2. Determine format, content, and order of information.
3. Identify objectives and target your audience.
4. Inventory your qualifications and achievements.
5. Analyze your competencies and capabilities.
6. Draft and critique your resume.
7. Duplicate it, post it, and distribute it.

Chapter 2 also outlined which steps are most important for certain job seekers. Pay particular attention to those steps, but don't ignore any of the steps.

Reviewing Samples

Break out the pens, highlighters, and sticky notes, and start examining the samples that appear throughout this book. Analyze them like a knowledgeable and focused job seeker, excited about the task at hand. Instead of thinking critically, like an editor, identify the qualities you like.

Prospective employers look for certain things as they review resumes. The first thing that employers and recruiters do when they want to fill a position is to list the qualifications the job requires—such as capabilities, areas of expertise, character qualities, employment history, and educational background. They list these traits in order of priority, according to which are essential, which are optimal, and which are merely desirable (or optional).

Once the employer decides on the qualities that he or she is looking for, candidates are sourced (or encouraged to apply), screened, and, ultimately, interviewed and selected. Sometimes job descriptions and postings include detailed qualification criteria. More often, however, these preferences are expressed vaguely, in broad descriptions.

FACT

> It is helpful to understand the employer's perspective, and it is a good idea to review other resumes. Just remember, this is *your* resume. You, and not anyone else, are responsible for success.

No matter how inaccurately they express their defined criteria, employers are always aware of them. Employers review resumes and cover letters, conduct interviews, and make their offers with those qualification criteria clearly in mind. In particular, they use written profiles of their desired qualifications for keyword scanning and behavioral interviews.

While the job seeker might wish otherwise, employers almost never share detailed qualification criteria. Nor do they thoroughly analyze the resumes they receive. The employer is not responsible for digging through a mass of poorly organized, badly written resumes to find the perfect job candidate. As the job seeker, you are responsible for conveying your goals, objectives, and a clear sense of job purpose. You must create a powerful resume that mirrors your qualifications, and follow that up with an interview that impresses the employers with your capability to perform the job.

Format, Content, and Order of Information

Pick out your two or three favorite sample resumes. Examine them from top to bottom. Here are some basic questions to consider as you review these samples:

- What first impression does the resume generate? How is it formatted?
- What appears first on the page?
- How does the resume identify the applicant? Does it include an e-mail address? Does it include both addresses, and all phone numbers, including a cell phone?

- Does it include a brief yet effective objective and a qualification summary?
- Does it present educational information before or after a qualification summary? Before or after experience? How would you present this information?
- How would you order information about your own work history, qualifications, and objectives?
- Based on your review and consideration of your own resume, how might you use as few lines as possible, reserving most of the page for critical content?
- Will you use columns, with dates on the left and descriptions on the right, or a block format?
- Will headlines be centered or left-justified?
- Will they appear under clearly phrased and focused headlines?

Reviewing others' resumes from a critical standpoint, as though you were the person reviewing the applications, can provide you with useful insights about how to present your own information most effectively.

ESSENTIAL

In elementary school you may have been told that it was bad to write in books. In this book, though, you should write your response to the sample resumes as you review them. Your first response to a resume is often purely visual, and ultimately, it's the human eye that reviews any successful resume. As you read, therefore, note the ways that you can give your resume a greater visual impact.

Formatting Basics

The font you choose is the key to a well-formatted resume. Fonts should be traditional, easy to read, and common. You don't want to create a beautiful resume in some obscure font that will be replaced on your reviewer's computer by an automatic bad font substitution (probably destroying all your careful line spacing and other formatting work as well).

THE BEST FONTS AND POINT SIZES FOR RESUMES

Bookman Antiqua 9 Point

Bookman Antiqua 10 Point

Bookman Antiqua 11 Point

Century Schoolbook 9 Point

Century Schoolbook 10 Point

Century Schoolbook 11 Point

Garamond 10 Point

Garamond 11 Point

Palatino 8 Point

Palatino 9 Point

Palatino 10 Point

Times 9 Point

Times 10 Point

Times New Roman 9 Point

Times New Roman 10 Point

Times New Roman 11 Point

ESSENTIAL

Consistency is the key to readability and effectiveness. Resumes are rarely read very thoroughly at all. Most employers say they review a resume for less than a minute before keeping it live or filing it. You want employers to be able to pick up important information just by scanning your page (visually and electronically). Review the samples for illustrations of effective and not-so-effective highlighting techniques.

For headlines, increase the font size two points at a time until the headline is emphasized but not disproportionate. You can highlight important elements with CAPITALIZATION, **bold face**, and *italics*, as well as with indentations, line spacing, and bullet points. At one time, e-mailed resumes had to be formatted so they could be easily scanned. Today, PDF is more common. PDF, or "portable document format," is a file format that anyone can read using special viewing software (free from software maker Adobe). Most current word processing systems let you save documents directly as PDFs. (Your software documentation should explain how you can do this.) The beauty of PDFs is that they allow you to use more creative formatting, such as graphics. Just keep in mind that a cluttered page will confuse your reader; use only those elements that help you present yourself effectively.

Identify Yourself

Maybe you don't need an eye-catching logo, but you do need to begin your resume—and your cover letters, and all other correspondence—consistently. Letterhead is the best and easiest way to do this. You can design your own very simply, using the features in any word processing program. Letterhead features your name on the first line. It includes your full mailing address, the telephone number(s) where you can be reached during business hours, and it should include your e-mail address as well. By the way, lose any cutesy or gimmicky e-mail moniker like Partyallnight@ or Muscleman@. It's hard to take such names seriously. Set yourself up with a free address at a major search engine such as Google.com to keep your job search correspondence easier to track. This keeps it separate from your personal e-mail or your work e-mail. Never use a current employer's e-mail address. You don't want your prospective employer to think (or know) that you aren't giving one hundred percent to your job while you're working. Also, take the time to review your voice mail messages on the phone numbers you include on your resume, both home and cell. While you're in the job market, refrain from including music, clever hellos, or other weird greetings. Try not to think of this formality as stifling your personality, but rather improving your chances for getting the interview.

The point is to make it as easy as possible for your reader to recognize you and to contact you with minimal effort. This is also part of creating your *Personal Brand*, as was defined earlier.

Summarize Yourself

Targeted resumes use qualification or achievement summaries to present objectives and goals. Summaries follow or even replace the statement of objectives, depending on what you learn in your self-assessment and goal research (steps four and five discussed later on in this chapter). Sometimes these sections come at the end, providing the resume with a solid "bottom line." Chapter 4 details issues related to objectives, as well as qualification and achievement summaries.

Put Your Experience in Order

The best resumes present the job seeker's most significant experiences first. Entries are grouped under headlines. They include undergraduate and graduate degrees, specialized training, and work history. Education can come at the top, as the first or second category, or you can present it last. Candidates with plenty of valuable on-the-job experience generally list that first, saving the bottom of the page for a summary of their education.

ALERT

Most recent graduates put their education at the top of their resumes. Your academic achievements may be significant, but you should think about where and how you want them to appear. Don't list education first just because you think you should; you might make important work history, projects, and other achievements look less important by bumping them farther down the page.

Academic achievements and honors can be presented in a bulleted list. To figure out what belongs on this list, think about courses, papers, and projects with special relevance to this field. You might also have pertinent extracurricular or community experience. In general, these activities should follow your education and employment entries. Most good resumes do not have a "personal interests" section. Include yours only if you're sure it emphasizes your goals and qualifications in the field.

Finally, it is important to note that your resume does *not* need to end with "References available upon request." That's a given.

Identify Your Objectives and Your Audience

This critical step is too often overlooked. You *must* identify your objectives and your target audiences. To do this, ask yourself what you aim to achieve with your resume. Answer that question, and you will define your goals. You must also define, as best you can, who will be reading your resume. Your reviewers belong to the field. They use particular words, phrases, and other field-focused terminology when they talk about their work. By using the proper language (or "talking the talk"), you project the sense that you can do the job (that is, "walk the walk").

Your resume should clearly state your career objectives, but not necessarily with what was once defined as a "Career Objective." Instead, your career objective should be conveyed by your content. Too often, old-fashioned Career Objectives were pure fluff. They were vague or said little to enhance the job seeker's qualifications or goals. Look through the samples in this book: When one is included it is very targeted, meaning it clearly focuses on a specific field and, within that field, on a certain job function.

Inventory Your Qualifications and Achievements

Why do so many resume writing and job search guides ask you to list your ten most significant achievements before creating your resume? The answer has to do with the power of positive thinking. With your greatest achievements in mind, you are more likely to think about—and represent—yourself as a valuable job candidate who is full of potential.

ESSENTIAL

It's not so easy to draft a summary of your qualifications, so don't worry if it takes some time. Start by asking yourself this question: "What skills have I demonstrated in the past that will make me valuable in my chosen field in the future?" Think of problems you have solved or instances of collaborative teamwork or projects that you managed with great success.

The best way to pick out your important achievements is to think in terms of the job or field you're aiming to enter. Freeform lists of random accomplishment are not as effective. You don't want to rely on your reviewer to figure out or analyze the significance of anything in your resume. It's your job to make your value clear.

Achievement summaries are the heart of any good resume. That's what makes a resume content-rich. They should be enough to convince the reviewer of your commitment, your qualifications, and your obvious value. It's important not to skimp on the time or energy you put into summarizing your past accomplishments. To a potential employer, your past has everything to do with the future.

Analyze Your Competencies and Capabilities

It may be *physically* impossible to look backward and ahead at the same time, but the world of resume writing follows different rules. Great resumes reflect past achievements and, via qualification summaries, project ahead to future roles and responsibilities. You are not limited to talking about what has been achieved. Instead, your resume is the perfect platform to express your confidence and competence to tackle the future.

Drafting and Critiquing Your Resume

Your first draft should be inspired by the sample resumes you've reviewed and analyzed. They will probably influence your choice of content and the order of your information. Let them. Later on, you can go back and determine the best order of presentation and omit unnecessary entries. Technology, of course, has made the task of creating a resume, and in multiple versions, far easier than in the "old days." There are some areas of caution to consider though.

Avoid Resume Software

You'll find plenty of resume-building software to tempt you as you create your draft. Resist the temptation and use a basic word processing application. Most, like Microsoft Word, come with resume templates. While attractive, these lock you into a format, and that can limit how you present yourself. Also, prospective employers have seen these templates used over and over again. You might eliminate yourself from consideration just because a hiring manager dislikes a particular format. Give yourself the greatest control over your resume by starting with a blank page.

FACT

The Internet has hundreds of listings for professional resume writers. Do your best to resist! Your resume is your responsibility; nobody can present you better than you can. If you are still dissatisfied with your finished product, you may want to consider a professional resume writer (see Chapter 4 for guidance). Your drafts will be a good basis for your consultation with an expert.

The First Draft

As you put your first draft together, don't worry about keeping it to any particular length. If anything, it is better to start long and edit it down later. Write as spontaneously as you can. Don't rewrite as you go. It's a sure way to inhibit your creativity and there will be plenty of time for that when your draft is complete.

When drafting, aim to just get the information down. Jot descriptive phrases to help you capture your thoughts quickly. For your final resume, you don't have to use articles ("the," "an," "a"), and you can leave the pronouns out. It's unnecessary to say, "I completed the survey"—in a resume, "completed survey" gets the point across. Without shocking your English teacher, you can also feel free to use sentence fragments.

Reviewing the Draft

Begin your critique only when you have a complete draft in hand. Some people like to see their resume on paper, and they edit with the old red pen technique. Others revise and edit onscreen. Work the way you're most comfortable, being sure that your method helps you polish your draft to perfection. Critiquing does not mean criticizing. Your revisions are meant to transform your resume into its most powerful form. Be positive. Make immediate changes as you need to, and be prepared to make future changes as your job search progresses.

Your finished resume should be concise. If, after your best editing efforts, it is still longer than one page, so be it! Employers do read two-page resumes, as long as they are well organized, with the most important information on the first page. One-page resume rules are part of the old way of job hunting.

Mass Production, E-mail, and Distribution

At one time people worried about things like typesetting and having a clean ribbon in the typewriter. Then it was a good laser printer, picking the right paper, and finding matching envelopes. That eventually moved into fax machines and now e-mail. Each era comes with its own advantages and pitfalls.

Most of your resumes will probably go out via e-mail or be posted to the web, though you will still need a printed version as well. In either case, it's important to keep making a good first impression in mind. Make your resume effective with strong format, very simple graphics (as long as they contribute to your statement), and an attractive design.

Most resumes are created or updated using word processing software and duplicated on paper using quality printers and photocopiers. And while you've probably seen creatively formatted resumes—horizontal style, fold-outs or brochures, for instance—it's really best to stick with the standard "portrait" orientation (with the resume reading top to bottom on the page). Why? Because this is the format that recruiters, HR professionals, and hiring managers are used to seeing. Because there are often many, many others applying for the same job you want to make their jobs as easy as possible and not create confusion or questions unnecessarily.

For paper copies, use a top-quality laser printer or photocopier, and use bond or linen paper. White, ivory, natural, and off-white are your best color options. The content and format of your resume will make your document "stand out," not the color of your paper. If you have your resumes copied, get extra paper and matching envelopes. Use the same paper for your cover letters and other correspondence. Brand yourself; a professional image contributes to your marketability.

QR Codes

QR, or quick-response, codes are an interesting development in the communication field and they have applicability for job seekers as well. QR codes are similar to bar codes and can be read by mobile phones through downloadable (and free) apps. They can also be created at no cost online through a variety of websites. Just enter a search time like "QR code generator" into a search engine and you'll receive a variety of options.

The code can be printed in black and white on any document, including resumes and, when accessed through a QR reader application, will take the user to the information. For job seekers, QR codes can provide additional information or link to samples of their work that potential employers can readily access. For instance, a graphic designer might want to create a QR code that takes interviewers to his online portfolio. A mechanical engineering job candidate might want to provide a QR code link to moving, 3D images of some completed projects.

While gaining in popularity, QR codes—like video resumes—are somewhat of a niche tool and not applicable or appropriate for all job seekers. For those in certain industries—e.g., media, entertainment or IT industries—though, they may provide some benefit.

CHAPTER 4

Goals, Qualifications, and Achievements

Your potential employer meets you for the first time in the first few lines of your resume. A strong statement of your professional objectives (your goals) and a convincing summary of your achievements to date assure your reader that you're worth the time it will take to keep reading. This chapter shows you how to give your resume the power it needs to hold your prospective employer's attention.

Meeting the Employer's Criteria

When an employer decides to fill a position, she must write up an accurate job description if she hopes to attract qualified candidates. That means listing job functions along with requirements such as years of experience, education, training, and any specialized skills or knowledge. As we've discussed, employers establish and use lists of essential, optional, and desired qualifications to identify, recruit, interview, and select candidates. Your potential employer will use your resume and supporting correspondence to determine how well you meet the defined criteria.

FACT

Career counselors say that lack of research is the reason why most job seekers can't articulate their professional goals. Even those professionals who rely on standardized tests to identify their clients' values, interests, personality traits, and skills agree that research is a key component to knowing your goals and what it takes to reach them.

It's important to know as much as you can about your chosen field and function. The more you know, the better you can focus your objectives. If you name a particular job title, or if a certain job function is your goal, be sure you know the responsibilities that come along with it. Some job hunters use the big job board sites to read employer job descriptions to help them better define their own positions on their resumes or to update their language and improve the way they relay their duties.

Field Descriptions

When it comes to an effective job search, the only question you have to answer is "What field do you want to enter, and what job are you looking for?" Many industry publications compile long lists of criteria to help workers assess their career compatibility and evaluate their potential goals. For you, as a job seeker, simplified field and functional perspectives are enough to help you check whether your qualifications meet an employer's qualification criteria. The following sections provide brief descriptions for some common fields. With this general idea of what comprises a field, you can more easily determine your particular focus and your qualifications for performing a particular function.

Administration

The administrative field involves general office management as well as oversight of facilities and systems associated with day-to-day organizational activities. No matter their titles, many employees in this field work in administrative, customer service, or general office positions. Those serving within these functions are also responsible for large operations and organizations. They generally supervise many individuals, projects, and resources. Job functions include office services, facilities, security, management, and project management roles.

Business

This sector includes almost any profit-driven activities. Most often, the business world is associated with large, publicly or privately held companies that provide services or market products.

Communication

The communication field involves writing, graphics, public relations, publicity, and promotions. It includes all activities associated with creating, distributing, and transmitting text and graphic information via varied print, video, audio, computer, and web-based media.

Education

The education field includes private and public preschools, elementary schools, middle and secondary schools, colleges and universities, and tutorial and training operations.

Finance

This field involves accounting, budgeting, treasury, auditing, and information systems activities. It includes collection, documentation, and analysis of financial data and the use of this data to make strategic decisions and share pertinent information with investors, regulators, and government entities. It also includes allocation and growth of capital required for annual operations as well as growth.

Government

Government includes all local, state, federal, and multinational organizations that pass legislation, offer and regulate services, lobby, and promote specific programs and resources.

Health and Human Services

Usually considered a part of the service sector, as in Health and Human Services as discussed above, this field includes both individuals and facilities that offer medical, psychological, social, and related services. Practitioners can be private, government affiliated, or have nonprofit status. Hospitals, clinics, residential treatment facilities, agencies, and special programs all fit within this field.

ALERT

In 2008, the popular job board website *www.careerbuilder.com* cited the following occupations among the top ten "cutting edge jobs" based on Bureau of Labor Statistics data, consumer need, changing technology, and shifting demographics: radiation therapist, nurse paralegal, genetics counselor, legal nurse consultant, art therapist, computer forensic expert, medical illustrator, veterinary physical therapist, nimal defense lawyer and animal assisted therapist.

Sales

The sales field involves direct sales, representative sales, distribution and arbitrage, and retail sales. It includes all activities associated with sales of raw materials used to create products or the sale of products directly to consumers. It can also involve sales of financial or other services.

Talk the Talk to Walk the Walk

Conversation is easy with almost anyone, as long as the people talking have something in common. In your job search—including your resume, correspondence, and interviews—you must speak the language that is common to your field of interest. The employer speaks to you in that language in the form of job descriptions and job postings. Your response is in the form of your resume and, later, your interview.

ESSENTIAL

You don't need to limit yourself to a single resume for one field. Objective statements are not difficult to create or update, and it is equally easy to recast your qualifications summaries to meet the criteria of different employers. Many candidates create multiple resumes and tweak them as needed based on the position they are applying for.

Courses and seminars are another way of learning the criteria for success in your field. If you can devote the time to an internship, or even arrange to spend time shadowing someone who performs your chosen job function (sometimes called an externship), you can learn through day-to-day experience.

Another good way to focus and state your goals to meet the employer's criteria is to check out a few professional publications. After just a few articles, you should start to notice some common factors. The terminology of the field should become clear, but you should also be able to tell something about individual job functions. Look for interviews or profiles of successful people in the field. What qualifications did they bring to their jobs? Even more general information, such as articles about processes or innovations in the field, should still contain clues. What you're looking for is the collection of characteristics that people who already work in your chosen field share. It is likely that those will be on your employer's list of qualification criteria.

Now is the time to think about the qualification criteria associated with job titles that raise your curiosity. Take out a pad or open a new Word document. For each job function that interests you, list the job title, field, and function. Think about the qualification criteria for each. If you were a prospective employer screening resumes, what would you look for? Jot down every qualification you think of. Don't write vague statements like "experience within the field and related education." Be specific and behavioral. **Figure 4-1** lists some sample criteria for an entry level Assistant Account Executive. Notice how each can be worked into a resume or used in follow-up correspondence and in your interview. Together, they form the basis of your common conversation with your potential employer.

ESSENTIAL

When you draft your statement of objectives and your qualification summary, think of them as messages that you're sending to potential employers. The message says, "I know what you need. I understand the job and its importance to your company. I am confident that I have the skills and ability to meet your needs and be an asset to your company."

Sample Statements of Objectives

Your professional objective does not have to state your long-term or lifelong career goals; it is simply a statement of the job title you are seeking. It provides focus for reviewers and influences how they perceive all subsequent content. Your statement of objectives is like a label that names the professional door you seek to enter. When you knock, seeking entry, you introduce yourself via a resume and cover letter. Ideally, after interviewing, you will receive an offer to stay.

As illustrated in samples throughout this book, resume objectives should be simple and stated in as few words as possible. They are best composed of a few nouns, not complex adjective- and verb-filled statements. No fluff. Top off your powerful page, literally, with the answer to the question: "What is the title of the job you seek?"

As you examine the format, content, and order as well as the objectives of the sample resumes in this book, think about their simplicity. Think about how they mirror a powerful knowledge of self and of a chosen career field and job function. Though the samples use different approaches, they still have much in common. Some probably have objectives and qualifications that match your goals, and it may be possible for you to adapt some of that content for your own resume. Your goal, here and throughout your resume

Figure 4-1: Sample Criteria

Qualification Criteria	Assets Sought and Interview Questions to Ask
Knowledge of the field	• Previous experience via internships or jobs • Courses in Advertising or Marketing • Vocabulary used in resume and cover letter • "What ads do you like the most and why?" question • "What agency has gained the most significant accounts last year?" question
Curiosity regarding consumer behavior and market research techniques	• Selected courses in Psychology, Anthropology, Marketing, or Sociology • Independent study or research, specifically in social sciences or marketing • Experience with questionnaire or survey development and analysis • "What ads do you like the least, and why?" question
Research and project management skills	• Diverse research or term paper topics, methodology, and outcomes • Multiple extracurricular roles or jobs while in school • Leadership within group projects • Examples of multitasking in internships, jobs, or academic roles • "When were you in charge of a project?" question
Blend of quantitative and qualitative analytical skills	• Diversity of courses, including mathematics, science, social sciences, and humanities • Economics, Business, Psychology, Anthropology, or Liberal Arts Curricula • Independent study or research experience revealed through papers and projects • "What are your strengths and weaknesses?" question
Group communication and task management abilities	• Extracurricular membership and leadership • Independent study, research support, or term-paper research experience • Semester-by-semester analysis of courses taken, motivation, and outcomes • "Describe your most impressive paper or presentation" query
Persuasive oral and written talents	• Majors and courses completed • Research and term paper topics • Cover letter and resume content • "Briefly describe your most impressive paper or presentation" query
Flexibility, curiosity, and ability to accept criticism	• Transcript analysis • Major choice, course selection, research, term paper topics • "Lessons learned from mistakes?" question • "What if I put you on the dog food account?" question • "What have you learned from your mistake?" question

writing and job search progress, is to show hiring managers that you know what it takes to succeed within your chosen field and function.

Think of a career objective like the thesis statement of a term paper or an "elevator speech" you might use when someone asks you about "what you do for a living." By adding keywords to your resume, you are trying to prove your knowledge of a particular area. Avoid pat phrases like "organizational skills" or "team player." Usually, the keywords you need to get your resume noticed are in the desired job description. Here is a sample objective:

Web management position encompassing marketing, design, development, and programming using Web 2.0 technologies including .NET, AJAX, J2EE, WebLogic, and traditional HTML and JavaScript.

Qualifications: The "Q" in You

Now that you have an objective, you can focus on the more nitty-gritty aspects of your chosen field. Here's another resume writing mantra for you to repeat: "I can get any job I can describe—as long as I can describe it well." The rest of this chapter explains the all-important skill of writing good qualification summaries that articulate and support your career goal. Qualifications are critical. In your work (or education or volunteer commitments), you have probably performed the very functions prospective employers are looking for.

FACT

> E-resumes are often analyzed electronically with database keyword searches. The more of these keywords you use, the more likely it is that your resume will make the cut. You can make a good start at figuring out the keywords in your chosen field by visiting any of the big online job boards, like *www.monster.com*, or *www.careerbuilder.com*.

Thinking about past achievements makes you take one step back so you can take two steps forward. Summaries of qualifications talk about the past, but they project your abilities and goals into the future. Plenty of your achievements are relevant to your goals. To decide which are important enough to include on your resume, think like a knowledgeable member of your target audience. From this perspective, you can see the criteria that will qualify you for the job. If the field is veterinary science, for instance, your volunteer work in the local 4-H Club teaching kids how to care for their livestock would count as a qualification. Review your achievements from a field-oriented perspective as outlined in the following section.

Bringing Out the "Q"

Take out three pieces of paper. Title each as follows:

- Employment Achievements
- Service Achievements
- Educational Achievements

Starting from the present and working back in time, list your achievements in each category using the following guidelines:

- Note when you accomplished this achievement, including month and year.
- For the employment category, think about full-time and part-time jobs, internships, and other project-by-project roles.
- The service category should include volunteer work and memberships in service organizations. In the education category, in addition to degrees earned, note important papers, publications, fellowships, or other awards of excellence.
- Think in particular about leadership roles you might have had. The proven ability to lead is an important achievement in any category.
- Name your title, if you had one. Be specific about the context of your achievement (were you an undergraduate when your paper was published or a busy grad student?).
- Phrasing should be brief. Edit later for style and to make your descriptions active.

When you finish, your three pages will list past achievements under each heading. But the lists on their own don't make for a thorough inventory, and it's an inventory you're after. The next step is to analyze your past by making a self-inventory.

Making a Self-Inventory

Take out a fourth piece of paper. Title it "Most Significant Outcomes and Accomplishments." Review the achievements you listed on your three earlier pages, and pick the ten that were most significant. Add them to this final page, and include the outcome that resulted from each one. For instance, perhaps one of your achievements was learning about HTML through a training program. A related outcome might be being asked to assist with modifications to your organization's web site.

Finally, transform these accomplishments into bullet points using an active, outcome-focused style (discussed in the following section and illustrated in the following samples). Refer to the samples for inspiration, if necessary. You can use these bullet points on your resume (under headlines like "Experience," "Community Service," and "Education"), or, with a little more work, you can transform them into your qualification summary.

Action Verbs and Action Statements

The following lists include action verbs and sample statements for describing qualifications. Boldface is used in the sample statements for emphasis, but it should not be used this way in your resume.

ESSENTIAL

Most keyword searches scan for achievement-focused nouns in addition to action verbs. Those might include the names of software applications, new technology, industry specific phrases, specialized techniques, conceptual models, or analytical tools.

Action Verbs			
Achieved	Adapted	Adjusted	Administered
Advised	Advocated	Affirmed	Analyzed
Applied	Appraised	Approved	Assessed
Assisted	Attached	Attained	Authorized
Balanced	Branded	Built	Chose
Classified	Combined	Communicated	Conceived
Condensed	Confirmed	Consolidated	Consulted

Action Verbs			
Controlled	Converted	Coordinated	Counseled
Created	Delegated	Delivered	Demonstrated
Derived	Described	Designated	Designed
Developed	Directed	Disclosed	Discovered
Displayed	Distributed	Documented	Drafted
Educated	Eliminated	Empowered	Encouraged
Engaged	Established	Estimated	Evaluated
Examined	Executed	Expanded	Extended
Formulated	Governed	Guaranteed	Guided
Highlighted	Implemented	Imposed	Improved
Increased	Initiated	Instructed	Interpreted
Introduced	Investigated	Joined	Justified
Lectured	Listened	Maintained	Managed
Measured	Minimized	Modified	Monitored
Motivated	Negotiated	Noted	Observed
Obtained	Operated	Organized	Planned
Produced	Programmed	Recommended	Reduced
Regulated	Reorganized	Reported	Represented
Researched	Responded	Revised	Solved
Strengthened	Studied	Supervised	Surpassed
Taught	Tested	Tracked	Trained
Transformed	Transmitted	Uncovered	Unified
Updated	Verified	Won	Wrote

Statements

- **Analyzed** procedures to **assess** overall efficiency and monitor outcomes relative to goals for Quality Assurance and Quality Control.

- **Assessed** proposals to determine accuracy of financial projections and prioritize strategies.

- **Applied** theories to research data, generated hypotheses, **analyzed** data, and then presented trends via written and oral reports.

- **Built** and **tested** actual and virtual prototype model of bridge and off-ramp.

- **Conceived**, **implemented**, and **improved** promotional campaign using web, direct mail, posters, and print media strategies.

- **Coordinated** the activities of more than 100 volunteers, focusing on serving approximately 5,000 meals.

- **Designated** specific tasks to individuals, **motivated** maximum performance, and **monitored** outcomes.

- **Described** products and services accurately over the phone, via e-mail, and in written proposals.

- **Evaluated** program effectiveness using predetermined criteria, then cited findings using PowerPoint presentations and written reports.

- **Formulated** and **implemented** questionnaire designed to clarify problem areas and assess attitudes.

- **Guided** families and prospective students, answered questions, and served as spokesperson for the university.[BBL2]**Improved** methods used to register clients, retrieve files, and initiate counseling sessions.

- **Investigated** past strategies, resources, and services to establish and implement improvements.

- **Listened** to concerns of customers and **responded** in ways to maximize loyalty and repeat sales.

- **Managed** time, personnel, and finances efficiently, maximizing impact with minimum resources.

- **Motivated** colleagues to complete program planning, implementation, and evaluation efforts.

- **Organized** projects to ensure accurate completion within existing deadlines.

- **Reported** findings in PowerPoint illustrated presentations and written reports containing charts, graphs, and spreadsheets.

- **Revised** training manual, including role-play interviews, interactive scripts, and inspirational quotes.

- **Simplified** client greeting and payment procedures to expedite check-in process.

- **Taught** new paralegals to use LexisNexis and other computerized search systems.

- **Trained** peer career advisors to greet students, conduct quick assessments, and address residence needs.

- **Verified** effectiveness of promotional strategies via attendance profiling and attitude questionnaires.

Back to the Future

With your inventory of significant accomplishments in front of you, it's time to create a timeline to link those past achievements to the present and on into the future, where your desired job awaits. Your significant accomplishments don't only belong to the past. They were significant because you made changes. Like a stone dropped in a still pond, the effects of your work create a ripple effect of energy that keeps moving, long after the stone has left your hand.

Your goal is to create a resume that, at a glance, gives a potential employer a powerful picture of your job worthiness. You do that in steps:

- A clear statement of objectives targets your resume.
- A summary of past achievements tells your employer about your abilities and qualifications.
- A description of outcome tells your employer about the continuing impact of your achievements.

You can see that it makes sense to talk about outcome. Your next employer is going to hire you as an outcome of your previous achievements and when you make outcome a theme of your resume, you help that employer think of a future that has you in it. That's exactly what you want your resume to do.

The following examples are taken from the action-verb statements, with outcomes in boldface. Review the examples to see how you might convey your achievements through the use of action verbs. Take a close look to see how an outcome description can add impact to your choose to proceed, ultimately lead to offers. Once you receive an offer, you will have the power to accept or decline; then and only then are you actually making a commitment.

ESSENTIAL

They say the eyes are the windows to the soul. Your resume, with its clearly stated objectives and qualification summary, is your prospective employer's window into your job goals. A resume allows you to display your assets; it also gives others a way of learning about your capabilities and interests. Don't underestimate the two-way powers of targeted resumes.

Create your resume as a Microsoft Word document. This will make it easy for you to share electronic copies, whether by uploading or by e-mail. Spell check your resume every time you make revisions. The grammar checking tool can be helpful, but remember that in resume style, you are allowed to use sentence fragments. You also commonly leave out personal pronouns (such as "I") and articles (the, a, an).

As you write, stay focused on the aspects of yourself that you want to present. Don't fall into the trap of trying to please some potential employer.

When you write your resume, and even when you send it out in application for certain jobs, you are not committing yourself to any field or job function. You might consider this a way of conducting research about the fields you are most qualified for. Any response you get from your resumes will tell you how professionals already working in that field judge your qualifications. If a resume lands you an interview, you can consider yourself a qualified candidate in that field for that position. This is important feedback for anyone just entering the job market who is unsure of how their talents and experience can be valuable. It's also good feedback for the job seeker who cannot decide on any one field. Often, the most attractive field is the one where others consider you an asset.

ALERT

Twenty-seven percent of human resources managers report receiving more than fifty resumes on average for each open position. More than one in ten (13 percent) say they receive more than one hundred resumes per opening. When evaluating resumes, these same HR managers indicate that *relevant experience* is the most sought-after consideration.

You are free to submit all the resumes you like and to take any interview offered you. But you should only accept an offer if you are prepared to take the job; in other words, research into that particular position ends when and if you are made an offer. If you cannot commit yourself to performing those job duties to the best of your ability, thank the employer for their consideration and graciously decline their offer of employment.

Special Issues for Special Circumstances

You can overcome limited experience by learning as much as you can about your target fields and functions. Research is key. It's difficult to take one logistical step back before taking two forward, but this is in many cases the best approach. Take the time you need to create very detailed qualification summaries and supporting correspondence that shows how much you really do know, whether your knowledge comes from on-the-job experience, school, volunteer work, or other means. Use the correct terminology to show your familiarity with the field.

This advice holds true for recent graduates, those preparing for graduation, people in the middle of a big career change, and for undergraduates looking for part-time job internships. Focus on making your resume show how much you do know, and don't worry about what you don't. Use your academic achievements to represent the experience you've gained in your field. Take the time to write a clear statement of your job objectives. Follow that up with a carefully crafted qualification summary, and you will have created a powerful resume.

ESSENTIAL

If you choose to include your volunteer work with your paid work experiences to save space and make your work history more continuous, make sure to title the section "Experience," rather than "Employment Background" or "Professional Experience."

Resumes for recent graduates must clearly project their goal-focused qualifications. If you wish, create and use one multipurpose and several targeted versions of your resume. But don't allow fear of focus to diffuse your goals or strategies. A job search can be frustrating. Don't lose the focus that you need to present yourself as a talented, committed employee. Continue to assess your strategies, and enhance your competencies when needed. It's amazing how one or two goal-specific courses taken at a local community college, in addition to a subscription to a field-focused professional or trade journal, can reignite a somewhat passive, if not dormant, job search campaign. Keep track of whom you contact in your job search. Follow up, then follow up again.

People in the underexperienced category of job seekers usually have an excellent record of success, yet they can be the most frustrated and easily overcome by self-doubt. A powerful, targeted resume is a sign to yourself and others that you are engaged in a serious job search. It is powerful as a direct contact tool and as a means of networking. Use it with pride.

Putting It All Together

Whenever possible, you should create or update your own resume, or at least attempt to do so. You will need to edit and revise until you are satisfied. It should read well to you, as well as to others whose judgment you trust. However, if you are not confident in your final version, or if the resume you have created does not generate interviews, a professional resume writer may help to increase your chances of success.

Working with a Resume Professional

The key to working with a good resume writer or resume service is finding someone whose finished product—your resume—positively reflects who you are in a way that you can also communicate verbally. A good resume can open doors, but you still have to go on the interview yourself. In other words, even if you outsource the writing of your resume to someone else, you still need to be able to articulate your experience and background as it appears on your resume on your own. A good resume writer will understand this concept.

The time needed for the finished product and the overall cost of working with a resume professional often depends on your work experience, career, marketplace, and other personal factors. Typically, you will help the writer by providing information on worksheets and via one-on-one communication, sometimes in person, online, or by telephone. Most writers provide a final resume in a digital file saved in Microsoft Word format that you can print and/or update as needed.

How can you find someone to do this job? There are two major reputable associations in this field. Check out The National Resume Writers' Association (*www.thenrwa.com*) and the Professional Association of Resume Writers & Career Coaches (*www.parw.com*). Both groups provide membership information to help you find the specialist that is best for you. A few things to consider in choosing your resume writer include:

- **Credentials:** how did this person become a Resume Writer? Does he or she have an employment background? What is their success rate? Ask for references and review samples before making a commitment. A great way to find a resume writing professional is often by referral, so ask around or call a staffing service and see if they can make a recommendation for you.

- **Methodology:** ask about the process. How will the two of you accomplish your goal? What will you be required to do?
- **Chemistry:** are you comfortable working with this person? This is a collaborative process. Do not work with someone who treats you condescendingly, displays poor customer service, or appears unprofessional.
- **Product:** ask about the end product. What will you receive? What format will your resume be in? Can you make changes or updates yourself, or does the resume writer require you to work only through them?
- **Delivery and Price:** Fees vary widely, but you should be quoted a price based on your experience and needs. Prices generally range from $150 to $1,000 and turnaround time is usually a week or more.

Take the time to carefully consider whether this individual is the right one to work with you to develop your resume. You are, after all, delegating a very important task!

Your Resume Checklist

Here is an actual step-by-step review of what you must do to create or update your resume today. This list simplifies the actions outlined and clarified previously. Have your legal pad or, better, your laptop or desktop computer ready. You should soon be writing or typing, not just thinking. The time for action is here. Without delay, you should be able to create or update your resume in less than a day.

❏ Identify at least two sample resumes to model.
❏ Reflect upon how and when these samples presented their information. Create a draft listing of headlines you might use, in the order you want them to appear.
❏ Concisely state your job search goal as it will appear in a statement of objectives or as the headline of a qualification summary.
❏ With this goal in mind, make a list of significant related accomplishments.

- Review significant related accomplishments to link past accomplishments with future potential via a qualification summary. It is recommended that you actually draft your entire resume, including the objective, before you take on this task. No matter whether this section is presented first or last, this section should be your last, most important, and perhaps, lengthiest, task.
- With model resumes in view, type a draft of your version. Don't think, just type. Later, you will complete self-critiquing and copyediting.
- Conduct software-linked spell checking and grammar reviews. Have someone else review for typos. Format questions, then make revisions and complete the final version. While you should respect comments of colleagues and friends, remain confident that you are the best and ultimate judge regarding what should appear in your resume and how it should be presented.
- Draft and finalize your cover letter. Distribute your resume. The time it takes to complete this step will depend on whether you e-mail your resume or deliver it by hand.

FACT

Sixty-three percent of human resources managers surveyed in a resume poll reported that *spelling errors* are the most annoying mistakes they see. Other gaffes include:

- Resumes that don't fit the position (30 percent)
- Lies (23 percent)
- Resumes that are more than two pages long (21 percent)

Remember, sending resumes is only one of the eight steps to job search success. These powerful pages must be used as part of a comprehensive strategy. You will use your resume to get interviews, and you will use it during your interviews. You will get offers and make good decisions. In behavioral and motivational terms, it's the person, not the page, that succeeds.

CHAPTER 5

Your Web Resume

"Recruiting" these days could just as easily be called "e-cruiting." It wasn't long ago that everybody mailed all their resumes through the U.S. Postal Service. Now we almost always e-mail them, send them as attachments, post them to a job board or website, or upload them into resume banks. It is vital to know how to create a resume suitable for the technology that dominates today's job market.

Resumes for the Internet

Electronic resumes are essential to the modern job search. For applicants the ability to submit resumes electronically represents both benefits and a few drawbacks. The big benefit is the speed at which your resumes can be received by the organizations in which you're interested. The big drawback is that, because electronic resumes are often first "viewed" by computers and not people, it can be difficult to break through electronic barriers to get your resume in front of a real person. In addition, a resume must be capable of being transmitted electronically so the reviewer can open it easily without jeopardizing your content or layout. After that, the concern is, as usual, with quality. The aim is to present yourself efficiently, so that no matter who (or what, in the case of a database search engine) opens your resume, it is clear that you are goal-oriented and qualified for the job.

Uploading Your Web Resume

Many potential employers use the Internet to list their job postings. Some use their own corporate websites. Many also use targeted recruiting sites that organize and display an employer's opening or advertisement and also make sure qualified applicants are brought to the employer's attention.

The process of uploading a resume from your personal computer is simple. Websites walk job seekers through the process step-by-step. The process may vary a little, but in all cases you are using your Internet connection to send the electronic file containing your resume directly to an employer or to the job board's online job bank.

File Format for the Web Resume

Uploading is easy, and it is a very effective way of making your resume easily available to many potential employers. However, the electronic file that contains your resume must be in the correct format. Your uploaded resume is useless if the database can't store it or your recipient can't open and read it.

All online job banks specify the file format you should use. Some common formats include:

- **Microsoft Word.** Almost everyone in almost all professional fields uses Microsoft Word. This is the application most preferred by hiring companies and job boards. If you create your resume using another software application, see if your software has the option to save your file as a Word document. One of the problems with Word formats is that the original formatting is not always maintained, resulting in "weird" symbols or spacing issues.
- **PDF.** This format is also very common on the web as PDFs cannot be edited or altered, making them a good way of keeping your content exactly as you created it. PDF files retain the formatting of the original file and they tend not to be corrupted in their travels across the Internet. You can create a PDF from almost any file format.
- **Webpage input.** Some job banks ask you to create a resume by filling in the fields of a resume form. In this case, you are not really uploading a file at all. The information you enter into the various fields is saved directly into the job banks database. Here, instead of storing resume files, this database contains the information directly.

No matter what format you use, you should do the following before uploading your file:

1. Make sure your resume file can be opened, and that it is formatted correctly. Word files can be corrupted, and when you change a Word file into a PDF, the change can substitute fonts and change things like font size or margins. Do not assume that just because you saved the file or created the PDF that it will meet your requirements.
2. Name your file correctly. Check the requirements of the job bank: They might have a system for naming files. In general, your filename should be short and descriptive. For instance: Your Name: Position.
3. If you are filling in a webform, take your time entering your information in the fields. Here, keywords, discussed in the following section,

are essential. You might need to edit your resume, aiming to keep things short while using as many keywords as possible.

4. Test it yourself. E-mail your resume to several friends or family members and ask them how it looks on screen and ask for a sample printed version to review yourself.

It's important to consider how your resume will ultimately be viewed. While technology provides us with many benefits, it can also throw curveballs your way. Take the time to ensure that what your prospective employer sees is what you intended them to see!

Search Engine Optimization Keywords

Many job seekers upload their resumes to job banks or job boards. These are true web resumes, sometimes referred to as e-resumes. The potential employer only sees this electronic version, only printing a paper version at his or her own option. Often, before any human being lays eyes on these web resumes, they are subject to review by a search engine that is loaded with certain keywords that the employer has defined as critical to any applicant's qualifications. Called SEO keywords (SEO meaning Search Engine Optimization), these words are "highlighted" by the search engine as being relevant to the position and more likely to get your resume to the top of the heap. This is where the challenge lies for job seekers.

Regardless of your abilities, if your qualification summaries or general content do not use these keywords, it is likely that you'll never make even the first cut. Consequently, it is very important that you pay close attention to the words and phrases that the organization uses in describing the position. And, most importantly, you need to incorporate these words and phrases into the copy you submit.

In addition, here is where your own research pays off. In defining your goals and drafting your resume, you learned the terms and phrases used in your chosen field. When possible, in your statement of objectives, you should name a particular title or use specific words and phrases that you know are used in your field. The verbs you use to describe your qualifications and experience should mirror those terms as closely as possible.

Here are two statements of objectives that could be used for the same resume. Which one do you think would be most likely to result in the more fruitful keyword search?

- Objective: Position designing logos and graphics for state-of-the-art websites.
- Objective: Position as Web Designer for software design firm, using skills in XML, DTML, streaming video, Flash animation, Oracle database design, and website maintenance.

Chances are, the second one will be of more help when it comes to getting your resume noticed. The more specific you can be with the use of words and phrases that mirror the requirements of the industry, the position, and the employer, the more likely your submission will be viewed as a match.

It is most likely that you are uploading your resume into a job bank in answer to a specific job posting. The smartest thing to do, therefore, is to compare the job description to your resume. Does your resume, particularly your qualification summary section, contain the keywords, terms, and phrases used in the job description? If this job description is short or vague, search the web for other descriptions of similar jobs. You will notice that they use a common vocabulary to define job functions and desired qualifications.

ESSENTIAL

Check the rules of the online job boards. Most allow you to regularly update your resumes. When you do an update, take the time to upload it so all potential employers always see the best and most accurate depiction of your job skills.

How Keyword Logic Works

It can be helpful to understand how keyword logic works and how the computer "looks" at your resume and decides (as a human would in the "old days") whether to pass it along to the hiring managers or HR professionals in the organization). Get it right and you'll move on to the next round of review. Get it wrong and real people will probably never see your resume.

A key point to keep in mind is that computers are much more "logical" than humans, which means that there won't be any interpretation of what you write. The computer will use algorithms to evaluate whether your resume is a fit. Based on that analysis your resume will be compared to the other resumes received and those that rise to the top will be forwarded on to a person in the organization.

Again, the job description provides initial clues as to the important keywords and phrases that are most relevant. These keywords and phrases will be matched to what you submit and the frequency of their use will also be evaluated. The computer will look for partial and completely matched keywords and then assign a rank based on the number of matches and their frequency.

There is no doubt that the increasing use of technology to ease the burden of hiring managers and HR managers of reviewing resumes themselves has benefited organizations in terms of efficiency. However, it is arguable whether this same technology might result in missed opportunities for both job candidates and employers. Regardless, if you find yourself submitting material online through these systems, it is very important that you understand the appropriate use of keywords to boost the chances that your resume will make the cut.

Keep an Inventory of Keywords

As you continue to search out new job postings, you will learn new industry specific ways of phrasing your qualifications and summaries. Rather than rewriting your resume every time you find a new, more appropriate term, keep a list and then update your resume when you have a collection of these terms. In this way, your update will not only be more efficient in terms of time, but you may come up with better ways of phrasing whole sections, instead of changing a word at a time.

Sample Web Resume

The following sample resume was specifically formatted and written for digital presentation.

Common elements of most successful web resumes include the following:

- E-friendly fonts
- Left-justified block text formatting, with minimal tabs or columns
- Detailed, comprehensive qualifications summaries containing key phrases and industry specific vocabulary
- Ability to be cut and pasted into e-mails or the fields of web-based forms

While a print resume and a web resume may differ, very often they are now one and the same. Acceptable formatting and technology have caught up with one another and employers now typically print a web resume as a candidate's official resume. Generally, it is a Microsoft Word document.

Advertising Account Executive Web Resume

CHRIS SMITH
123 Main Street, Hometown, NY 00000, (555) 555-1234, csmith@company.com

ADVERTISING ACCOUNT MANAGEMENT QUALIFICATIONS
Marketing research, strategic planning, promotions, customer service, and sales talents nurtured by in-depth and diverse advertising, promotions, retail internships, and employment. Technical skills gained via courses including: Principles of Marketing, Marketing Projects and Cases, Psychology of Human Motivation and Emotion, Business Administration, Public Relations Writing, Advertising, Mass Media, Persuasion, and Consumer Behavior. Confidence serving on account team and interacting with client colleagues. Special interest in using and enhancing talents associated with market research, segmentation, demographic and media planning, business forecasting, break-even analysis, product strategy development, pricing analysis, financial planning, and publicity concept creation. Capacities to understand four Cs: context, company, consumer analysis, and competitor analysis; and the five Ps: people, product, price, place/distribution, and promotion. French, Dutch, and Farsi fluency, and conversational Spanish capabilities. Word, Excel, PowerPoint, Quark, PhotoShop, and Internet skills.

ADVERTISING AND MARKETING EXPERIENCE
DAYS ADVERTISING, INC., Pittsford, NY
Account Management Intern: Assisted with design of television and radio ads and proposals for varied clients, including Wegmans and Bausch & Lomb. Summer 2011

ADEFFECTS, Rochester, NY
Account Management Intern: Researched and developed promotional materials for retail, manufacturing, and restaurant clients. Suggested changes in advertising materials, consumer outreach strategies, and marketing literature. May 2010–July 2011

PEARLE VISION CENTER, Pittsford, NY
Sales Representative, Summer 2011

IT HAPPENS, Antwerp, Belgium
Marketing Intern: Determined target markets and developed advertising budget for concert, event planning, and entertainment agency. Conducted and analyzed surveys to determine market penetration. Assisted artists with ads, posters, and brochures. Summer 2008

BUSINESS, ECONOMICS, AND LANGUAGE STUDIES
UNIVERSITY OF ROCHESTER, Rochester, NY
Bachelor of Arts, French, with a major GPA of 3.5, May 2010
Bachelor of Arts, Psychology, with a major GPA of 3.3, May 2010
Minor: Economics, with a minor GPA of 3.4
Management Studies Certificate, Marketing and Finance/Accounting Tracks, May 2010

FINANCE EXPERIENCE
THE FINANCIAL GROUP, INC. DISCOUNT BROKERAGE FIRM, Pittsford, NY
Operations Management Intern, January–May 2010

E-mailing Your Web Resume

Some job postings ask you to e-mail your resume directly to a contact person. The process here is very simple: Your e-mail message is your cover letter, and your resume should be included as a file attachment. An e-mail cover letter should be short and direct. The first line should state your purpose ("I am writing in response to your posting for an experienced Web Designer"). Any subsequent text should state your qualifications bluntly ("I have five years of freelance experience designing websites for independent movie studios, sometimes using GoLive and Adobe Design software but mostly writing my own code to incorporate movie clips and other complex elements").

The simplicity of email communication doesn't mean that you should treat this process casually. Details matter!

QUESTION

How much information should I include in my e-mail?
It's a good idea to say what made you respond to this posting ("I use links to your site to give our own web visitors access to real-time industry news, and I would love the opportunity to work for you"). E-mails are quick and informal by nature. You know from experience that an overwritten e-mail is hard to read. Be polite, but don't be stuffy and be specific so that the recipient knows that your e-mail is not generic.

E-mail Etiquette

When sending your resume via e-mail, the question of file formats is particularly important. Pay attention to the stated format requirements, and do not bother submitting a resume that doesn't meet them. You may think PDF is much better than Word, but if Word is what the contact person requests, he or she will not appreciate your substitution and it immediately signifies that you don't take direction well.

The common question with an e-mailed file of any kind is whether the recipient received it in a legible form. If your resume file is huge, with graphics or other special features, it will take a long time to transmit and to open.

Nobody appreciates being made to wait, so for e-mailed resumes, it's a good idea to keep things very simple.

Addressing the E-mail

Job postings often ask you to reference a job number in your subject line. Be sure you include this information, as it is unlikely that your e-mail (or resume) will reach its destination without it. In addition, most job postings include a link to the contact person's e-mail. All you have to do to address your e-mail properly is to click on the link. You must also use a personal address, however, in your cover e-mail. Online job postings are notorious for giving little to no information about the contact person. Sometimes all you have is an e-mail address and no name at all. Use whatever information you have. If you don't have a contact name, start the letter immediately after the address, using no salutation at all.

Web-Based Research and Job Search

The web is full of all the information you could ever need to know about your chosen career. Chances are that your dream job is out there somewhere, too. If only you could find it.

In doing research on the web, it's best to start with what you know. It doesn't matter whether you start off in the exact right place. The web is a job seeker's paradise because it is so easy to follow any trail in whatever direction you choose. Here's an example. We'll let our web designer friend Chris Smith take a quick look around the Internet to see what's happening in the working world.

1. Chris is just beginning a job search, so he starts at his favorite all-purpose search engine (we'll say that's *www.google.com*).

2. Chris types in his chosen job title, "web designer," in the search field and narrows the search just a little by adding "employment."

3. Google returns nearly 2 million websites that are related somehow to the phrase "web designer employment." Some of these sites belong to other web designers looking for employment. Chris ignores these for now, although later they might be a good way of networking with others in his field. He wants actual job postings and doesn't have to look very hard to find them. The second listing on the page lists a job board specializing in web designer and other graphic oriented opportunities. These are sometimes known as "niche job boards."

4. In the next five minutes, Chris finds the following information, just by clicking links that look promising:

   - Dozens of job postings for web designers, containing plenty of keywords.
   - Several big job boards or niche sites specific to graphics and web professionals. These contain not only job postings for web designers, they give Chris an idea of which companies are hiring, what industries in his part of the country are seeking web designers, and what qualifications employers currently expect.
   - Salary information. Some job postings include a salary range. But these are not often reliable, so Chris clicks around a little and finds salary statistics on an employment-related government website, as well as on salary sites.
   - Sites of individual companies with pages devoted to current openings, all with contact people listed.
   - Online forums and blogs maintained by people just like himself, experienced web designers of all kinds. Their discussions cover topics ranging from "Freelance Survival" to "Making It Big in the Corporate World."

These are the results of a real web search, using these keywords, conducted during a quick coffee break. As you can imagine, the real key to getting useful information from the web is knowing when to stop. Five minutes can easily yield more information than anyone could use in a week as one page links quickly to another. The web is a huge, chaotic haystack of information, but as long as you don't worry yourself about hunting for one needle in particular, you'll find more info there than you can possibly use.

Vistas for a Web-Based Job Search

Here are a few avenues for beginning your online job search:

- Check with your local librarian to see whether your state or geographic region sponsors a job bank or whether individual listings can be found online.
- Check the websites of companies in your chosen field or marketplace.
- Use a search engine to visit the three current major job boards: *www.indeed.com, www.monster.com*, and *www.careerbuilder.com*.

Your local newspaper may also list its help wanted ads online. Online listings are usually much easier to search than the printed version. Also, ads often include a link to the company's website, where other suitable postings may be found.

Reactive and Proactive Web Strategies

It is easy to think of the web as a giant fishing pond. You as the job seeker have a certain kind of bait on your pole, and you dangle your line in hope that the right fish is out there, waiting to bite. This is a reactive job search strategy, where, as a job seeker, you react to postings and try to model yourself as the best candidate for the job. Sometimes that's all it takes, but a truly effective job search campaign incorporates proactive techniques as well.

You have already begun using the web in a proactive manner. When you research your chosen field, for instance, to find the websites of the top companies, you are engaging in proactive research. Maybe the company you would most like to work for has several postings that are close to what you're looking for, but nothing that you feel qualified to apply for. You plan to keep checking back, but in the meantime, why not write a quick e-mail to the contact person listed for that job. Tell him or her of your interest. Explain briefly how you believe you could be a real asset to the company. Close by saying you will keep in touch, and do it.

Another proactive technique on the employment e-frontier is a twist on our old favorite, networking. Online forums and bloggers cover almost any topic imaginable. They are easy enough to search out (try Yahoo!'s e-group listing, at *http://groups.yahoo.com*) and to join. You may not get any job offers, but you are likely to learn a lot about your chosen field and the function you hope to perform in it.

FACT

The 2012 User's Choice Awards, compiled from an online poll by the Internet Recruitment site, *www.weddles.com* named thirty favorite job boards as chosen by job seekers and recruiters. Among them *www.careerbuilder.com*, *www.flexjobs.com*, *www.indeed.com*, *www.military hire.com*, *www.net-temps.com*, and *www.topusajobs.com* (see list of additional career websites in Appendix B).

Job Board Giants and Niche Sites

The job seeker who fails to make use of the Internet's most popular job boards and niche sites is doing his or her job search a major disservice. These Internet resources have become a major source of recruiting for almost all employers. A job board is a website that lists job postings by employers and resumes offered by job seekers. Although each site has different methodologies, both the employer and the candidate can identify good prospects based on their need. Some job boards are generic and offer a wide range of employment opportunities by industry, job title, location, and earnings.

Job Board Giants

At the time of this writing, the top two most popular general job board giants continue to be: *www.monster.com* and *www.careerbuilder.com*. Two other popular sites—*www.indeed.com* and *www.simplyhired.com*—are job aggregators. They pull listings from across the web together into one place to make it easy for you to search for jobs based on your areas of interest. There are also a number of niche-related boards that focus on specific types of jobs and careers, so take the time to do an online search to find out what resources may exist in your area of interest. In addition to these you may also have access to job boards through any groups or organizations you may be a member of, or through your alma mater.

Many job seekers choose to set up a search agent at the boards, which means they are regularly e-mailed openings that match a specific criteria according to parameters they set up for themselves. If you see a position that appeals to you, click the link that allows you to reply to the opening and send your resume. Do not rely on the job board or the employer to find you on the site, even if you have a resume posted there. Be proactive and go after the openings that seem the best match for your skills and career goals.

Niche Sites

Niche sites are exactly what they sound like: sites that are devoted to an industry, earning capacity, or geographic region. Some popular niche sites include: *www.healthjobsusa.com*, *www.allretailjobs.com*, *www.hrjobs.org*, and *www.talentzoo.com* (this last one for advertising and media professionals). If you want to make your job search more focused, you might find greater success with the niche boards.

Online Networking

Everyone knows about networking face-to-face. You meet someone, you chat, and you build contacts and learn about employment leads or the names of other people who can assist you with your career goals. Online networking is very proactive and means you actively seek out and introduce yourself to someone who might work at a company you aspire to be part of. You can also seek people with a certain title to learn more about their professional duties or their company and perhaps give you an inside edge on getting your foot in the door at their firm.

Now social networking sites on the Internet are changing how people communicate and gain information about employers and job candidates. Sites such as Facebook and LinkedIn—the two sites most used by both job seekers and recruiters—provide personal webpages and personal and professional information about individuals that can include their job titles and where they work.

Typically, you can join a social networking site on your own, or someone already a part of the network invites you to join. Joining simply means you set up a profile viewable to others who then have the opportunity to contact you as well. Social networking sites that are not business oriented, such as Facebook or Twitter, often showcase an individual's hobbies and lifestyles. Be careful what you include on such sites since many employers now go to these sites to see if a candidate is profiled there. There have even been reports of hiring managers asking candidates to show them their social media sites during the job interview. On some occasions, individuals have included inappropriate photographs or comments that may reflect poorly on their consideration for employment. So watch what you include on such sites, since you do not want to be blind-sided by digital dirt.

FACT

Estimates regarding how many resumes are stored on or transmitted via web-based resources vary. Some believe that the numbers of resumes stored in resume banks and connected to postings via mega job search sites doubled each year over the past five years. While actual totals are difficult to confirm, almost all agree that millions of resumes are stored annually and tens of thousands are transmitted by e-mail daily.

With all of these social media sites you should make sure to:

- Only include information and images that you will be comfortable having potential employers see.
- Think carefully about the information you include to accurately reflect your own personal brand.
- Reach out and make connections that represent your professional interests.
- Connect with the companies and individuals (e.g., recruiters) that you are interested in.
- Use keywords that are related to your areas of career interests to boost the odds that you will come to the attention of job seekers.

Additionally, do yourself a favor and Google your name, or visit *www* *.google.com/images*. Simply type your name into the search engine and see if you or others with your name show up. Also check for images that might be out in cyberspace—you may be surprised. You can remove anything of your own that might jeopardize your search. This also allows you to discover if there are others with your name that might be mistaken for you if an employer goes through this same process. Unfortunately, it can be far more difficult to remove information and images that have been posted and, potentially, shared by others. Social media and social networking have become very powerful tools for job seekers in the twenty-first century, with one site in particular standing out.

Your Resume and LinkedIn

LinkedIn has become the go-to resource for HR professionals and recruiters and having a profile on LinkedIn is a must-have for any job seeker. A profile serves as your online resume, allowing you to list your work experience, educational background, achievements, and interests. Most importantly, it allows recruiters to find you through searches on LinkedIn that will take them to your profile. As when you think about keywords to include in your resume for online use, you should be thinking of and including keywords that others might use when looking for employees with the type of skills, background, and career aspirations that you have when you create your LinkedIn profile.

FACT

While Facebook is the most popular social networking site, with more than 500,000 users around the globe in 2011, its more social nature makes some job seekers uncomfortable using it as a career tool.

An added benefit of having a well-developed profile on LinkedIn is that your LinkedIn profile is likely to come up very high in search results for you on the web. Companies that you're applying to these days are very likely to search for you online. When they do, they'll come across your profile.

You can also search for jobs through LinkedIn. There is a link at the top of the page that allows you to do simple and advanced searches based on the types of jobs you're interested in, geography, etc. Once you've found some jobs you may be interested in, check to see if you have any connections who may be connected to people at those companies. It is that "friend of a friend" capability of LinkedIn that really adds value to your online job search efforts. You can also search for people you may know, but are not yet connected to, through the Companies link at the top of the page.

LinkedIn's basic services are free and, for most job seekers, there will be no need to upgrade the account, although benefits include the ability to reach out to people who are not your personal connections.

Your Resume and Facebook

As hard as it may be to believe, Facebook has only been in existence since 2004. It was founded and launched by Mark Zuckerberg, as a means of connecting college students on the Harvard campus. Today, Facebook is the world's largest social network.

Facebook, like LinkedIn, is free and, as with LinkedIn, you have the ability to set up and begin connecting with others immediately. Primarily a social tool, Facebook lends itself to the sharing of information and images among a group of affiliated people whose network grows exponentially as they begin to connect with "friends of friends of friends."

For your job search it's important to know that "friends of friends" can also include companies. Facebook users can "like" companies that they are interested in monitoring for job opportunities, learn more about those companies and the people who are involved or connected with them, and get a sense (through the postings and images) of the culture and personality of the company.

ESSENTIAL

Don't mix business and pleasure on any of the social networking sites. If need be, consider setting up separate accounts for personal and professional use. You don't want prospective employers to see photos or read posts that reveal too much about your personal interests.

While Facebook emerged initially as a very social site, it has changed over the years since its introduction and does offer some opportunities for job seekers. A new service geared to professional networking called BranchOut was recently added and quickly grew to about 25 million members. Through BranchOut you can find where your friends work and find connections at the companies that you're interested in. Facebook has positioned the service as a competitor to LinkedIn and says it provides "a professional profile for the Facebook generation."

Your Resume and Twitter

While Twitter allows more limited opportunity to brag about your accomplishments through your profile, the popular microblogging service (called micro because your posts must be 140 characters or less) can provide opportunities for networking and is another way to keep tabs on what's happening at employer organizations that you're interested in. By following others in your desired industry you can stay on top of trends and, after you become comfortable in this forum, join the conversation to begin building connections and credibility. Again, though, always keep in mind that what you post reflects on you and may impact potential employers in both positive and negative ways. Twitter's

www.twitjobsearch.com is a search engine designed specifically for twitter to help users quickly learn about job opportunities. Popular searches included "marketing in New York," "pharmacy technician jobs," and "social media assistant." Typically, more than 870,000 new jobs are posted each month.

CHAPTER 6

Job Search Correspondence

You've heard all your life that, "You can't tell a book by its cover." While this may be metaphorically true for some publications and people, it's not the case for resumes. Every piece of communication that you use in your job search makes an impression. That includes your cover letter, any element of an email message you might send, and, of course, your resume itself. This chapter examines the relationships between your resume and the communications that may accompany it.

Always Send a Cover Letter

It's easy to focus too much of your job search attention on resumes, but the cover letter that you send out to prospective employers is just as important. Regardless of the means you use to submit your resume, and regardless of who the person is, *never* send your resume without a cover letter. While a complete letter may not be necessary in all circumstances, at the very least a quick note should accompany your resume, especially if you are sending your resume via e-mail.

Your cover letter represents you. It tells your readers what you most want them to know about you and your goals. Just like your resume, your cover letter mirrors your knowledge of self and your knowledge of the qualification criteria associated with specific positions or functional areas.

In the old days, a standard cover letter asked readers to "assess your candidacy and determine the most appropriate fit." Today, you must quickly and clearly state your goals, briefly present your qualifications, and then refer your reader to the resume. While cover letters are most definitely written for others to read, they are, in many ways, personal tests of your ability to state and support your job search targets. They are the pre-assessment tools that help you make it to the job interview.

ESSENTIAL

Always cover your resume with a letter or a note. If you are told to, "Just send a resume," what you should hear is, "Send a resume and a supplemental document focusing the reader's attention on your desired goals." While you may not actually hear that lengthy phrase, you should always send some form of letter. Resumes should, in good taste, never be naked.

Ideally, every cover letter you send will be addressed to a particular person. "To whom it may concern" or "Sir or Madam" are never appropriate salutations. If you don't know the recipient's name, start the letter immediately following address information, or use a memo format. Correspondence-style or memo-formatted documents can be faxed, e-mailed, or actually mailed. Know your target readers and write accordingly.

E-mailed cover letters can and should be shorter than traditionally mailed cover letters. An e-mail recipient expects correspondence to be brief and to the point. Be sure to note in your subject line something like: Marketing Exec w/10+ years in B2B for Director of Marketing Opening. The body of your message should generate immediate interest by indicating experience and relevant skills. Reference your attached resume. Do not be overly friendly or use any instant messaging abbreviations or smiley faced emoticons.

The best cover letters and resumes can stand alone, soliciting and supporting consideration. Readers can look at either one independently and have enough information to judge your worthiness for an interview. But when they're combined, the impact of the two is much greater. See some sample cover letters at the end of this chapter.

Other Types of Job Search Correspondence

There are many other kinds of letters you will be called upon to write as you progress through your job search campaign. The following sections describe a few of them, and you can find samples of each at the end of this chapter.

Letters of Introduction

A letter of introduction does just what it says; it introduces you and your circumstances to readers. You also clearly identify what you would like the reader to do next and what you will do next. You can seek assistance, specific information, or referrals. Readers are, most often, prospective network members and advocates, or persons who can offer answers to specific questions. They are, less often, potential employers from whom you solicit consideration.

Letters of introduction are most effectively used as research and information-gathering tools. They ask readers to conduct information conversations or for referrals to persons, organizations, or websites that might be of assistance. Always phrase your requests in ways that require more than "yes" or "no" responses. They should inspire readers to forward names, e-mail addresses, phone numbers, websites, or other desired information. In closing, note whether you will "patiently wait for an e-mail response" or "follow-up by phone to discuss your reactions to this request."

Don't ever ignore the power of the brief message you might send through email to introduce the documents you are sending. Effective communication does not always have to be formal nor lengthy. You can first briefly ask for some very specific information, and then follow up with more detailed documentation. In fact, people today may respond better at first to a number of quick e-bites, rather than one lengthy multiparagraph document. While it is always a good idea to attach resumes to any job search letter, you do not have to do so with these briefer messages. Eventually, through follow-up efforts, you will send resumes to everyone you contact. Less formal communications designed to introduce yourself to others are particularly helpful when you utilize social networking websites. They may help you gain critical information or provide entrée to prospective employers of interest.

Letters of Application

A letter of application is a reactive tool used specifically to apply for a posted position. Within this letter, you first state the job title (and number when given), where you saw the posting, and your desire to interview for the position. Later, you support requests for consideration by offering an accurate assessment of your qualifications. These two, or at most three, subsequent paragraphs show readers that you know the field, function, and title in question and that you have thought about what it will take to succeed.

These middle sections are where you very thoroughly share with readers what you learned through inventorying your qualifications and achievements and analyzing your goal-focused competencies and capabilities. This can be done simply by rephrasing your resume's qualification summary. You are the one required to look back, then look forward, and, most importantly, share your confident, future-focused views. After reviewing these paragraphs, readers must sense that you are worthy of an interview.

Be prepared to reflect your knowledge of the job, and use phrases from your resume that reflect upon past achievements, with a preference for those that project knowledge of the future along with words contained in the announcement and from websites and articles written about the firm. Show prospective employers that you have more than the minimum qualifications. Refer to your attached resume, and expand upon the qualification summary. Again and again, the more you talk the talk, the more likely you will walk the walk, down the path toward job search and career success.

Maintain and share your always-improving target vocabulary in letters of application. Through this targeted letter of application, you are applying for a particular job with a specific organization. Give them a clear sense of your focus.

FACT

Career professionals believe that sending your resume directly to a recruiter's inbox is up to twenty times more effective than posting your resume to a job board. Once you've e-mailed your resume to a recruiter, it is perfectly permissible to follow up via e-mail.

For creative fields, including public relations, advertising, and publishing, you can take more creative approaches, but for others, goal-directed, yet formal, phrasing will do. Some jobs allow you to take a more humorous approach, while others may require you to illustrate your abilities to create and send formal business communications. Know your audience, and keep in mind that you can share creativity in follow-up letters, rather than in first contacts.

Whenever possible, close letters of application with a statement like "I will call to confirm receipt of this letter and to discuss the next step." You must remember to follow up initial correspondence with phone calls and, if needed, with e-mails, then phone calls again. Do leave voice mail messages if you don't get through when you call. Don't call too often. Be persistent, yet not obnoxious.

Later in this chapter, samples illustrate a very user-friendly and quick approach to creating effective letters of application.

Letters of Inquiry

A letter of inquiry is a proactive tool, used to inquire regarding current opportunities and, most often, to inspire individualized consideration for future ones. In order to gain consideration, you must reinforce the sense of focus represented in your resume. In fact, the more effective you are at revealing your knowledge of the field, the more likely it is that you will get an interview. Show reviewers that you have done your homework about the field, function, and firm. Ironically, the last is very much the least important.

If readers are impressed with your knowledge of the field and with your abilities to serve within specific functions, you don't need to impress them with your knowledge of their firm. You'll have the opportunity in the interview to show how much you know about the particular organization.

A letter of inquiry is your opportunity to state in very clear terms what field and within what functions you are focusing your search. Ideally, you can cite some commonly used job titles, but they don't have to be specific to any particular organization. Like letters of application, the middle two or, at most, three paragraphs show readers that you have analyzed what it will take to succeed. You support your request for consideration by offering your summary of qualifications.

Address queries like the following:

- Why have you chosen this particular field?
- What does your background have to do with the field and the function you wish to serve within?
- What are the key qualities required to serve within the desired day-to-day roles?

Answer these questions proactively, and you will have the opportunity to answer others reactively, via the phone, or in person, via an interview. Use phrases and vocabulary that are field specific, and you will truly have the chance to talk the talk more and more as you continue to walk the walk on the path to offers and career success.

ESSENTIAL

Some "inquiry and referral notes" can be brief, and followed by a more detailed letter, but you should always be clear regarding the focus you possess. A very brief, three or four sentence expression can close with "a more detailed letter will soon follow" statement, but always include what functions you are interested in.

Some letters of inquiry begin with, "I'm contacting you at the suggestion of (a specific person who is serving as an advocate or network member)." A name recognizable to the reader at the very beginning of your correspondence should ensure that it will be thoroughly read and, hopefully, that an interview will follow. Close all letters of inquiry with, "I will call to confirm receipt." You might also wish to copy your contact person to generate some behind-the-scenes supportive communication. Don't hesitate to identify the option of, "meeting to discuss current opportunities or informally discussing future options."

Networking Requests

Requests for networking assistance should be clear and concise. Not everyone shares a common definition of this term. With a letter, you can seek information about your career biography, advice regarding how to gain consideration within your organization, or referrals to others who can provide information or consideration. At the pre-research (research before job search) stage, you might focus on the first and third requests. When in job search mode, you might focus on the second and third.

When communicating with alumni, family, or friends, do not be vague in your requests. If you want the names and e-mail addresses of specific people, ask for them. If you want to know, "How do I break into your field?" or whether they will forward the attached resume to the right person, ask. Regardless of your request, be appreciative in tone and in words. Be sure you say thank you. Then say it again, for good measure.

To simplify, "networking" involves clearly stating your goals, then asking for specific help of others to attain these goals. These requests can be of persons you know or of those you would like to know. They can follow or be included in letters of introduction to individuals who are at first just names gained via articles, professional association directories, or search engine referrals. As with all communications, the impact will come from follow-up efforts.

Follow-Up Letters

Ideally, everyone you contacted would respond promptly and positively. But, as you know, job search undertakings are most often far from ideal. Effective campaigns involve follow-up communication. While patience is a virtue in some circumstances, it is not a characteristic of a strategic job search. Your challenge is to figure out what to say next and when to say it.

In the cover letter you sent with your original resume you may have indicated your intent to call and confirm receipt of your resume. Now is the time to make the call! Don't expect much out of this exchange. Very few of them will result in any kind of positive response. Most likely, you will leave a message with a receptionist or via voice mail. Do leave voice mail messages. State your name, identify that you sent a cover letter and resume and that you wish to "confirm receipt and, ideally, set up a phone or in-person interview."

You should alternate your communication approaches—phone calls, e-mails, and social media contacts—and be sensitive to how often you are contacting potential employers. Because most resumes today are e-mailed or sent through social media channels like LinkedIn, your initial confirmation call can take place within twenty-four hours. The old, "I will call within a week," standard closing phrase is most definitely passé. If next-day calls get through, that's great. If they lead to interviews, wonderful. Most likely, they will yield a polite, "Please be patient." If you talk to an actual person, ask when you should call back. Then follow the suggested time frame. If you're told next week, don't call before. In general, one contact a week for the first three weeks, then one contact a month after is a good rule of thumb.

FACT

Whenever you make a revision in your resume, you have a good reason to send a brief follow-up letter. Whether it's because you've changed your address, added a new course or seminar, or have seen another posting on a website, after you've updated your resume, send it accompanied by a cover note. Refer quickly to past contacts, yet focus on what is new and directly related to your job objectives on the resume.

You can follow calls with brief telegram-style, follow-up e-mails. A message like the following is appropriate:

"Tried to call today, but could not get through. Understand how busy you are. Just wanted to confirm receipt of resume and cover letter. Can we talk by phone or in person? Thanks."

For the first follow-up contact, you can include another copy of the cover letter and resume. For the following two (maximum) follow-up contacts, you can include just a copy of your resume.

Thank-You Letters

Expressing appreciation is a very effective form of job search communication. While it may sound trite, you can say thank-you at every step along the way. Everyone knows to send a thank-you note after interviews, but too few communicate their gratitude before then. A thanks for confirming receipt of your resume, including an expression of continued interest and a clearly expressed wish for a telephone or a face-to-face interview, is usually the first of these efforts.

A thanks for clarifying status, including an expression of continued interest, with a statement regarding when you might follow up again, is most likely the second. Too often ignored, a thank-you for a rejection letter or e-mail is also appropriate. Respond to a "your background does not match" letter or e-mail with an, "I remain very interested in your firm, hope at a future date my qualifications might be appropriate for other opportunities," statement. Be careful of tone, but do seek continued consideration as well as some additional focus.

Appreciation should always be expressed to network members and advocates who have referred you to postings or persons. By keeping these individuals informed of your efforts, you are subtly, or directly, inspiring their own follow-up efforts. Follow-up calls or e-mails by network members to their contacts, requesting "special consideration," often lead to interviews and speed up an otherwise slow process. In many ways your follow-up networking letters are as important as those to organizations you wish to work for.

Confirmation, Acceptance, and Declining Letters

While it's usually not legally or logistically required, it is a good idea to confirm most activities and decisions in written form. Whether these expressions are transmitted via electronic means or mailed is not important. But it is important that you communicate continually and effectively. The use of e-mails has made this process quicker, easier, and less awkward for most.

You should call or e-mail a few days before each interview to confirm the time and date and to assist with your preparation for this important series of conversations. When making decisions regarding offers, you should continue to communicate enthusiastically. After you have made a decision, you will accept or decline via a brief note, or e-mail.

These continued communications are good habits to get into and they set the scene for future positive interactions. Pre-interview contacts facilitate critical next steps, and post-offer communications impact salary and other discussions. In many cases, they can lead to consideration and offers years from now.

E-mail Versus Snail Mail

Those who remember record albums and rotary telephones also remember that the job search was different in the "olden days." Today, e-mail is the most common and accepted way to send resumes and all follow-up letters. But do not forget that alternating media can diminish the potential for over-saturation and negative consequences and might even give you a competitive advantage for standing out from other job seekers.

"Snail mail" is the phrase used for the slow, but sure (we think) U.S. Postal Service. At one time the only persons who delivered resumes, cover letters, and all other correspondence were the men and women in red, white, and blue. Today we have wearers of the brown (UPS), blue and orange (FedEx), and others who can guarantee delivery in one or two days. Don't ignore the impact of express delivery on specific individuals, particularly those with whom you have spoken over the phone, but remember that e-communication is now the most cost-effective, immediate, and (in this "sad, but true" security sensitive world) safe forms of delivery.

ALERT

If you think recipients may be concerned about virus-carrying e-mails, copy and paste your resume straight into the e-mail text box. Do not identify it as an attachment. Remember to note the title of the job desired and the words "enclosed resume" in the e-mail subject heading.

You can follow some electronically transmitted letters with hard copies, just to be safe and traditional, but do not depend solely on paper, envelopes, and stamps as your job search tools. When you do send items by mail, make sure you have the correct postage. Match your resume and cover letter paper, and use large mailing envelopes so you don't have to fold your contents.

Phone and Fax

These communication and transmission techniques are underused, but not obsolete. With the preferred method of e-mail, fewer people use phone and fax as follow-up tools. You are encouraged to use the phone whenever possible and, when the situation warrants, a faxed resume is acceptable as well. While at first awkward for most, phone skills and confidence enhance with each call. Do call to confirm receipt of documents, to identify next steps, and to make a clear, "Can I schedule an interview?" request. Leave brief, slow, and clear voice mail messages whenever you call. Don't appear to be a pest, but do be persistent and professional.

After you have left a message or two, e-mail a note. Always briefly and clearly state who you are, when and how your earlier contact was made, and what you would like to happen next. Don't be afraid to state, "I would like to meet with you," or more assertively, "I would appreciate an interview." Also, ask if they would like another copy of your resume to refresh their memory regarding your background. It is okay to provide one with the first two follow-up letters, particularly those that are faxed.

Sample Letters

The following samples are offered to share insights into the job search efforts of our fictional friends. Through a longitudinal glimpse at these initial contact and follow-up letters, you should be inspired to create or update effective documentation.

To maximize the effectiveness of your resume and correspondence, make them personal. Whether you are a soon-to-be or recent college grad, an experienced candidate or someone seeking a promotion, the content and style of your communication will impact success. Be inspired by the samples that follow, but make sure the documents you use are perceived as yours and that they clearly connect to your goals. Your written and spoken voice during your job search must sound like you.

Advertising Account Executive Letter of Application

- This letter of application may be used when applying for a web posting or a classified advertisement.

- Addressed to actual contact person. Name gained via company website, then confirmed by phone.

- Document first uses abbreviated qualifications summary from resume to present overall candidacy.

- Second set of bullets paraphrases qualifications in actual ad. These must be changed for each letter of application, depending upon the job and requirements.

- This "copy and paste, then change" technique can be used when applying for almost any posted job. Make sure the specific qualifications highlighted match the position sought and contain keywords used in the posting and within the field. This is crucial for keyword searches associated with web-based resume collections.

- In some cases, the specific qualifications may appear before the general ones.

CHRIS SMITH
123 Main Street • Hometown, NY 00000 • (555) 555-1234 • csmith@company.com

August 23, 20–

Jamie Stenson
Account Supervisor
Saatchi and Saatchi
8765 Broadway
New York, NY 14623-0450
FAX (555) 555-5555

Ms. Stenson:

I would like to interview for an Assistant Account Executive position. Relevant courses in Marketing, Finance, and Accounting, as well as independent marketing projects have enabled me to develop practical skills and perspectives. Knowledge of strategic planning, marketing research, budgeting, advertising techniques, and related report-writing and presentation skills have been fine-tuned in varied settings. In general, I offer:

- Marketing research, strategic planning, promotions, customer service, and sales talents nurtured by in-depth and diverse advertising, promotions, and retail internships and employment.
- Technical skills gained via courses including: Principles of Marketing, Marketing Projects and Cases, Psychology of Human Motivation and Emotion, Business Administration, Public Relations Writing, Advertising, Mass Media, Persuasion, and Consumer Behavior.
- Confidence serving on account team and interacting with client colleagues.
- Blend of research, analysis, writing, and presentation talents.
- Proficiency in Word, Excel, PowerPoint, PhotoShop, and Dreamweaver.

Specific qualifications that match those cited on your website as required include:

- Marketing research, strategic planning, promotions, customer service, and sales talents nurtured in advertising and promotions internships.
- Blend of quantitative, analytical, and creative problem-solving talents.
- Capacities to conduct and analyze research, and then translate data into persuasive proposals, reports, and graphics.
- Intense curiosity regarding consumer behavior, varied products and industries, and the nature of market segmentation.

I graduated from University of Rochester with dual majors, a minor in Economics, and, most significantly, a Certificate in Management Studies in Marketing. As my resume indicates, I have had a number of related internships with local as well as international firms. I would welcome the chance to discuss my qualifications. I will call to confirm receipt of this fax (originals to follow by mail) and, at your convenience, to arrange a brief meeting.

Sincerely,

Chris Smith

Advertising Account Executive Follow-Up E-mail

CHRIS SMITH

123 Main Street • Hometown, NY 00000 • (555) 555-1234 • csmith@company.com

August 23, 20—

Jane Green
Recruiter
jgrecruiter@company.com

As shared with Jamie Stenson via the attached letter, my post-graduation objective is to begin a career in advertising. It is with focus and enthusiasm that I seek to interview for an account management-focused position at Saatchi & Saatchi. After speaking with Ms. Stenson's assistant, Kim, I understand that you coordinate all requests for consideration, and that recent graduates can be considered for internships as well as post-baccalaureate opportunities.

Relevant courses in Marketing, Finance, and Economics, as well as many independent marketing projects, have enabled me to develop practical skills and perspectives. Knowledge of strategic planning, marketing research, budgeting, advertising techniques, and related research, report-writing, and presentation skills have been fine-tuned in varied roles and settings.

As my resume indicates, I have had a number of internships in the past five years. Each has taught me much and nurtured advertising-related skills. I would welcome the chance to discuss my qualifications with you and your Saatchi & Saatchi colleagues as soon as appropriate. I will call to confirm receipt of this e-mail (originals to follow via mail) and, at your convenience, to arrange a telephone or in-person interview.

Trips to New York are easy to arrange. Perhaps we could meet when I am next in the city? I am committed to this field and I will persevere to succeed through job search and beyond. Thank you for your consideration.

Sincerely,

Chris Smith

- E-mail used as initial contact via referral from original communiqué.

- Font as per e-mail setting.

- This follow-up supplements a "letter of inquiry" for general opportunities within a particular field or a "letter of application," in specific application for a posted job.

- The candidate is making first contact with a person whose name has been referred by another.

- E-mail is a quick way to transmit follow-up communiqués.

- Document covers original letter as well as resume. It is copied and pasted into the actual e-mail text box, with other documents sent as attachments.

Letter of Introduction and Networking E-mail

- E-mail introduction sent to initiate networking activities with alumnus.

- Expectations clearly cited.

- Candidate's background only briefly noted.

- Illustrates a "letter of introduction" and a "networking letter," used to gain information and referrals within a particular functional area.

- The candidate is making first contact with a person who might serve as a network member or advocate. Initially, contact was gained through online alumni directory.

- This document seeks specific consideration for a position with the alumnus's firm as well as general referrals.

DANA JOHNSON
123 Main Street • Hometown, NY 00000 • (555) 555-1234 • djohnson@company.com

August 23, 20–

Marty Jones
Account Manager
DDB Needham
mjones@company.com

Mr. Jones:

The advice and support of a University of Rochester alumnus would be much appreciated. My post-graduation objective is to begin a career in advertising. It is with focus and curiosity that I seek to learn about your own career path and, respectfully, request referrals to persons within your firm and other agencies who might grant me an interview.

Through telephone or, if convenient, in-person discussions I would welcome learning about your background to gain insights regarding how I can perhaps enter the field of advertising. Ideally, I would do so as an assistant account executive. Specific suggestions regarding how to network and successfully solicit interviews would be well received.

The attached resume is offered to quickly familiarize you with my background. A more detailed cover letter can follow if you judge my candidacy worthy of consideration by you and your DDB Needham colleagues. As the resume indicates, I have had a number of related internships over the past five years, and my academics have given me strong conceptual foundations upon which I have built field-specific skills. I will call to confirm receipt of this e-mail and, at your convenience, to arrange a phone conversation or a meeting. In advance, thank you for your assistance.

Sincerely,

Dana Johnson

Advertising Account Executive Letter of Inquiry

FRANCIS WILLIAMS
123 Main Street • Hometown, NY 00000 • (555) 555-1234 • fwilliams@company.com

August 23, 20–

Marty Jones
Human Resources Manager
Ogilvy and Mather
123 West 49th Street
New York, NY 14624
FAX (555) 555-5555

Ms. Jones:

I read with great interest your career profile on ZoomInfo.com. If I may be so bold, I would like to interview for an entry-level account management position with O&M. Independent marketing projects, related internships, and relevant courses in Marketing, Finance, and Accounting have enabled me to develop practical skills and hands-on experience in the advertising industry. Knowledge of strategic planning, marketing research, budgeting, advertising techniques, and related report-writing and presentation skills have been fine-tuned in varied settings.

Diverse account management qualifications and capabilities include:

- Marketing research, strategic planning, promotions, customer service, and sales talents nurtured by in-depth and diverse advertising, promotions, and retail internships and employment.
- Technical skills gained via courses including: Principles of Marketing, Marketing Projects and Cases, Psychology of Human Motivation and Emotion, Business Administration, Public Relations Writing, Advertising, Mass Media, Persuasion, and Consumer Behavior.
- Confidence serving on account team and interacting with client colleagues.
- Blend of research, analysis, writing, and presentation talents.
- Knowledge of International Business approaches gained living and working in varied North American, European, and Middle Eastern settings.
- German, French, Dutch, and Farsi fluency, and conversational Spanish capabilities.
- Proficiency in Word, Excel, PowerPoint, PhotoShop, and Dreamweaver.

I graduated from University of Rochester with dual majors, a minor in Economics, and a Certificate in Management Studies in Marketing. As my resume indicates, I have had a number of significant advertising-focused internships. During an interview, I can expand upon internships as well as the above bullets, learn more about the nature of opportunities at Ogilvy & Mather, and support my candidacy for account management-related positions. I will call to follow up this e-mail to see if you will consider an exploratory interview. I will make myself available at your convenience. Thank you.

Sincerely,

Francis Williams

- Times New Roman font and header match resume.
- Recipient was identified on a social networking business site. A good way to network online.
- This illustrates a "letter of inquiry," for general opportunities within a particular field.
- The candidate is making first contact with a person on his "hit list." Initially contacts are identified via directories or websites, and then confirmed through phone conversations.
- This document uses the qualification summary as an easy and effective way to present overall qualifications.
- Letter writing doesn't have to be difficult to be effective. Qualifications highlighted must match positions sought and targeted fields.

Advertising Account Executive Thank-You Note

- This is a simple thank-you note. It was e-mailed immediately following interviews to the recruiter who coordinated a series of meetings. All others involved were named. Additional notes will be sent. It's not important that they all be different. But it is important that they all receive quick positive and appreciative reactions.

- The middle and last paragraphs refer briefly to particular points addressed during their particular meeting. While some use thank-you notes to reinforce qualifications, they can also just be simple expressions of appreciation.

- Also, this note reminds the reader that supplemental materials will soon be forwarded.

Corey Davis
123 Main Street • Hometown, NY 00000 • (555) 555-1234 • cdavis@company.com

September 17, 20—

Jane Green
Recruiter
Saatchi & Saatchi
jg@company.com

Ms. Green:

I appreciate the opportunity I had to share qualifications for an account assistant position. The more people I meet, and the more I learn from enthusiastic professionals like you, Jamie Stenson, and Bill Burton, the more eager I become to join you and your colleagues on the Saatchi & Saatchi team. I do look forward to hearing soon regarding the outcome of the interview. The writing sample we discussed will be forwarded shortly by e-mail.

Thank you again for your time and consideration. I sincerely hope to begin an achievement-filled career with Saatchi & Saatchi. As a dedicated account assistant, I will contribute to the multifaceted research, analysis, campaign development, and client-relations roles associated with this critical area. It was exciting to see how enthusiastic your colleagues were about their particular accounts, particularly those who have Hershey as a client.

As discussed during the interview, I will strive to personify the blend of creative, quantitative, analytical, and communication talents required to add value to the account team, the client, and the firm.

Sincerely,

Corey Davis

Advertising Account Executive Acceptance E-mail

CHRIS SMITH
123 Main Street • Hometown, NY 00000 • (555) 555-5555 • csmith@company.com

September 27, 20–

Jane Green
Recruiter
Saatchi & Saatchi
jg@company.com

Ms. Green:

It is with great pride that I confirm through this e-mail that I accept the account assistant position. I understand that my immediate supervisor will be Bill Burton and that my starting salary will be $35,000 annually. The start date of October 1st seems ideal, and I will visit your office within the next few days to complete all required forms. I am eager to join the Saatchi & Saatchi team and begin an achievement-filled tenure as an account assistant. Ideally, this will mark the beginning of a long and productive career with the firm.

As we discussed after the offer was extended, I do appreciate your agreeing to a performance and salary review after six months, and another one year after my start date. This will allow me to prove my value and hopefully offset the financial burden of my relocation to the New York City area. Of course, the relocation allowance of $1,500 is most generous and will be used appropriately.

My personal thanks go out to you for your efforts throughout all stages of the consideration and interview process. I will see you soon, when I visit to complete paperwork. If you wish to contact me for any reason, please do so via the phone number or e-mail address above.

Sincerely,

Chris Smith

- This e-mail confirms verbal acceptance of an offer. While not a legal document, it does clarify key points. Some employers continue to send formal offer letters, detailing all aspects of compensation and related matters, but not all maintain this practice. Candidates who don't wish to offend by asking for something in writing can send messages like this one.

- It details issues covered in discussions.

- If any questions are raised regarding the details cited, it's best that this occur immediately following receipt of this note. Then clarifications can be immediately addressed.

CHAPTER 7

Resumes as Interview Preparation and Motivation Tools

Somewhere you've read this advice: "Use resumes to get interviews, and interviews to get offers." An even more accurate statement would read: "Use your resume to get interviews *and* during interviews; then you'll definitely get offers." This chapter identifies how to use resumes as both interview preparation and motivation tools.

The Resume, Interview, and You

Never interview without a copy of your resume in your hand, in your heart, and in your head. The interviewer will refer to this document to inspire questions. You can use it to inspire answers as well as attitudes. While it may seem simple and somewhat silly, read the following statement aloud: "As you can see on my resume." Yes, aloud! Listen to yourself saying these seven words. Do so with enthusiasm and confidence. This phrase is the verbal and strategic foundation for planning and maintaining interview communications.

Interview preparation begins with a thorough, job-specific review of your resume. With a job title and job description clearly in mind, develop a list of qualification criteria. Highlight the most relevant experiences on your resume. Identify at least three things on your resume that you must discuss in the interview. Select the bullet points from your qualification summary, accomplishments from your experiences, or educational achievements that you must cover. This is your general review. Later in this chapter, a step-by-step pre-interview regimen takes you through the process in detail.

Your resume should act as a psychological security blanket that nurtures confidence and diminishes anxiety, as well as a guide to the key points to cover. Your resume is not just for the interviewer. It is a preparation and implementation tool for you. To maximize your interview performance, use your resume before your interview to identify and link qualities and accomplishments to the job you are interviewing for. Use the resume during your interview to guide the conversation and ensure that key points were covered.

Your Resume as a Guide for Interview Day

As qualification criteria were used to review resumes and identify whom to interview, these same qualities are the yardsticks by which all interviewers will measure you. To determine your potential to walk the walk to success within a particular job, your interview talk will be heard and analyzed. Those you interview with will be listening for verbal cues that reveal how strongly you match their predetermined criteria. As they listen, they will process what they hear and create an overall impression of your potential to succeed within the specifics of the job.

Focus your thoughts first, and then your statements, on roles and responsibilities of the job. Prospective employers have already identified connections between your resume and their desired and required competencies. All you now need to do is reinforce these resume-linked connections while sharing information on your communication skills as well as your personality style.

ESSENTIAL

Interviews can flow as conversations, but you should figure out ahead of time what key points you want to address. You don't go into academic exams without focusing on specific topics. You don't conduct presentations without some notes or presentation tools. Pre-interview resume review activities focus on topics and provide needed visual cues.

It is easy to use this process-oriented knowledge. Before each interview, create a list of qualification criteria for the position. What specific criteria would be associated with an ideal candidate for the position you will be interviewing for? Identify the basic qualities sought and how one would determine who possesses these traits. Most importantly, use your resume to create a carefully conceived strategy and list of discussion points.

Pre-Interview Resume Review Inventory

Before each interview, complete the following exercise on the back of a resume. This will organize your thoughts, identify what last-minute information needs to be collected, and clarify what to highlight during the discussion. Using these notes, you will be able to focus the interview into a target-specific conversation. Review your notes beforehand, but avoid using them during the interview.

What, When, and Where

Answer the basic questions first. Briefly note the organization and describe the position you will be interviewing for. If you can do it in, let's say,

100 words, you are ready to move on from this exercise. If you cannot, you have some fact-gathering or thinking to do.

If you have not yet reviewed a detailed job description, request a copy and do so. Then summarize what you have read in your own terms. Describe the job as if you were speaking to the fifteen-year-old son or daughter of a friend or neighbor. In this way, you will force yourself to simplify and describe actions and outcomes associated with the job in basic behavioral and functional terms.

Define Qualifications

Second, cite three key points that make you qualified for the position in question. Review your resume's qualification summary section, then identify three of those cited or define broader connections that clearly match qualifications for the position you are interviewing for. In general, you are completing the statements, "Thinking about this job, specifically, my three key assets are . . ." or "Thinking about the job, the three key points I want to raise in the interview include . . ." Ideally, these will match some of the phrasing used on the qualifications criteria list that you have already created for the job. Each of the three bulleted points should be no more than fifty words.

Illustrate Your Abilities

Third, note three anecdotes that illustrate your capabilities to succeed on the job. Stories should support the three key points cited, linking skills used when taking goal-directed actions and, ultimately, to achieve results or finish a project. Start out by very briefly noting the story. Then, identify actions, results, and tasks that were associated with your accomplishments. Last, cite the key skills used and enhanced as a result of each particular experience. Interviewers are particularly interested in problem situations and how you solved them or participated in the resolution process.

Also, list three questions you would like to ask the interviewer. Ask one question in the first five minutes of the interview and another in the second five minutes so that you can use your interviewer's response in the discussion as it progresses. These initial inquiries should focus on day-to-day job responsibilities and on how performance will be judged. Clarifying and confirming shared expectations early in the conversation will ensure that you raise appropriate issues. Often, the answers you receive inspire immediate re-establishing of key points you wish to discuss later. If three questions won't do, prepare a list of additional questions to ask during and at the end of the interview session.

ALERT

While you should definitely prepare for interviews by identifying key points and reviewing typical questions in advance, do not memorize them. Have some anecdotes to share, but don't attempt to deliver previously written soliloquies or word-for-word responses. The oxymoronic phrase "planned spontaneity" describes the best results.

By writing all of the above on the back of your resume, you will have used existing printed text to create new supporting documentation. You will have a handwritten focal point containing well-conceived key points, anecdotes, and employer queries.

Easy Job Search Conversations

Preparation is how you avoid perspiration. By being prepared, you will skillfully facilitate conversation. Conducting pre-interview preparation builds your confidence, provides focus for communication, and enhances outcomes. Too many candidates spend hour after hour researching historical facts and obscure figures associated with an organization, unnecessarily increasing their anxiety. These individuals research companies too much and pay too little attention to their own backgrounds and job descriptions. They don't review resumes, and they limit qualification criteria analysis to a quick perusal of brief, oversimplified job announcements. Here are some easy to follow guidelines for last minute prepping.

Call Ahead

Two or three days before your interview, e-mail or call the employer to confirm your meeting and to request a copy of the job description if it's not already available on the company's website. Offer to stop by to pick up the information or ask if it can be e-mailed or express mailed. Specifically ask this question: Are there questions or issues I should focus on to prepare for our meeting? Imagine how well you can prepare if you receive a list of potential questions or critical issues to examine. You would be surprised how often interviewers will provide this information when asked.

Clarify logistics of the day, particularly for callback interviews arranged after initial telephone or in-person screening discussions. Know how many people you will be seeing and what to expect of your visit. Don't fear stupid questions, including asking for directions; the more information you have, the smarter you will appear on the day of the interview.

Queries can be made by phone. If you can't get through to the appropriate person(s), leave a voice mail message, followed quickly by an e-mail or faxed note, and then, later in the day, by another call. If you start a few days prior to the interview, you have a greater chance of receiving a response.

Conduct Specific Research

Conduct an Internet search or visit a reference librarian, seeking information on the firm and, most importantly, on general current events articles on the field involved. If possible, enter a few keywords into a general search engine or into search options within the company's website. Don't dwell too long on researching the prospective employer. Basic and topical information on the field involved is often much more valuable.

You should be able to discuss industry trends, major players, and what's hot and what's not within the field. While somewhat retro, reference librarians are still competent problem solvers. They thrive on the challenge of locating hard-to-find information under the pressure of a pending deadline. Also, just as a sports fan regularly reads the sports section of the newspaper, don't forget to read the business or related sections of local papers and professional publications.

Do Some Online Networking

A website such as *www.zoominfo.com* or *www.linkedin.com* can lead you to others with the same job title you are interviewing for or the one you desire. If you care to be bold, you might consider e-mailing one of these members to ask for some insight into their position's highlights and challenges. Many people are flattered by this kind of communication, the same way they are flattered to be contacted by a recruiter. This kind of pro-active job searching can give you critical knowledge that will set you apart as the candidate of choice.

Timing Is Everything

Arrive approximately twenty minutes early, check in, and, if you haven't already done so, ask if you can review a copy of the job description as well as literature describing the nature of the organization and significant events of the past year. Sit down in a comfortable area and review your resume and cover letter. It's amazing that most job seekers forget this very simple preparation activity. Think about it. What do interviewers review when determining whom to meet? What do they review immediately before and during the interview? Most definitely, the answer is your resume and cover letter.

ESSENTIAL

Bring a favorite photo with you to relieve any stress. It's hard to stay tense when looking at a smiling face of a friend or beloved pet. You cannot help but calm down a bit by glancing at a picture of someone or something that always makes you feel better. Do this discreetly while you are waiting for your interview, not during the interview.

So, don't forget to review these documents before your interview. Mark critical points or make notes on the back. This one-page personal note sheet can be very effective. Have extra copies of your resume available in case you meet with someone who doesn't have one.

Questions and Answers

Ask two questions within the first ten minutes of the interview, and bring copies of your work to show. Questions should be variations on, "What are the qualities you are seeking for this position?" and "What specific expectations in terms of output and outcomes do you have for the person who holds this job?" This will allow you to gain a greater understanding of the position and reflect qualifications later in the interview. The more you learn early in the conversation, the better. Remember, an interview is simply a conversation with a purpose. It is not an adversarial right or wrong or "the interviewer is out to get me" process. Be enthusiastic, optimistic, and inquisitive.

Put It All Together

Sweaty palms, knotted guts, and beads of sweat are too-frequent physical and psychological symptoms on interview day. But, if you prepare and have the proper attitude, interviews can be fun. When else is it okay to brag and speak about yourself in positive ways for an hour or two? After creating and reviewing your resume, you should be very appropriately egocentric, focusing on you. You're a great candidate, or you would not have been invited to interview. Enjoy the chance to share your pride in your achievements as well as your personal visions of your future.

Two Key Phrases You Must Think or Say

Interviewers constantly use your resume as a point of reference for forming particular questions. You can and should do the same, by stating things like, "As you can see on my resume," or "As my resume illustrates." Refer interviewers to key experiences or education, and use the phrase specifically in advance of anecdotal discussions. Let the interviewer's eyes focus on specific sections, and don't be surprised if they highlight text or take notes while you speak. This key phrase perks interest and invites magnified attention. Use adaptations, or proceed with a simple, "Again," but do refer to your resume regularly. In response to questions, do state aloud or allow your internal voice to focus thoughts on the phrase, "Thinking about the job." These four words will inspire you to connect past achievements and related qualities to job-specific requirements. Find creative ways to restate this phrase. Creatively, you might change it to, "Thinking about your answers to my questions about the job," or "Thinking about the job description." Or, you might refer to your past answers by stating, "Thinking about job-specific issues I addressed earlier." This is a very effective technique.

ESSENTIAL

Consider members of your personal and professional networks who may have experience with interviewing and will be willing to offer you specific and constructive feedback. Even if some of their toughest questions don't come up during the actual interview, you'll find that the preparation makes you feel more relaxed. You will be amazed at how powerful these two simple phrases can be and how using them in various forms can improve your interview skills. At first, do so via role-play interviews. Have someone ask you typical interview questions, and then respond aloud, as you would in an actual interview. This is perhaps the best way to complete final preparation efforts. While the person asking the questions will be playing the role of interviewer, you will remain yourself and answer as you would in a real interview. Be yourself! Don't be the person you think the interviewer wants you to be. Sincerity during the interview will yield honesty based relationships as well as the personality and capability required for on-the-job success.

Common Questions and Universal Themes

Almost every job search resource contains a list of common interview questions. What makes this book unusual is the emphasis it places on using the resume as your foundation for identifying themes to address when answering these and all questions.

Basically, interviewers determine through very special questions and answers whether you have the potential to succeed. Because potential can be a mercurial concept and very difficult to measure, much of the interview process is subjective. No matter how difficult to predict, it is a process that is easy to prepare for. You just have to translate past actions into words and, using appropriate tone, project confidence as well as your knowledge of self and of job-specific qualifications.

Behavioral Interviews

Past behaviors are cited on your resume. Your ability to connect your past to the future and to your desired goal will be the basis upon which your interviewing skills will be judged. In fact, a popular interviewing trend these days is called behavioral interviews. This technique allows interviewers to quantify and objectify a traditionally subjective process. It is based on the principle that states that past behavior is the best predictor of future performance. Moreover, more recent behavior is a better predictor of future performance than older behavior, and trends in behavior are better predictors than isolated incidents.

Interviewers present "what did you do when" scenarios or ask you to identify past incidents when you used certain behaviors to reach a goal. Before the interview, a behavioral interviewer determines the behaviors that are desired. Basically, the interviewer arrives with a pre-established checklist for determining if you have the qualities associated with success in a particular job. Be prepared for this, and don't get rattled by any open-ended questions. Note taking by the interviewer is not unusual, so don't interpret it as negative or positive. Interviewers may seek clarification of or contradiction in your statements by continually probing, so don't become rattled or express frustration.

Behavioral questions include the following:

- Describe what happened when you faced problems at work that tested your coping skills. What did you do?
- Give an example of a time when you could not participate in a discussion or could not finish a task because you did not have enough information.
- Give an example of a time when you had to be relatively quick in coming to a decision.
- Tell me about when you used communication skills in order to get an important point across.
- Tell me about a job experience when you had to speak up and tell others what you thought or felt.
- Give me an example of when you felt you were able to motivate coworkers or subordinates.
- Tell me about an occasion when you conformed to a policy even though you did not agree with it.
- Describe a situation in which it was necessary to be very attentive to and vigilant about your environment.
- Give me an example of a time when you used your fact-finding skills to gain information needed to solve a problem; then tell me how you analyzed the information and came to a decision.

- Tell me about an important goal you've set and tell me about your progress toward reaching this goal.
- Describe the most significant written document, report, or presentation you've completed.
- Give me an example of a time when you had to go above and beyond to get a job done.
- Give me an example of a time when you were able to communicate successfully with another person, even when the individual may not have personally liked you.
- Describe a situation in which you were able to read another person effectively and guide your actions by your understanding of his or her individual needs or values.
- Specifically, what did you do in your last job in order to plan effectively and stay organized?
- Describe the most creative work-related project you have completed.
- Give me an example of a time when you had to analyze another person or a situation in order to be effective in guiding your action or decision.
- What did you do in your last job to contribute toward a teamwork environment? Be specific.
- Give an example of a problem you faced on the job and how you solved it.
- Describe a situation when you positively influenced the actions of others in a desired direction.
- Tell me about a situation in the past year when you dealt with a very upset customer or coworker.
- Describe a situation in which others within your organization depended on you.
- Describe your most recent group effort.
- Describe the most challenging person you've interacted with and how you dealt with him or her.

Behavioral interview questions are very common in today's interviews. In preparation for your interview and for these types of questions, consider what sorts of situations the employer might be interested in assessing you on. Who are the people you are most likely to interact with? What specific challenges might the job hold?

Traditional Interview Questions

During a traditional interview, the interviewer will use your resume as a starting point to ask you for additional information and clarification about your background and experiences.

To maximize your use of this list, after you review the general as well as behavioral queries, identify a top-five list of questions that relate to a specific job matching your goals. Then conduct a practice session, having a friend or family member ask you these questions. Remember, there are no right answers to particular questions. Responses during an interview must seem well conceived, yet spontaneous. Think of this interaction as a conversation, not an inquisition. It is best to complete this exercise aloud, even if you are doing so alone.

- Why are you interested in this particular field of employment?
- What academic or career achievements are you most proud of?
- Why did you choose your major, and how does it relate to your goals?
- What classes did you find most stimulating, and did they nurture job-connected skills?
- What would you like to be doing in five years?
- What are your greatest strengths and weaknesses?
- How would you describe yourself and how would others describe you?
- How would you characterize career-related success?
- What are your three most significant employment or school-related achievements?
- When did you use persuasive skills or sales talents?
- Why should we hire you?
- What are your long-term career goals?
- How have your academic experiences to date prepared you for a career, and what are your future academic goals?
- What would you do differently with regard to academic or career experiences?
- What was your most difficult decision to date, and how did you go about making it?
- Why did you attend your alma mater?

- What do you think it takes to succeed in the job you are being interviewed for?
- What lessons have you learned from your failures or mistakes?
- What are your geographic preferences, and are you willing to relocate?
- What concerns do you have with regard to this job/academic program and our organization/school?
- How would you describe this opportunity to friends and family members?
- What additional information do you need to determine if this is the right opportunity for you?
- What motivated you to first contact us?

Your resume can give you a good indication of the types of questions you may be asked during a traditional interview. Make sure you have reviewed and are thoroughly comfortable with the content of your resume and consider the types of questions you might be asked.

Nontraditional Interview Questions

Some interviewers like to rattle candidates a bit to see how they think on their feet. They may even want to assess whether you have a sense of humor or how creative you can be. While offbeat questions often seem totally irrelevant, some interviewers feel they gain a better sense of the individual by asking someone what their favorite book was as a child or how their clothes closet is organized at home. There really is no right or wrong answer to these wildcard questions, so just be yourself.

- Who would you want to play you in a movie about your life?
- If you could pick someone from history to have dinner with, who would it be?
- If you won the lottery, what would you do next?
- You become shipwrecked on an island. You have food, water, and fire. What other three things would you want to have with you?
- If you were a superhero, what superhuman powers would you have?

No matter the style, whether it's nontraditional, traditional, or behavioral, a review of common questions is extremely helpful. Attempting to memorize answers can do more harm than good, so please use the list to stimulate your thoughts and inspire you to share ideas effectively during interviews. Ask a friend, family member, or peer to select five and ask them aloud, initiating a role-play interview. Hearing the questions as well as your answers, rather than just thinking about responses, is valuable.

Questions You Can Ask Potential Employers

Questions you might ask potential employers during an employment interview or during a pre-interview information conversation include the following:

- How would you describe the job in terms of day-to-day roles and responsibilities?
- What qualities are you seeking in a candidate?
- What type of person would most likely succeed in these roles?
- What kind of performance or production level would exceed your expectations for this position?
- What should I expect of myself over the first few months on the job?
- How will my performance be judged, and by whom?
- Whom should I use as a role model for this position and would it be appropriate to contact this person?
- What characteristics does it take to succeed within this organization and within this position?
- What are the best things about the job and the most challenging requirements of the position?
- Who would have highest expectations of me, or be the one(s) who would be most difficult to impress?
- What is the typical career path and time frame associated with career development?
- How will I be trained, and how can I appropriately seek skills enhancement?
- Who last served in this position, and what is he or she doing now?
- What goals do you have for the person who will serve in this job?
- What project would you expect to be completed first, and what would be involved?

Asking questions of your potential employer reiterates your interest in the open position. It shows you are trying to visualize yourself in this position and determining whether it will be a good fit for you.

Conversations, Not Cross-Examinations

Each interviewer has a personal style, but most interviews can be identified using a few common labels. Many interviews will be conversational or traditional, in which interviewers chat with candidates and ask fairly typical interview questions. Some are behavioral, in which interviewers ask about past achievements, seek details regarding the behaviors and skills that contributed to these undertakings, and ask candidates, "What would you do in this situation?" questions. Occasionally, particularly for consulting firms, interviews are case studies, in which interviewers ask candidates to analyze specific situational cases and problems; revealing how candidates think on their feet in response to specific analysis-driven cases.

Let's take a look at the differences between these types of interviews and how to best prepare for each.

ESSENTIAL

Interviews should not be thought of as simply a series of questions and answers. They are conversations with a common purpose for you and the interviewer. Both use qualification criteria to assess the other's potential to succeed. During the exchange, the more verbally inspired images of success that are sent and received, the more likely an offer will be made.

What You Say

Don't be shy! Talk about your achievements with pride. Interviewers have limited time to get to know the real you. Don't think there are right answers. When asked a technical question, if you don't know the exact answer, talk the interviewer through how you would find the correct information. Don't wait to do so; always ask questions when invited.

Each interview opportunity will provide you with important insights that you can use to adjust and improve future interviews. But, don't overanalyze or dissect your performance after each interview. Decision making is very subjective. The process changes from initial screening through call-back stages and, ultimately, through selection interviews. If your style and strategies remain sincere, no matter the interviewer's style, technique, or temperament, you will find a good fit. If you don't receive an offer, never stop to ask why. Instead, you should, via follow-up contacts, seek consideration for the next available similar opportunity. Remain confident and enthusiastic. Remember to smile and be friendly, yet professional. More often than you think, you can transform someone who rejected you into a strong advocate and network member who might interview you again very soon.

ESSENTIAL

Bring extra resumes with you in case you unexpectedly meet additional interviewers. You might also wish to bring supporting materials to serve as illustrations of your work. Some fields, specifically publishing, public relations, and journalism, require writing samples or portfolios. Be ready to detail what samples you have included and why they demonstrate specific talents.

What You Wear

We talked about attire in Chapter 1, but it's worth noting here that what you wear also influences interviewers perspective about your resume. Consistency is key; remember you are conveying your personal brand through every interaction you have and every impression you leave.

When preparing for the interview, inquire about the appropriate mode of dress. Some situations and organizations are business casual. Neatly pressed slacks, an ironed shirt, and a tie (a sport coat is optional) would be appropriate for men. Slacks or skirt and an ironed shirt or sweater would be appropriate for women. Others are business formal, and suits, ironed shirts, polished shoes, and ties are a must for men, and suits are required for women.

What was once known as casual Friday has become confusing Monday through Friday for contemporary candidates. Old-fashioned rules regarding power suits, colors, and ties may not seem to apply today, but because what you wear may impact what you say and how others perceive your professionalism, in truth, they still do. Your interview image, revealed by your attire, is a projection of common sense rather than fashion sense. It's always recommended that you remain conservative and traditional with the clothing you select for interview days.

FACT

According to a joint survey conducted by the job board Yahoo!, HotJobs, and retailer Banana Republic, the majority of employees wear either business casual or casual outfits to work, indicating that more companies are relaxing office dress codes. As a result, 34 percent of job seekers said that, on the night before an interview, they spend most of their time deciding what to wear.

Ties can be loosened, jackets removed, and sleeves can be rolled up. It's easy to transform business formal into something more casual, but the opposite is not possible. Unless specifically told otherwise, dress more formally. Suits are always appropriate and required for banking, financial services, consulting, and conservative fields. For other settings, blue blazers, gray or khaki slacks or skirts, crisply ironed shirts, and appropriate neckwear may seem like prep school uniforms, but these basics are always good bets for interviews.

Remember potential red flags. Tone down jewelry, ditch the backpack, temporarily remove nose, eyebrow, or tongue piercings, go easy on perfume or cologne, and wear polished shoes (no flip-flops or backless). Ladies should watch cleavage and hem length, and men should go with long-sleeved shirts rather than short.

After reading this chapter, you are ready to use your resume as an interview preparation and implementation tool. You have learned how to use this document to focus preparation prior to and during these crucial conversations. On interview days, simply looking at your resume should instill confidence and generate effective communication. Resumes contribute to your chances for landing a job well beyond the initial contact stages. Used effectively, they impact all actions and outcomes.

CHAPTER 8

Resume Review and Critique

This chapter reveals details that will inspire you to maximize your efforts to create or update great resumes. As you read, it will be as if you have your own resume coach at your side. This word-for-word review will inspire you to immediate actions. We'll also discuss the role of the resume coach and then provide some examples of resumes with evaluations that can help you consider how you might change these resumes if you were in the applicant's place. Most importantly, the advice you read—although not directed toward your own resume—may give you some ideas about areas of your own resume that you should review with an eye toward making changes.

The Heart and Head of the Resume Coach

The job seeker uses both his heart and head while writing a resume. These two different perspectives yield different resume writing and job search strategies. You've learned how emotional perspectives and hopes must blend with intellectual and strategic thoughts to yield success. Step-by-step strategies inspired you to unite attitudes and actions in order to conduct comprehensive job search campaigns. Resume writing and job search coaches possess and share contradictory yet complementary views as well.

The Heart of the Resume Coach

The heart of the resume coach is often very traditional, encouraging you to write resumes its way. While appearing optimistic to some, heart-driven advice can be unrealistic for most and even damaging to your career. It is characterized by statements, queries, and often impractical hopes that include the following:

- Keep your options open. Do not limit yourself by placing goals on resumes.
- Send out as many multipurpose resumes as possible; respond to almost every posting.
- Even if you don't have any experience, just send out multipurpose resumes and let employers judge your potential to succeed.
- The broader the entries on your resume, the better. You want to appear well rounded.

The impact your resume will have on a resume coach and, ultimately, a hiring manager or HR professional is often qualitative, or heart-driven. These qualitative assessments are important, though, and create initial and sometimes lasting impressions of you.

The Head of the Resume Coach

The head of the resume coach has had to change its old-fashioned way of thinking and adapt to the philosophies unique to targeted resumes. These views guide you to take active and proactive steps in logical sequence. The related advice and strategies are realistic and logistically sound, yet they are also inspirational. This view is characterized by statements, queries, and realistic hopes that include the following:

- Focus your proactive efforts on three fields and two functional areas within each, but respond reactively and creatively to as many postings as you wish, using targeted resumes.
- Complete goal identification, qualification inventorying, and analyses needed to create targeted qualification summaries for all of your resumes and many letters.
- Be prepared to clearly articulate realistic goals, maintain awareness of qualification criteria associated with related jobs, and always use field-focused phrasing in documentation, conversations, and interviews.
- Take responsibility for projecting goals as well as qualifications through effective resumes and job search communication.
- Complete the assessment and research needed to set and share realistic goals and to mirror qualifications via targeted resumes and very focused supplemental documentation.

Both the heads and hearts of resume coaches agree that you should, if possible, create your own resume. While some professional resume writers do create effective documents, especially for very experienced candidates, it is always best to personally go through the resume writing steps. If you still are dissatisfied you can bring your resume to a professional for review and critique, but you will have benefited from the writing and thought process.

FACT

Most believe that only 20–25 percent of all jobs are posted. Maximum estimates for the "posted versus hidden job market" are one-third hidden to two-thirds posted. But no matter the numbers, all agree that you should never limit efforts to postings. Proactive actions are the only way to uncover hidden opportunities.

A Few Detailed Reviews

The following multipurpose resume review represents a detailed word-for-word, step-by-step critique as it was conducted by a resume coach. First you will be privy to the thoughts and actual changes associated with transformation of one "before" version into an effective multipurpose "after" model. Then you will learn how this one broad resume can become three, much more effective, targeted versions.

The sample that follows was that of an actual soon-to-be graduate, but the lessons learned from the detailed critiquing are applicable to all resume writers. Recently laid-off workers, soon-to-be and recent college grads, inexperienced workers, experienced executives and mid-managers, and those seeking basic employment will become educated and motivated by these detailed resume reviews. If you haven't hired a resume coach, don't worry. All job seekers can gain much from the words of the resume coach who will critique these documents. Someday soon, your internal voices will echo the knowledge of these concepts and phrases. You will become your own strongest resume coach and, perhaps, support the efforts of others.

Multipurpose Resume Before Critiquing

Chris Smith

123 Main Street   987 Centre Avenue
Apartment 13   Philadelphia, PA 11111
Hometown, NY 00000   (555) 555-5678
(555) 555-1234   csmith@company.com

EDUCATION

Bachelor of Arts, Political Science, University Of Rochester, Rochester, NY,
anticipated May 2008
Dean's List. Completed cluster of three thematically linked courses explor-
ing the natural sciences in physics and astronomy. Completed cluster of
three thematically linked courses in Spanish. As member of Student Senate, organized campus activities and worked to ensure a maximal educational
experience.

EXPERIENCE

Server, Burgundy Basin Banquet Hall, Pittsford, NY
Greeted customers. Took orders. Maintained accurate records of receipts and
gratuities. 2012–Present

Research Assistant for Professor Harry Smart, University Of Rochester,
Rochester, NY
Scheduled subjects, conducted interviews, input and analyzed data, and
completed library research. Completed comprehensive interview assessing
husband-and-wife relationships. Scored, coded, then input data, ensuring
easy retrieval and data analysis by graduate students and faculty. Conducted extensive library and Internet research, identifying studies related
to husband-and-wife relationships. Spring 2011–Present

Intern/Assistant to the President, The Ardmore Group, Ardmore, PA
Reported directly to the president of a multidivisional enterprise that
included political consulting, special-interest lobbying, bidding on and
awarding state government contracts in health care, social work, and welfare administration. Organized luncheons and various meetings for political
operatives and office holders. Conducted research as to what contracts were
available for bid and what resources would be necessary to produce that
bid. All research with recommendations submitted in written report to the
president. Work involved independent trips to the state capitol and attendance at networking sessions to procure clients. Summer 2012

Assistant to the CFO, Philadelphia Physicians Associates, Philadelphia, PA
Reported directly to Medical Records Supervisor and CFO of regional medical
practice. Audited medical records for accuracy. Distributed those records
to doctors, attorneys, and insurers. Organized records for depositions. Distributed work to clerical staff. Part time and summers 2010–2011

Coach's Comments, Queries, and Quick Corrections

Here's what the resume coach has to say:

- **First, visually this resume is organized and easy to read, yet it lacks something.** The Monaco font is basic, often used as a default setting for e-mails, and it does not really project a professional image.
- **Are you looking for jobs in the Philadelphia area?** If yes, then leave both addresses, but do not use as many lines to present this information.
- **Do you have a job search goal? A general field of interest? Particular functions in mind?** It's okay to start with a multipurpose document, but you should use targeted ones for each of those areas you stated. The format, content, and style of this one are not presented effectively for some of those goals. Create one general resume and then a few targeted versions.
- **You use two very clear and appropriate headers, but don't you want to tell readers a bit more about some of your educational and practical achievements?** Think about themes you want readers to be aware of as you create a better multipurpose resume and the targeted versions. How would you characterize your education? If you used a multiword headline for education, what would it be? What words best describe the type of education you received? Would the header be different for different targeted resumes?
- **You highlighted your degree using bolding and position on the page, but what about the school?** Isn't University of Rochester one of the top schools in the country? Doesn't this school have a unique cluster-oriented curriculum? Shouldn't you proudly highlight the school's name?
- **The information under education and experience headers is well written, but it isn't highlighted.** Have you thought of other ways to present both degree and school as well as employer and position?
- **The header for experience is also very traditional, but it doesn't allow you to break away from the reverse chronological order rule.** You've blended some very interesting and sophisticated experiences with other less significant experiences. In fact, your first job is a waitress position. What experience themes do you want readers to quickly recognize as you create the better multipurpose resume and targeted versions? How would you characterize your experience? If you used

multiword headlines for groupings of experience, what would they be? What are the two most significant and sophisticated experiences? Is there any way to present them more prominently? Would the headers be different for different targeted resumes?

- **You highlighted your experience titles using bolding and position on the page, but what about the employer?** Some of the organizational titles might focus the reader's review of descriptions cited.

- **Look at all of your academic as well as practical experience.** What are your most significant achievements? What skills and abilities yielded related accomplishments? Can you make a profile containing your greatest assets?

- **Okay, let's review a bit.** We're first going to create a better multipurpose resume. Later, we will create targeted resumes for each of your stated goals. These fields include consulting, advertising, and law. Let's not worry about it now, but you will very soon have to review the newly updated multipurpose resume and think about specific qualifications for these fields and what entries to highlight. We'll use order of presentation as well as headlines to highlight the selected skills.

- **Now, we will proceed from top to bottom.** Use one line for each address, rather than five. We most likely will need those extra three lines somewhere else. Place bullets in between entries, graphically creating separation for what was on individual lines before.

- **Next, we will create a general summary of qualifications.** This will contain four or five bulleted phrases that reveal to readers some of your basic qualities and characteristics. Again, look at all of your academic and employment experiences.

Which are most important? Your courses were all research-oriented, and your research assistant position, political consulting, and medical practice management experience all required strong research, data analysis, writing, and presentation skills. One of your summary statements will reflect this.

Oh, you think of yourself as a good writer. What kind of documents have you written for academic or other purposes? Can you detail how you did so? Do you have samples?

Yes, computer competencies are important. What software can you confidently use? Can you teach others to use these systems?

Course titles are often left off resumes, but they can reinforce some of the qualification statements. For the multipurpose resume, you can list a few general ones, but later, think about including only those related to particular goals.

- **Changing your headers to headlines should be relatively easy.** The education headline can now reveal that you've had some liberal arts, science, and political science studies. Better, the headline can reveal that your academics seemed research focused. The experience section can reinforce the same themes. It can show you have had research-driven achievements. Let's think about distinct categories for your research experience, project management, and general business experience.

- **For education, using all caps to highlight the name of your school, and presenting it first, followed by city and state, would be effective.** On the next line you can still use bold for the degree. If you have enough room, use bullet points to highlight extracurricular achievements. Let's see if everything fits. So far, so good. How many semesters did you make the dean's list? What were your overall and major GPAs? Let's not include those, nor enter dean's list if it was for your first semester freshman year.

- **Now, let's focus on headlines for experience.** The most important experience should go first. The way information now appears, you highlight titles and not organizations. We'll use the same format for experience used for education. Make the organizations all caps, followed by city and state. Then, bold the title. Ideally, describe overall responsibilities under the title and follow with bulleted accomplishments. And the dates can go on the same line as the title, justified to the right margin. Cities and states should also be justified on the right margin.

- **Let's create headlines and divide up your experiences by importance and nature of roles.** Okay, the two most important experiences are the research assistant position and the one with the governmental firm so you should definitely group these two and then add the medical practice management position to this section. The three will appear under a headline that clearly notes the research, writing, and time management skills you possess. Let's leave off the waitress entry. Yes, it does show that you work hard and contributed to educational expenses.

But did you gain significant skills? If you have room, list it at the end of the page. If space permits, it'll stay. If not, it'll go. Okay?

- **Let's focus a bit on the actual job descriptions, particularly on the accomplishment bullets.** After we do, we'll revisit the qualification summary to ensure that it reflects the skills used to achieve these outcomes. Now, are the most significant achievements noted for each position? Is anything missing? Would someone who worked with you in these settings approve? Action phrasing does not require embellishment or deception.

- **Okay, the first draft is complete.** Let's play with the font and spacing a bit to fit on one page. Times, Times New Roman, and Bookman Old Style are fine, but Garamond looks like it will allow the most information to fit. Let's also play with some of the blank spacing between headlines and entries, and between entries. Shrinking it from ten point to four point does add a line or two.

- **Now that we're close to being finished, let's try something dramatic.** Put education last. Your experience is so strong that it deserves to be more prominent. The fact that courses are in the qualification summary serves the purpose of introducing specific topics. The degree and school don't carry as much weight as your significant work experience. What do you think? I know every one of your friends lists education first. Do they have strong GPAs and academic honors? Are their majors directly related to targeted goals? Remember, this is your multipurpose document. The targeted ones might have a different order of presentation.

- **Will you be uploading this resume to job boards or corporate home pages?** After we're done, you should conduct some web and library research to focus on the vocabulary and keywords used within your three fields of interest. Consulting, advertising, and law do have their own lexicons, and when your resume is reviewed, they must be identified. No matter whether the keyword scanning is done electronically or visually, by a person or machine, these words and phrase will be key! After your research, we'll transform your multipurpose document into three targeted ones.

- **Finally, let's think about all visual and content issues.** I know, it's not that easy. Let's look at the following questions to determine if your resume is ready to distribute to potential employers.

Before-and-After Checklist for Determining Distribution Readiness

The queries on the following before-and-after checklist formalize those that would informally or intuitively be asked by a resume coach before drafts are considered final versions. Visually scanning the resume from top to bottom inspires the following questions of both coach and resume writer. What would your answers be for the sample that immediately follows? Is it ready for duplication and distribution? Do you like the before-and-after transformation of this multipurpose document? What about the experience phrasing and bulleted accomplishments? How would you change it into targeted versions?

- Is the identifying information accurate, including your e-mail?
- Is just one address and phone enough? Consider including your cell phone number.
- Is it easy to read and visually appealing with information presented in a logical format?
- Can you identify a logical pattern for headline, content, and highlighting techniques?
- Can it be copied and pasted into an e-mail?
- Is the objective brief, and does it use field-specific phrasing?
- Does the summary of qualifications section support the stated objective?
- Does this summary of qualifications paragraph or bullet point listing reveal that you possess the qualification criteria for target jobs?
- Does this summary of qualifications section project to the future as well as reflect upon the past?
- Are most significant goal-related qualification statements presented first?
- Do special headlines for experience and education project objective-related focus?
- Does the order of appearance effectively portray significance?
- Does the education section present school(s), degree(s), area(s) of concentration, courses, and honors?
- Do courses, papers, and projects appear somewhere?
- Is specialized training presented under a special headline?

- Do headlines project knowledge of targeted fields and draw attention to related achievements?
- Do headlines, quickly reviewed, identify the nature of entries that follow?
- Are all entries described using active and accomplishment-oriented phrasing, including facts and figures?
- Are goal-specific experiences grouped under appropriate headlines, presented in order of significance?
- If entries are simply cited, with no descriptions, are they obviously of less importance than others?
- Are organizations, titles, and dates easy to see, revealing an obvious pattern?
- For space as well as goal-directed purposes, are only the most significant experiences thoroughly described, with most important appearing first?
- If listed by soon-to-be or recent college grad, are leadership roles and achievements cited?
- Are most important headlines presented first, with most significant information appearing under each?
- If your resume is more than one page, is the most important information on the first and does the second page have your name and a page number header?
- If you have more than one targeted resume, are objectives for each very clear?
- Did you change order of presentation for each resume and are your summaries of qualifications target-specific?
- Can you elaborate upon the resume in a well-crafted cover letter or brief cover note?
- Would readers sense goal-oriented competence and confidence without an accompanying letter?
- Can you use the resume as a clear guide during an interview?
- Are you definitely ready to duplicate and distribute your resume?

Hopefully the previous questions provided you with some new insights about your resume and some ideas on changes you might make to improve your resume's impact.

Coach's Final Words on the Multipurpose Resume

- **While your responses to the before-and-after checklist were not 100 percent positive, because we're working on a multipurpose document, I think it's ready to go.** What do you think? Yes, you can upload it into your school's resume collection and on-campus recruiting system. You can now begin responding to postings and networking with alumni. But, we have to finish those targeted versions if you are to maximize your efforts. Of course, we need to work on cover letters as well.

- **Targeted resumes with objectives and qualification summaries are best.** While you should be proud of yourself and your newly created general resume, it's not quite the best document. You must support your targeted reactive and proactive efforts with clearly focused resumes found later on in the chapter. No, focus is not bad. It does not limit you. You will be using appropriate resumes and supplemental documents for each field. You can use this wonderful multipurpose version to get the process started and whenever something "unique" might arise. Remember, it's your responsibility to share and support goals, not the employer's responsibility to interpret resume content and magically identify goals for you.

Multipurpose Resume after Critiquing

Chris Smith

123 Main Street, Apartment 13 • Hometown, NY 00000 • (555) 555-1234 • csmith@company.com
987 Centre Avenue • Philadelphia, PA 11111 • (555) 555-5678

Qualification Summary

- Confidence conducting detailed research using library and Internet resources.
- Data collection, trend analysis, and writing talents nurtured via practical experiences, as well as academic papers and research projects.
- Confidence in research, writing, editing, proposal development, presentation, event planning, and project management roles.
- Windows, UNIX, HTML, Word, Excel, PowerPoint, PhotoShop, and Internet utilities.
- Skills, interests, and perspectives gained from courses including: Applied Data Analysis, Economics, Debate, Psychology of Business, Arguments in Politics, Political Theory: Politics in the Mass Media, Political Systems, Social Psychology, and Adolescent Psychology.

Research, Writing, and Project Management Accomplishments

UNIVERSITY OF ROCHESTER | Rochester, NY
Research Assistant for Psychology Professor Harry Smart | Spring 2011–Present
- Conducted extensive library and Internet research, identifying studies related to husband-and-wife relationships. Summarized findings and developed detailed listings of citations. Presented findings at weekly faculty-led research team meetings.

THE ARDMORE GROUP | Ardmore, PA
Intern/Assistant to the President | Summer 2012
- Reported directly to the president of a multidivisional enterprise that included political consulting, special-interest lobbying, bidding on and awarding state government contracts in health care, social work, and welfare administration.
- Conducted research regarding contracts available for bidding and what resources would be necessary to produce that bid. All research efforts were transformed into written recommendations submitted in reports to the president. Yielded about one hit per month.
- Work involved independent trips to the state capitol, attendance at networking sessions and sharing of information with colleagues and supervisor to determine appropriate next steps.

PHILADELPHIA PHYSICIANS ASSOCIATES | Philadelphia, PA
Assistant to the CFO | Part-time and Summers 2010–2011
- Reported directly to Medical Records Supervisor and CFO of regional medical practice.
- Audited medical records for doctors, attorneys, and insurers.
- Organized records for depositions in specialized formats facilitating access by attorneys, arbitrators, and judges addressing specific points of law.

Research-Oriented Studies

UNIVERSITY OF ROCHESTER | Rochester, NY
Bachelor of Arts, Political Science | anticipated May 2013
- As member of Student Senate, effectively interacted with peers, administrators, and others, transforming goals into decisions to implement freshman housing model.

Coach's Internalized and Verbalized Before-and-After Review

This chapter has already revealed a detailed critique, illustrating the transformation from a before draft to a finished after version. Step six of the seven required to create or update resumes involves drafting and critiquing. Questions on the before-and-after checklist reveal for you, with great confidence and closure, whether a resume is ready for distribution.

Resume coaches think about and ask these questions aloud of those creating or updating documents. Silent or spoken answers inspire attitudes needed to stop drafting and start distributing. What would your answers be for the new multipurpose version and, more importantly, for the targeted versions that follow? For each sample on the pages that follow, see if you can you identify obvious and subtle changes made from one resume to the others.

ALERT

If after you have sent a cover letter or resume, you have updated the resume or wish to add additional information, do not hesitate to send follow-up documentation. Refer to earlier communications, yet highlight in your follow-up communiqué all critical new issues and assets on your revised resume.

As you recall, when all responses to the before-and-after checklist are "yes," a resume is ready for distribution. If some answers are "no," the document can be revised or used until changes are made. While questions asked by coaches, advocates, and others do help, you now have a written script that they might use. In many creative and confidence-building ways, you now have what can be viewed as the very best coach's queries printed on just a few pages. To inspire continued re-evaluation, you might wish to photocopy the before-and-after checklist and post it in a clearly visible location whenever you are creating or updating resumes.

One Multipurpose Resume Equals Three Targeted Resumes

As the resume coach's reactions revealed, targeted resumes will be created to match stated goals. Many job seekers should do the same. One resume cannot do all things for all candidates. The first step to updating and creating resumes involves reviewing samples. This section offers annotated reviews of three resumes created from one. Comments offered by the coach should inspire you when you create one, two, or three targeted resumes.

Coach's Comments for an Advertising Resume

- **So, the multipurpose resume is finished.** Oh, you have a new research position. Yes, it's too early to cite many accomplishments, but let's describe it now and you can add more as you progress. Let's add it. No, don't worry about room until we've drafted again. We'll think of some space-saving approaches later.
- **Now let's get to the targeted versions.** Have you done your homework? Did you research the fields? We'll start with advertising and then go to the others. Continued research will reveal information and, most significantly, key phrases that will be added to updated resumes and supplemental letters. Let's not delay. You need some targeted documents to maximize posting responses as well as self-initiated contacts with prospective employers.
- **Now, let's focus on advertising.** Is there a particular job title or functional area of interest? Can you describe it in terms that anyone will be able to understand? Can you describe it using specialized terms? That's good! So, account management in the advertising sector is your objective. We'll first create a distinct objective statement, but we might have to blend the objective with a qualification summary to save space.
- **The qualification summary is now the most critical component of your resume.** Targeted versions must reveal that you know your goals and that you know what is required to succeed within these roles. In many ways, the rest of the resume will stay the same. But, we will think about order of presentation, headlines, and specific descriptions.

- **Thinking about your newly found knowledge of the field, what are your most significant academic or employment accomplishments?** Have you had directly related experiences that should be highlighted via the qualification summary? The summary must show that you know about this field and that you know about particular skills you possess that are related. You'll show more in your cover letter, but the qualification summary must quickly reveal your goals and basic qualifications.
- **We do have some space issues, so we must get very creative.** Let's just use one line for identifying information. You can add the second line to cover letters targeting Philly firms. Also, let's make sure that your course listing is as concise as possible and presents most important classes first.

Coach's Final Words on the Advertising Resume

- **Your responses to the short and long list of questions were close to 100 percent positive.** That's great. You should research the field more and constantly improve the qualification summary, but I think it's ready to go. Of course, you must convey much of the knowledge already gained through research in your cover letters as well. With advertising, you can be a bit more creative and add humor to these cover letters. Also, for each firm you can refer to some particular clients and recent awards or sales gains. For this field the cover letter may be as important as the resume.
- **Definitely start sending resumes and cover letters to the many, many firms on your hit list.** Also, network with alums. Learn about their career biographies. Increase knowledge-of-field appropriate phrases and terminology. Ask if they can consider you for positions on their client teams, or if they can forward your resumes to someone who can.
- **Targeted resumes with objectives and qualification summaries are best, but starting with a headline like the one you used takes the place of an objective statement.** Remember, you had some space issues, and this allowed you to save a line or two.
- **This one is ready to go.** Keep in mind that the focus does not limit you. You will be using different resumes and cover letters for each field. I

realize that you don't truly know what you want to do, yet advertising is one of your top choices. This resume clearly reveals your goals. Additional documents and, eventually, interviews will show how much you have learned about advertising and how easy it is for you to speak using field-focused vocabulary.

- **If you can, sign up for a marketing or advertising course or seminar.** Local chapters of professional associations might offer brief seminars. You don't have to take courses for credit, and they can be offered at a local community college. The more you demonstrate true interest in the field, the more your actions will speak as loudly (or more) than your words on this great resume.

FACT

The terms *cum laude, magna cum laude,* and *summa cum laude* are all lowercase and should be put in italics.

Chris Smith

123 Main Street, Apartment 13 • Hometown, NY 00000 • (555) 555-1234 • csmith@company.com

Advertising Account Management Qualifications

- Curiosity regarding consumer attitudes and behaviors and confidence using data collection, trend analysis, and writing talents to develop client-focused campaign strategies as well as proposals, and to assess campaign effectiveness.
- Experience in roles requiring attitude assessment, brainstorming, persuasive communication, and creation of reports, presentations, and proposals.
- Confidence independently or as a team member developing proposals and presentations, planning events, and completing special projects.
- Interests and perspectives gained from diverse courses including: Psychology of Business and Industry, Applied Data Analysis, Economics, Debate, Arguments in Politics, Politics in the Mass Media, Social Psychology, and Adolescent Psychology.
- Abilities to use Word, Excel, and PowerPoint for quantitative analyses, reports, proposals, presentations, and related campaign support documents.

Political Consulting

THE ARDMORE GROUP   Ardmore, PA
Intern/Assistant to the President   Summer 2012
Reported directly to the president of a multidivisional enterprise that included political consulting, special interest lobbying, bidding on and awarding state government contracts in health care, social work, and welfare administration.

- Conducted research regarding contracts available for bidding and what resources would be necessary to produce that bid. All research efforts were transformed into written recommendations submitted in reports to the president. Yielded about one hit per month.
- Attended networking sessions to procure clients, and shared information with colleagues and supervisor to determine appropriate next steps.

Research, Proposal Writing, and Project Management Accomplishments

UNIVERSITY OF ROCHESTER   Rochester, NY
Research Assistant for Psychology Professor Harry Smart   Spring 2011–Present

- Conducted extensive library and Internet research, identifying studies related to husband-and-wife relationships. Summarized findings and developed detailed listings of citations. Presented findings at weekly faculty-led research team meetings.
- Scheduled subjects, conducted interviews, input and analyzed data, and completed library research.

Speech and Hearing Center Research Assistant   Fall 2012–Present

- Identified methodology to be used to measure effectiveness and target criteria impacting therapeutic outcomes.

Education

UNIVERSITY OF ROCHESTER   Rochester, NY
Bachelor of Arts, Political Science   anticipated May 2013

Coach's Comments for a Consulting Resume

- **So, now the advertising version is finished. See, it didn't take long to adapt the multipurpose resume to a specific purpose.** In fact, each adaptation should take much less time than the original process, not much longer than thirty to forty-five minutes. The next two probably won't take much more than twenty minutes each.

- **Okay, consulting is the next field.** Again, have you done your homework? Did you research this particular field? I understand it's not an easy one to enter for undergrads. Yes, it's that selective, but you don't know if you have what it takes to get an interview if you don't try. Continued research will reveal more information and additional key phrases that will be added to updated resumes and supplemental letters. But let's get the first ones out soon. This field screens candidates and completes initial interviews early in the on-campus and off-campus recruiting cycles.

- **Let's focus on consulting.** Is there a particular job title or functional area of interest? Each firm has a variation on the titles used for entry level opportunities, some call them Associate Consultants, some use Analysts, and others use Research Analysts. So, instead of an objective statement, we'll use the headline and summary of qualification strategy again. Can you describe what these first post-baccalaureate jobs are all about? What do recent grads who work for consulting firms do? Continue your research even after you've sent your first group of resumes and cover letters. Follow-up letters can reveal when you've gained additional insights.

- **The qualification summary remains the most critical component of this targeted resume.** This section must reveal that you know your goals and what is required to succeed within these research and analytical support roles. Like before, the rest of the resume may stay the same, but you might change order of presentation, headlines, and specific descriptions.

- **Now, for the qualification summary, you must project knowledge of self, knowledge of the field, and knowledge of particular job functions.** What are your most significant consulting-related academic or employment accomplishments? Yes, you did work for a consulting firm already. Even though it wasn't exactly a management consulting firm, it was a consulting firm so let's include that in the qualification summary and bring that entry as high up on the document as we can. You'll want to use a good headline as well.

ESSENTIAL

Order of presentation is crucial and the first two entries on your resume must be impressive. You do want to de-emphasize education if it's not your greatest strength. Leave it last on the page, but make sure to highlight specific courses and concepts in the summary.

- **The summary must show that you know something about consulting and that you know about the particular skills you possess that are related.** In the cover letter you will show more, but the qualification summary must effectively reveal your goals and basic qualifications. With a selective field, it may be the most important section of the resume. Because it is read first, if it doesn't grab the attention of the reader, the rest of your resume might not be read.

Consulting Targeted Resume after Critiquing

Chris Smith

123 Main Street, Apartment 13 • Hometown, NY 00000 • (555) 555-1234 • csmith@company.com

Management Consulting Qualifications

- Confidence developing proposals and presentations and completing special analytical projects within a consulting firm's deadline-driven and detail-oriented environment.
- Knowledge gained via Economics, Applied Data Analysis, and Psychology of Business courses.
- Experience using economic models, Excel, statistical analyses, and other approaches to quantify data, identify trends, and present findings to colleagues, supervisors, and clients.
- Curiosity regarding strategic planning, profit profiling, industry trending, and competitor analysis.
- Experience in hypothesis testing, brainstorming, and creating reports.
- Abilities to use Word, PowerPoint, and Excel for financial and marketing analyses, reports, presentations, and case documentation.

Consulting Accomplishments

THE ARDMORE GROUP   Ardmore, PA
Intern/Assistant to the President   Summer 2012

Reported directly to president of multidivisional $10 million annual billing enterprise that included political consulting, special-interest lobbying, bidding on and awarding state contracts in health care, social work, and welfare administration.

- Conducted research regarding contracts available for bidding and what resources would be necessary to produce that bid. All research was transformed into written recommendations submitted to the president.
- Involved independent trips to the state capitol, attendance at networking sessions to procure clients, and sharing of information with colleagues and supervisor to determine appropriate next steps.

Research, Analysis, and Project Management Accomplishments

UNIVERSITY OF ROCHESTER   Rochester, NY
Research Assistant for Psychology Professor Harry Smart   Spring 2011–Present

- Conducted extensive library and Internet research, identifying husband-and-wife relationship studies. Summarized findings and developed listings of citations. Presented findings at weekly faculty-led research team meetings.
- Scheduled subjects, conducted interviews, input and analyzed data, and completed library research.
- Completed comprehensive interviews assessing husband-and-wife relationships.

Speech and Hearing Center Research Assistant   Fall 2012–Present

- Identified methodology to be used to measure effectiveness and target criteria impacting therapeutic outcomes.

PHILADELPHIA PHYSICIANS ASSOCIATES   Philadelphia, PA
Assistant to the CFO   Part-time and Summers 2010–2011

- Audited medical records for accuracy prior to distributing records to doctors, attorneys, and insurers.
- Organized records in formats facilitating ease of access by attorneys, arbitrators, and judges.

Education

UNIVERSITY OF ROCHESTER   Rochester, NY
Bachelor of Arts, Political Science   anticipated May 2013

Coach's Final Words on the Consulting Resume

- **Your responses to the questions will reveal some anxiety associated with the selectivity of the field, but they also showed that you think the resume is ready.** You can now begin responding to postings, sending self-initiated contacts to firms, and networking with alumni.

- **For this field, networking will be most crucial.** When selectivity is involved, it's often the name of someone stated at the beginning of the cover letter or, better, the fact that this person forwards your documents to the resume screener that impacts success. Use your past consulting employer as a source for referrals. Don't be shy about leveraging his name and his network of colleagues and associates. He can help you identify some other smaller, entrepreneurial and privately held firms. Make sure, though, to always ask for permission to use individuals as references so they are prepared in the event that they receive a call or email asking for their impressions of you.

- **Now work on your cover letters.** In this case you must first show that you have the research, analysis, and presentation skills required to effectively fill the roles desired. Read and think about some Harvard Business School case studies and refer to this activity within your correspondence. Pick up and read one of those books on introductory business management. A liberal arts student like you can very quickly pick up appropriate phrases and concepts applicable to consulting. When you do, quickly update both resume and cover letters. Oh, and you can follow up with firms who may have already rejected you. You have nothing to lose.

- **While this resume is ready for distribution accompanied by a great cover letter, you can and should enhance both as your job search progresses.** Continue to read about consulting and network with individuals in the field. Enhance your business-related knowledge and lexicon as you read. Update both documents whenever you wish. Send them anew or again when strategically appropriate.

Coach's Comments for a Paralegal Resume

- **This should be the easiest version to complete:** You've done two already, you have some significant experience, and you are sincerely interested in the field.

- **Of course, you've thought a great deal about the field already.** Yes, it's a very attainable goal. Many large and a few small firms regularly hire legal researchers and paralegals with academic backgrounds similar to yours. They appreciate the breadth and depth of research skills gained as a liberal arts student, specifically a political science major with a career interest in law. In your case you have also had directly related experience and a strong skill set.

- **The qualification summary remains the most critical component of your resume.** This targeted version will reveal that you are seeking a paralegal or legal research position and that you have all of the competence and confidence required to succeed within these roles.

- **The qualification summary must effectively reveal your goals and basic qualifications.** To save space, use the headline approach again. The words selected for this first headline will clearly state your goals. The bulleted statements that appear next, with the most important first, will summarize what you have to offer. They will serve to preview as well as review all of the qualities and capabilities you possess. You cannot use the same statements as you used for consulting, although some might remain. Think specifically about those experiences and skills that relate to paralegal and legal research.

- **A revised order of presentation will make this resume most impressive.** You do want to emphasize the law-related experience immediately following the qualification summary. Add to the description or accomplishment list to make sure readers understand how much of this job was law related. The rest of the resume will look very much like the consulting one, except with a new header for education. You are interested in someday applying to law school, right? Many of your courses were taken as an exploration of law, government, and political science topics, correct? So, let's use "Pre-Law" in the headline.

- **It may seem too quick, but we're done.** It's time again to ask aloud the questions we covered earlier in this chapter to determine if the resume is distribution ready.

Paralegal Targeted Resume after Critiquing

Chris Smith

123 Main Street, Apartment 13 • Hometown, NY 00000 • (555) 555-1234 • csmith@company.com

Paralegal and Legal Research Qualifications

- Confidence conducting research using library and Internet resources as well as interview techniques.
- Experience in roles requiring detailed collection and review of documents and creation of reports and indexes.
- Confidence developing proposals and presentations, planning events, and completing special projects.
- Knowledge gained from courses including: Applied Data Analysis, Economics, Debate, Arguments in Politics, Political Theory, Politics in the Mass Media, Political Systems, and Social Psychology.

Legal Research and Litigation Support Accomplishments

PHILADELPHIA PHYSICIANS ASSOCIATES — Philadelphia, PA
Assistant to the CFO — Part-time and Summers 2010–2011
Reported directly to Medical Records Supervisor and CFO of regional medical practice, supporting day-to-day business, law, and insurance-related functions.
- Audited medical records for accuracy prior to distributing records to doctors, attorneys, and insurers.
- Organized indexes and record packets for depositions in specialized formats, facilitating ease of access by attorneys, arbitrators, and judges, and focusing on specific points of law in question.

Research and Project Management Accomplishments

UNIVERSITY OF ROCHESTER — Rochester, NY
Research Assistant for Psychology Professor Harry Smart — Spring 2011–Present
Assisted with study assessing perceptions impacting husband-and-wife relationships.
- Conducted extensive library and Internet research for husband-and-wife relationship studies. Summarized findings and detailed listings of citations. Presented findings at weekly faculty-led research team meetings.
- Scheduled subjects, conducted interviews, input and analyzed data, and completed library research.

Speech and Hearing Center Research Assistant — Fall 2012–Present
Assisted with planning and implementing study assessing effectiveness of speech and language therapy services.
- Scheduled home visits, explained services, helped clients complete assessment questionnaires.

THE ARDMORE GROUP — Ardmore, PA
Intern/Assistant to the President — Summer 2012
Reported directly to president of multidivisional enterprise that included political consulting, special-interest lobbying, bidding on and the awarding of state government contracts in health care, social work, and welfare administration.
- Conducted research regarding contracts available for bidding and resources necessary to produce bids. All research was transformed into written recommendations submitted to the president. Yielded one hit per month.
- Developed and distributed detailed pre-event and post-event documentation and correspondence.

Political Science and Pre-Law Studies

UNIVERSITY OF ROCHESTER — Rochester, NY
Bachelor of Arts, Political Science — anticipated May 2013

Coach's Final Words on the Paralegal Resume

- You should be very proud of this targeted resume. It will easily and effectively support reactive and proactive efforts. You can respond to postings and send this out immediately to firms of interest in New York, Philadelphia, and Washington, D.C.
- But just because the resume is strong, don't undervalue the potential impact of your cover letter. Within this supporting document share qualifications as well as motivations. Reveal that you know the ideal profile of paralegal candidates and those who serve within these roles. State that you wish to apply to law school only after the appropriate tenure with the firm. If confidentiality allows, within these letters note the firms involved and a summary of some of the cases that were related to your experience with the medical practice.
- Make sure you add the Philadelphia address to the letterhead used for letters targeting firms in your "home city." This will enhance your chances to be invited to interview.

An Actual Resume Success Story

Many of the sample resumes in this book are adaptations of those used by actual job seekers. Ideally, these real-life documents reveal the most effective use of concepts and themes presented within the preceding pages. Most significantly, the final versions presented in this chapter were, in somewhat different forms, used by a successful recent graduate.

This clearly strong, yet typical, candidate used all of the varied formats that were examined here. They won him several interviews. He used the resumes in preparation for and during these discussions. He got several offers. Ultimately, this talented individual accepted an offer to work as a paralegal.

This chapter revealed how a draft can become a more powerful finished resume and how one multipurpose resume can, with coaching support, be transformed into targeted versions. You have learned to become your own resume coach.

CHAPTER 9

What They Say about Your Resume

We solicited the comments of recruiting and human resources professionals to get an idea of their thoughts on the resumes they review. Many responded to a brief, open-ended query: "What are some best practices that you would point to for those who are preparing resumes as part of their job search?" Their comments were edited for length, not content. The fields represented are diverse, and views varied (and were sometimes contradictory).

Eugene R. Boffa, Jr.

▶ Eugene R. Boffa, Jr., Esq., is an attorney with Schumann Hanlon in Jersey City, N.J.

- Resumes should not be more than one page if you are applying for a job right out of college or grad school. Do not tell me about fishing or high school football days—I don't care! List the items that relate to the job you are applying for.
- If you are making a lateral move, the resume can be longer but should deal with your expertise. Always send a cover letter. Do *not* send it to "To Whom It May Concern," as I throw those out. If you can't find my name, try to make it somewhat personal, i.e., "Hiring Partner, Schumann Hanlon"; it shows effort on your part. Use the cover letter to make points. It tells a lot about you.
- My best tip . . . if you do get an interview, *always* write a thank-you note.

Kat Krull

▶ Kat Krull is Associate Marketing Manager at Résunate, an online firm with a web-based tool that helps you build customized, job-specific resumes. Most employers now use an applicant tracking system (ATS), which makes tailoring your resume specifically to each job the best way to ensure your resume is noticed and makes it through the system. Job seekers can do this by comparing their resume to the job description and using relevant key-words from the description on their resume. They need to show why they are the best match for the opening in order to be one of the top-ranked candidates. Here are other tips for helping your resume make it through an employer's ATS:

- Get rid of graphics and special characters. The ATS is breaking down your information and sorting it into different categories, and it won't be able to understand these when parsing your info.
- Choose web-safe fonts like Arial, Georgia, Impact, and Tahoma.

- Make your skills section as comprehensive as possible. Most employers use their ATS to search by technical or specialized skills. Spell out skills and also include industry specific abbreviations or acronyms.
- Avoid spelling errors. The ATS will miss an important keyword if you've misspelled it!

Conrad Martin

▶ Conrad Martin has been in the recruiting and staffing industries since 1998; he is Founder and Principal of OnPoint Search Group Inc., in the Boston area.

When I review resumes I look for three things before I present someone to one of my clients.

- How long have you been with your current employer and what is your track record with past employers? If you move from one job to the next every year, you will likely only spend a year at your next landing spot.
- What have you done in the past to help your employer achieve their goals and how would you quantify that in tangible results? For example, if you increased productivity in your department by 45 percent, I would be very interested in hearing about that.
- Is your resume concise and well written? Everyone is busy so get to the point.
- Hiring managers are interested in "what's in it for them." If your resume can clearly define what it is you can do for a potential employer, you will most certainly get a second look.

Patrick Lynch

▶ Patrick Lynch is the President of The Frontier Group, a career coaching and consulting practice with offices in Atlanta and Charlotte.

What we coach our clients on in starting their resume is to have a very clear objective statement. Your objective statement should let the decision-maker know what primary functional areas and marketable skills you want to use to enhance the organization. Remember you want to put the company's interests before your own! You must tell the decision-maker:

- The type of role you can play (by not specifying the exact level of responsibility and providing a variety of functional areas you are giving them options as to where you can fit into the organization). For instance, your objective could state: A management position in a customer driven organization utilizing my leadership skills in Sales and Marketing Management, Channel Development and Consultative Selling in order to increase sales for your organization.
- What you will do for the organization. For example, can you:
  - design/direct strategies to improve top line revenue and bottom line profitability;
  - identify/capitalize on opportunities to increase market penetration and capture greater market share;
  - establish relationships, build trust as subject matter expert and innovate solutions to close business and retain customer loyalty.
- By creating a clear objective, you have already defined the "product" that you want to take to the job market. A good resume can play a strong supporting role in your search by setting you apart from others and helping to communicate your strengths and capabilities.

Amanda Augustine

▶ Job Search Expert for TheLadders job-matching service, based in the New York headquarters.

- The resume is not about you—it's about how your skill set can provide value to a potential employer. Quantify your accomplishments whenever possible to show the reader how you can help their business cut costs, generate more revenue, become more efficient, etc.
- Don't assume the person viewing your resume knows your industry and line of work. Include a line in your resume that describes each company you've worked at so the viewer has a sense of how your role and title fit in the overall company.

- Incorporate keywords and phrases found in the job description into your resume so you'll make it past the computer and on to someone in recruiting or HR.
- Tailor your resume and cover letter so that you've clearly highlighted how you meet the primary requirements of the role. Recruiters only spend six seconds looking at your resume. If it's not obvious why you're a fit for the job, then chances are you won't receive a response.
- If you're looking to relocate, include the following at the end of your executive summary, "Willing to relocate at personal expense."
- Only apply to opportunities where you meet all the "must-haves" in the job description. If you apply to a job where you only "sort of" meet the requirements, you're not only wasting your application time, you're wasting the recruiter's time and losing credibility.
- Don't forget to follow up! The majority of job seekers do not attempt to follow up after a job application. By taking the time to track down the recruiter or hiring manager and send a follow-up message, you are setting yourself apart from the crowd.

Lisa Chau

▶ Assistant Director of Public Relations, Tuck School of Business at Dartmouth

- LinkedIn has become the new standard in corporate recruiting. It's more important than ever to make sure your online profile is updated and comprehensive.
- A focused summary is also important because it gives recruiters a quick overview of your credentials. If your background doesn't generate interest within a minute, it's unlikely you will be granted an interview.
- It's always advisable to use specifics, for example:

International marketing and public relations professional with a highly competent, results-oriented attitude and over six years' experience in the field, including four years of experience in higher education.

is better than simply:

International marketing and public relations professional with a highly competent, results-oriented attitude and over six years' experience in the field.

- Definitely quantify when possible by being able to answer questions like:
  - How much money did you save the company?
  - What was your annual sales record compared to the staff average?
  - How many people did you supervise?
- Every detail in your resume should be up-to-date and verifiable.

Now comes the tricky part: recommendations.

Recommendations are the most powerful piece of your virtual ecosystem. They will also take the most time and patience to cultivate. However, the reward is worth the effort.

- Try to get recommendations from people you reported to, people who report to you, and peers. Ideally, get three recommendations per position that you have held.
- I have found that the best time to ask for an endorsement is at the time of initial contact, when you ask to connect. After the person has agreed to write something for you, use LinkedIn's built-in tool for your request. The system auto-generates a link for your connection to follow and complete their testimonial of you.
- Always make the process as easy as possible for the other person.
- That said, the best method to help yourself is to help the other person by writing a draft for them to edit. When you send the draft, provide your connection with the information they will need when writing your endorsement, like how and when did you meet, the kind of work you did together, and what you'd like to have them emphasize. Also, write a sincere and unique recommendation for the other person. (Don't call everyone a "rock star." Be specific!) This will give them an idea of what you expect them to write for you. It will also make them feel good. Good luck!

Bill Belknap

▶ Bill Belknap is an Executive Career Coach (*www.billbelknap.com*) who has coached over 800 managers and executives in the last ten years. He has been working with resumes for more than thirty years.

- The first time around, the reader gives the resume about a ten-second scan. It is critical that your resume is structured to attract their eye to your accomplishments.
- Hiring managers are interested primarily in what you can do for them. "How many home runs will you hit, and how many bases will you steal?" It is all about performance.
- The resume becomes doubly critical in a tight market because the buyers can afford to be choosey.
- Well-written accomplishments, good appearance, user-friendly (lots of white space), no typos can mean the difference of making it into the "A" pile versus the "C" pile or worse, the "round file" or garbage can.
- Attention has to be paid to what makes you different; an accomplishment bullet does just that.
- Every accomplishment bullet must answer the simple question, "So what?" For example saying: "Developed a software program to improve the order entry process" doesn't tell the reader if it did or not. Said another way, what was the *business* impact for each of your accomplishments?

Jonathan Bujno

▶ Jonathan Bujno is a Senior Clinical Recruiter with Clinical Resource Network.

- The resume, like the diary or journal, is an introspective look at a person's past and present life. One major difference is that the resume's intent is often to lead you to employment, to money, and to success. Perhaps this is why it is such a difficult process. One thinks, "If this is no good, I won't be interviewed and I won't earn this job." This is generally true in my opinion. Initially, resumes are relied upon to screen candidates in or screen them out. It is often impossible to screen every candidate by phone, and managers will rely on the resume to represent skills and accomplishments. You may be the most qualified for the position; however, if your resume is a poor representation of your background, you may not be considered for the position. Therefore, one must take a careful approach to resume writing to ensure that they accurately portray potential.

- Writing a resume can be a lot easier than most people make it. The problem is, people tend to update it at the last minute and it's hard to remember what you did on the job for the last four years. Here are a few tips: If your human resources department gives you a job description when you're hired, keep it and file it somewhere. Also, buy a notebook and take it to work with you. Each time you do something new or accomplish something on the job, write it down. Updating your resume will now be much easier. Instead of trying to remember what it is you did, you can calmly refer to these resources and piece together your resume. Also, include examples of work-related initiative, diligence, and character on your resume. If you filled in for someone at the last minute and saved the company $30,000, include that.

- Your resume will be used as an interviewing tool. A good recruiter will probe everything you put on there. Know your information well and be careful of inconsistent information.

- Regarding format, keep it simple. Simple fonts, simple paper, simple color, and simple bulleted facts that are relevant to the position you are applying for. Design your own resume rather than using the standard Microsoft Office template. This will help your resume stand out. Include a summary of professional objectives, education, experience, and technical skills. From there, you may add (to name a few): certifications, publications, accreditations, involvement with community organizations, and additional education.

- Proofread, and when you think your resume is perfect, give it to someone else and let them look it over. Finally, we all know "references will be available upon request," so you don't need to include that.

- Preparing your resume doesn't have to be a frustrating experience. But if you do feel yourself becoming a bit heated, then pound the table, take a walk, scream, and yell, do what you do; just don't rush to get done! Remember, your resume can screen you out or screen you in. The latter is the goal.

Danilo Minnick

▶ Danilo Minnick was the Senior Recruiter for the Peace Corps Regional Office for five years and a retired Peace Corps volunteer who worked in Gambia.

I have viewed tons of resumes—not only volunteer applicants but also for staff positions. Believe me, I have gotten good at recognizing poor versus well-constructed documents. It really is the most important element of one's job search, and—along with a professional cover letter—it's the first step to "selling" yourself with the hope of being called for an interview. The essential "basics" and extra "frills" that do get my attention include:

- One page, especially for "newbies" (students or inexperienced workers). Of course, midcareer professionals or execs can go beyond that, but when a twenty something submits three pages, it's probably formatted with a lot of white space and has little substance and relevant detail.
- Bold and bullets recommended (no underlines or abbreviations except for the U.S. states).
- No salary or personal information.
- Identification includes name, address, phone, and even e-mail, centered on the page.
- Education and training are musts, even if just listing high school or certificates. If that is all they have, then this would be appropriate. The earlier you are in your career the more you might need to rely on high school records, for instance.
- When describing job responsibilities, use action words and accomplishments.
- Use bullets or concise three- to four-line paragraphs; a big block of type takes too long to browse quickly.
- Use a "Professional History" or related subheading to summarize many jobs. Through this section, expand upon qualifications that don't quite belong as detailed descriptions under each listing.

- Concise, consistent, dynamic phrasing that stresses results and accomplishments.
- Include a targeted or generalized skills summary.
- Avoid pronouns, use proper verb tenses, and check many times for spelling and mistakes. We do ask for revised resumes if an applicant isn't represented professionally, because documents are shared with the host before they decide whom they want to work in their countries.
- Don't ever lie.

Linda Matias

▶ Linda Matias is the president of CareerStrides, a nationally Certified Resume Writer (CRW), and the former president of The National Resume Writers' Association.

- Statistics indicate that the majority of hiring managers glance at resumes instead of reading them fully. It's hard to blame them, since most receive hundreds of resumes for every open position. With this statistic in mind, use bullet points sparingly—to bring attention to your most notable accomplishments. If the whole document is bulleted, it is difficult for the reader to know what is important and to quickly grasp your achievements. It's best to include responsibilities in paragraph form and only use bullets for special highlights.
- When developing your resume give thought to the person who will be reading it. What are his or her immediate concerns? How will you be able to solve that person's problems?
- Since the resume serves only as a synopsis of your accomplishments, you won't be able to include everything you've ever done. However, it is important that you identify all your achievements and then take great care in determining which ones you will include.
- Chances are, if your current manager was impressed by a specific accomplishment, your next employer may also be impressed. Therefore consider including the observations made by your current/previous manager.

- If you send a resume that lacks focus, the hiring manager will assume that you are unfocused and ready to accept any job that comes along. In the meantime, your competition is submitting focused resumes that speak to what the organization is looking for. Who do you think will be the one called in for an interview?
- It's okay if you have more than one focus. Most job seekers do. However, if you fall into this category, this means that you will need more than one resume. There really isn't any way around this. If you want to get noticed, the resumes you are submitting have to hone in on what the hiring organization is looking for.

Nancy D. Miller

▶ Nancy D. Miller is Executive Director of VISIONS: Services for the Blind and Visually Impaired.

I am most impressed with resumes that are:

- Neat, twelve to fourteen point font (ten point is too small).
- Clearly organized, simple to read, not in color so that copying is easier.
- Chronological with dates of employment starting from most recent.
- No more than two pages (preferably one); includes talents, hobbies, specialties.
- Neat and typo-free and without whiteout.

I am most impressed with resumes that include:

- Computer or software expertise.
- Languages spoken and/or written other than English.
- For recent grads, part-time and/or volunteer work statements that specify which jobs were paid.
- Education, with university, date, and degree received.

Because a cover letter is as important as a resume:

- Write to me and refer specifically to the job I am advertising or specify that you are conducting a general search.

- It should be personalized to the organization you are approaching.
- Let your personality show through without being cutesy.

Barry Goldman

▶ Barry Goldman is Critical Skills Internship Manager at Lawrence Livermore National Laboratory.

While the first half of my career was as a recruiter, the latter part has been administering internships—including placing students in projects at an R & D facility. I have over thirty years of experience in human resources, ranging from recruitment, staff relations, compensation, and education. Past employers include McGraw-Hill, Stauffer Chemical, Exxon, and Westinghouse. The following are my thoughts on the topic of resumes:

- A resume is not intended to get you a job. It is intended to get you in the door to be interviewed. As a result, resumes should be targeted to the specific opening for which you are applying. The initial reviewers of a resume may very well be just screeners without any technical expertise. The resume will be reviewed against established criteria for the posting. Therefore, use the same wording as the ad—otherwise, a nontechnical person might not recognize your match and screen you out instead of in!
- There are many kinds of resumes or formats for resumes. Determine the format that is appropriate for the application. Keep in mind there are also differences in resumes that will be hand submitted or included with a cover letter versus one that may be sent electronically.
- Every word on a resume should have meaning. If it doesn't, omit it.
- While not about resumes, it's okay if you're able to interview with others based on family and contacts of friends. Remember, if you are offered the job, it is not usually because of whom you know but because of your skills and what you will bring to the job.
- If you are applying in response to an ad, as mentioned previously, use the language from the ad. If applying as a cold call, it is even more important to research the company. Check out their home page. Maybe there is a search engine that will allow you to research your interests in line with company programs. Check out their organiza-

tional chart and job postings. Postings will give you a flavor for their needs and types of openings. Possibly they have hyperlinks to publications that are available externally?

- The more you can identify project or employee names that can be referenced on your application, the more you will increase your chances of being successful by getting it to the attention of the right people.
- As a past recruiter, a thank-you letter after an interview is advised. Anything to keep visibility on your name, availability, and on what makes you different than other applicants. Managers also like this form of follow-through as they would like to see this characteristic also in their employees.

Timothy G. Wiedman, DBA, PHR

▶ Timothy G. Wiedman is an Assistant Professor of Management and Human Resources in the Division of Economics and Business at Doane College in Crete, Nebraska.

- For many types of jobs, employers require a cover letter along with the Applicant's resume. In this situation, the written documents supplied should be concise, grammatically correct, error-free, and sufficiently customized to address the specific requirements of the position as advertised. Further, the cover letter should give screeners a reason to thoroughly review the resume, so it needs to make a good "first impression." Thus, a rambling, multiple-page (boilerplate?) cover letter that largely provides information unrelated to the position will not be well received. Further, if the position in question requires good communication skills, errors in punctuation, grammar, spelling, or clarity will likely remove the application package from further consideration.
- A well-written cover letter states why an applicant might be a good fit for a specific position rather than why a person might generally make a good employee in any (un-named) job that might be available. So specifically address the position and its stated job requirements, be clear and concise, proofread for errors, revise as needed, and proofread again.

- If possible, have all documents proofread by somebody else who has good communication skills. A second set of eyes will often see mistakes that the author overlooked. Finally, when it comes to cover letters, shorter is usually better. A lot of information about an applicant's background and experience can be condensed when it is put into a bullet format. The bullets act as headlines for the more detailed information contained in the resume. Thus, a one-page cover letter can often address all of the specific job requirements as advertised, and entice the screener to read the resume as well.

Use This to Your Benefit

Clearly the perspectives of the hiring managers and HR professionals you will encounter in your job search vary. Yet the basics of effectively presenting your background and qualifications through your resume remain consistent: focusing on those items that present you in the most positive light based on the specific organization you are contacting, maintaining professionalism in terms of your approach and the accuracy of the information you present as well as how it's presented, and considering how you can most effectively capture the attention of those who will be making decisions about whether or not you will move on to the next step in the hiring process—an interview.

PART 2

Sample Resumes

CHAPTER 10

Sample Designs

This chapter contains seven common resume formats and designs. Look each one over carefully and experiment with combining different formats to get the results you feel best match the image you wish to convey.

Chris Smith

123 Main Street • Hometown, NY 00000 • (555) 555-1234 • csmith@company.com

Consulting Qualifications

- Specialized knowledge of e-business models and techniques related to market segmentation.
- Skills gained conducting real and academic focused case analyses related to Wal-Mart and Dell Computers and projects investigating marketing and distribution strategies.
- Capacities to research, analyze data, identify trends, and create proposals, plans, and documents.
- Word, Excel, PowerPoint, InDesign, Netscape, Explorer, and Internet talents.
- German and English fluency and conversational French and Swedish talents.

Economics, Business, and Mathematics Studies and Honors

2009–2013   UNIVERSITY OF ROCHESTER, Rochester, NY
Bachelor of Arts, Economics, with Mathematics Minor, anticipated May 2013
Economics GPA of 4.0 and **Overall** GPA of 3.92 and **Mathematics** GPA of 3.91
- John Dows Mairs Economics Prize for a Junior achieving the best in the field
- Golden Key International Honour Society and Omicron Delta Epsilon International Honor Society for Economics
- Courses at Uppsala University, Uppsala, Sweden, Fall 2011

2009–2013   WILLIAM E. SIMON SCHOOL OF BUSINESS ADMINISTRATION, Rochester,
NY

Management Studies Certificate, with Marketing Track, May 2013
- Simon Scholar tuition scholarship applied to future enrollment at Simon School

Selected Business, Economics, and Mathematics Courses

Financial Accounting, Statistics, Principles of Economics, Intermediate Micro- and Macroeconomics, Economic Growth in America, Economic Thinking, Teaching Assistant for Microeconomics, Probability and Statistical Inference, Advanced Microeconomics, Econometrics, Marketing, Economics of the Organization, International Organizations.

Research and Policy Analysis Experience

2012   EUROPEAN PARLIAMENT, Brussels, Belgium
Intern: Supported efforts of German SPD delegation and 35 MEPs. Performed competitive analysis of German parties impacting federal elections of 2012. Researched and wrote paper on topic of emissions trading from environmental, economic, and industrial standpoints.

Business, Strategic Planning, and Quantitative Experience

SAATCHI & SAATCHI ROWLAND, Rochester, NY
Summer 2012   **Freelance Media Assistant:** Assisted media team with DuPont 2012 and 2013 media planning.
Winter 2011   **Account Management and Media Intern:** Assisted with customer profiling and competitive ad spending runs for DuPont Teflon.
Summer 2011   **Account Management and Media Intern:** Performed product research and customer profiling, interviews with sales representatives to construct marketing plans for various Bausch & Lomb products, such as ReNu, Purevision, and Ocuvite.

Block Text, Caps Headlines, Paragraph Descriptions, with Right Justified Timeline

Chris Smith

123 Main Street • Hometown, NY 00000 • (555) 555-1234 • csmith@company.com

CONSULTING QUALIFICATIONS

- Specialized knowledge of e-business models and techniques related to market segmentation.
- Skills gained conducting real and academic focused case analyses related to Wal-Mart and Dell Computers and projects investigating marketing and distribution strategies.
- Capacities to research, analyze data, identify trends, and create proposals, plans, and documents.
- Word, Excel, PowerPoint, InDesign, Netscape, Explorer, and Internet talents.
- German and English fluency and conversational French and Swedish talents.

ECONOMICS, BUSINESS, AND MATH STUDIES AND HONORS

UNIVERSITY OF ROCHESTER   ROCHESTER, NY
Bachelor of Arts, Economics with a Mathematics Minor   **anticipated May 2013**

- Economics GPA of 4.0 and Overall GPA of 3.92, and Mathematics GPA of 3.91
- Recipient of John Dows Mairs Economics Prize for a Junior achieving the best in the field
- Golden Key International Honour Society and Omicron Delta Epsilon International Honor Society for Economics

WILLIAM E. SIMON SCHOOL OF BUSINESS ADMINISTRATION   ROCHESTER, NY
Management Studies Certificate, with Marketing Track   **anticipated May 2013**

- Courses include: Financial Accounting, Statistics, Principles of Economics, Intermediate Micro- and Macroeconomics, Economic Growth in America, Economic Thinking, Probability and Statistical Inference, Econometrics, Marketing, and International Organizations
- Recipient of Simon Scholar tuition scholarship applied to future enrollment at Simon School

BUSINESS, STRATEGIC PLANNING, AND POLICY ANALYSIS EXPERIENCE

EUROPEAN PARLIAMENT   BRUSSELS, BELGIUM
Intern   **2012**

Supported efforts of German SPD delegation and 35 MEPs. Performed competitive analysis of German parties impacting federal elections of 2012. Also, researched and wrote paper on topic of emissions trading from environmental, economic, and industrial standpoints.

SAATCHI & SAATCHI ROWLAND   ROCHESTER, NY
Freelance Media Assistant   **Summer 2012**

Assisted media team with DuPont 2007 and 2008 media planning.

Account Management and Media Intern   **Winter 2011**

Assisted with customer profiling and competitive ad spending runs for DuPont Teflon.

Account Management and Media Intern   **Summer 2011**

Performed product research and customer profiling, as well as assisting sales representatives with constructing marketing plans for various Bausch & Lomb products, such as ReNu, Purevision, and Ocuvite. Expanded knowledge of marketing, strategic planning, account management, and client relations. Nurtured project management, writing, communication, and team skills.

Block Text, Caps Headlines, Bullet Descriptions, with Right Justified Timeline

Chris Smith

123 Main Street • Hometown, NY 00000 • (555) 555-1234 • csmith@company.com

CONSULTING QUALIFICATIONS

- Specialized knowledge of e-business models and techniques related to market segmentation.
- Skills gained conducting real and academic focused case analyses related to Wal-Mart and Dell Computers and projects investigating marketing and distribution strategies.
- Capacities to research, analyze data, identify trends, and create proposals, plans, and documents.
- Word, Excel, PowerPoint, InDesign, Netscape, Explorer, and Internet talents.
- German and English fluency and conversational French and Swedish talents.

ECONOMICS, BUSINESS, AND MATH STUDIES AND HONORS

UNIVERSITY OF ROCHESTER   Rochester, NY
Bachelor of Arts, Economics, with **Mathematics** minor   anticipated May 2013
Economics GPA of 4.0, **Overall** GPA of 3.92, and **Mathematics** GPA of 3.91
- Recipient of John Dows Mairs Economics Prize for a Junior achieving the best in the field.
- Golden Key International Honour Society and Omicron Delta Epsilon International Honor Society for Economics.

WILLIAM E. SIMON SCHOOL OF BUSINESS ADMINISTRATION   Rochester, NY
Management Studies Certificate, with Marketing Track   anticipated May 2013
- Courses include: Financial Accounting, Statistics, Principles of Economics, Intermediate Micro- and Macroeconomics, Economic Growth in America, Economic Thinking, Probability and Statistical Inference, Advanced Microeconomics, Econometrics, Marketing, and International Organizations.
- Recipient of Simon Scholar tuition scholarship applied to future enrollment at Simon School.

RESEARCH AND POLICY ANALYSIS EXPERIENCE

EUROPEAN PARLIAMENT   Brussels, Belgium
Intern   2012
- Supported efforts of German SPD delegation and 35 MEPs and performed competitive analysis of German parties impacting federal elections of 2012.
- Also, researched and wrote paper on topic of emissions trading from environmental, economic, and industrial standpoints.

BUSINESS, STRATEGIC PLANNING, AND QUANTITATIVE EXPERIENCE

SAATCHI & SAATCHI ROWLAND   Rochester, NY
Freelance Media Assistant   Summer 2012
- Assisted media team with DuPont 2012 and 2013 media planning.
Account Management and Media Intern   Winter 2011
- Assisted with customer profiling and competitive ad spending runs for DuPont Teflon.
Account Management and Media Intern   Summer 2011
- Performed product research and customer profiling, and interviews with sales representatives to construct marketing plans for various Bausch & Lomb products, such as ReNu, Purevision, and Ocuvite. Expanded knowledge of marketing, strategic planning, account management, and client relations.

Jamie Brown

123 Main St. • Hometown, MN 00000 • (555) 555-1234 • jbrown@company.com

BUSINESS AND FINANCE EXPERIENCE

June 2011–
Present

RBC Capital Markets (formerly Dain Rauscher Wessels), Minneapolis, MN
Analyst, Investment Banking, Healthcare Group
- One of fifteen investment banking professionals serving life sciences companies.
- Advise clients on M&A candidates and perform strategic analysis; conduct due diligence; determine valuation parameters; evaluate pro formas; and identify potential acquirers/targets.
- Assist in the execution of equity, debt, and private placement offering process.
- Identify potential clients; develop presentations; participate in introductory meetings; evaluate company, analyze sector- and market-related issues affecting a transaction.
- Manage documentation; support Equity Research, Capital Markets, and Sales & Trading; and assist in transaction committee approval process.
- Perform company valuation including discounted cash-flow analyses, comparable company analyses, and precedent transaction analyses.
- Develop models to analyze mergers, equity, debt, and private placement offerings.
- Assist Research Analysts and advise Investment Bankers on technology and product assessment, applying industry knowledge gained via education and experience.

RESEARCH EXPERIENCE

Summer 2010

Vaccinex Inc., Rochester, NY
Research Intern, Cellular and Molecular Immunology Department

Summer 2009

University of Rochester Medical Center, Rochester, NY
Laboratory Assistant, Department of Pharmacology and Physiology Peracchia Lab

Summers 2007
and 2008

Harvard Medical School, Brookline, MA
Department of Epidemiology Research Assistant

BUSINESS AND ENGINEERING STUDIES

2007–2011

William E. Simon School of Business Administration, Rochester, NY
Management Studies Certificate, May 2006
- Certificate for completion of courses in Financial Markets, Financial Accounting, Marketing Management, Economics, Computer Programming, and Statistics.

2007–2011

University of Rochester, Rochester, NY
Bachelor of Science in Chemical Engineering, May 2006
- Emphasis on Life Sciences systems; including courses in Biochemical Engineering, Biotechnology, Biochemistry, Clinical Diagnostics, Reactor Design, Separation Processes, and Organic Chemistry.

Side Headlines, Block and Justified Text and Descriptions, Right Justified Timeline

DANA JOHNSON
123 MAIN STREET • HOMETOWN, NEW YORK 00000 • 555.555.1234 • DJOHNSON@COMPANY.COM

OBJECTIVE

Pharmaceutical sales representative position.

QUALIFICATIONS

- Experience building and maintaining relationships with physicians, surgeons, and nurses.
- Ability to interface with individuals at all levels of health care organization.
- Results oriented and ready to implement marketing strategies that meet and exceed goals.
- Adept at processing and conveying complex terminology via written and verbal communication.
- Timely and assertive follow-up skills to handle inquiries and reinforce existing relationships.

MARKETING AND COMMUNICATION ACHIEVEMENTS

Albert Einstein Hospital   **New York, NY**
Assistant Director of Public Relations   *May 2004–Present*

Function as PR account representative for medical center and 750-bed hospital. Develop and maintain relationships with physicians, surgeons, and nurses. Generate publicity for urology, orthopedics, neurology, neurosurgery, blood/marrow transplant, emergency medicine, dermatology, radiology, anesthesiology, and otolaryngology. Proactively and effectively pitch stories to news media. Serve as spokesperson and liaison to local/national news media, on-call 24/7 as needed. Write news releases and speeches. Assist news crews and direct press briefings. Develop text for brochures, fundraising pieces, and Web sites. Write op-ed pieces and letters to the editor. Direct, write, produce, and edit videos. Develop and implement strategic publicity plans.

New Jersey Corn Cooperative   **New Brunswick, NJ**
Communications Manager   *June 2000–December 2003*

Directed all aspects of corporate communications/public relations for 600-member cooperative. Managed production of monthly member newsletter, quarterly employee newsletter, and annual report. Served as spokesperson and liaison to local and national news media. Wrote news releases, pitched stories, created print ads/brochures, and assisted with speech writing. Directed public relations events at fairs, schools, and festivals. Performed all in-house photography.

Princeton Vineyards & Winery   **Princeton, NJ**
Sales Representative   *Summers 1997 and 1998*

Served as tasting room sales representative and tour guide for 30,000-gallon winery. Managed all tasting room operations and represented winery at festivals and other events.

EDUCATION

New York University   **New York, NY**
Bachelor of Science, Communication   *May 2000*

184

Side Headlines, Indented and Paragraph Descriptions

DANA JOHNSON

123 MAIN STREET • HOMETOWN, NEW YORK 00000 • 555.555.1234 • DJOHNSON@COMPANY.COM

PHARMACEUTICAL SALES QUALIFICATIONS

- Experience building and maintaining relationships with physicians, surgeons, and nurses.
- Ability to interface with individuals at all levels of health care organization.
- Results-oriented and ready to implement marketing strategies that meet and exceed goals.
- Adept at processing and conveying complex terminology via written and verbal communication.
- Timely and assertive follow-up skills to handle inquiries and reinforce existing relationships.

MARKETING AND COMMUNICATION ACHIEVEMENTS

Albert Einstein Hospital, New York, NY
Assistant Director of Public Relations, May 2004–Present
Function as PR account representative for medical center and 750-bed hospital. Develop and maintain relationships with physicians, surgeons, and nurses. Generate publicity for urology, orthopedics, neurology, neurosurgery, blood/marrow transplant, emergency medicine, dermatology, radiology, anesthesiology, and otolaryngology. Proactively and effectively pitch stories to news media. Serve as spokesperson and liaison to local/national news media, on-call 24/7 as needed. Write news releases and speeches. Assist news crews and direct press briefings. Develop text for brochures, fundraising pieces, and Web sites. Write op-ed pieces and letters to the editor. Direct, write, produce, and edit videos. Develop and implement strategic publicity plans.

New Jersey Corn Cooperative, New Brunswick, NJ
Communications Manager, June 2000–December 2003
Directed all aspects of corporate communications/public relations for 600-member cooperative. Managed production of monthly member newsletter, quarterly employee newsletter, and annual report. Served as spokesperson and liaison to local and national news media. Wrote news releases, pitched stories, created print ads/brochures, and assisted with speech writing. Directed public relations events at fairs, schools, and festivals. Performed all in-house photography.

Princeton Vineyards & Winery, Princeton, NJ
Sales Representative, Summers 1997 and 1998
Served as tasting room sales representative and tour guide for 30,000-gallon winery. Managed all tasting room operations and represented winery at festivals and other events.

EDUCATION

New York University, New York, NY
Bachelor of Science, Communication, May 2000

DANA JOHNSON

123 MAIN STREET • HOMETOWN, NEW YORK 00000 • 555.555.1234 • DJOHNSON@COMPANY.COM

PHARMACEUTICAL SALES QUALIFICATIONS

- Experience building and maintaining relationships with physicians, surgeons, and nurses.
- Ability to interface with individuals at all levels of health care organization.
- Results-oriented and ready to implement marketing strategies that meet and exceed goals.
- Adept at processing and conveying complex terminology via written and verbal communication.
- Timely and assertive follow-up skills to handle inquiries and reinforce existing relationships.

MARKETING AND COMMUNICATION ACHIEVEMENTS

Albert Einstein Hospital, New York, NY
Assistant Director of Public Relations, May 2004–Present
Function as PR account representative for medical center and 750-bed hospital. Develop and maintain relationships with physicians, surgeons, and nurses. Generate publicity for urology, orthopedics, neurology, neurosurgery, blood/marrow transplant, emergency medicine, dermatology, radiology, anesthesiology, and otolaryngology. Proactively and effectively pitch stories to news media. Serve as spokesperson and liaison to local/national news media, on-call 24/7 as needed. Write news releases and speeches. Assist news crews and direct press briefings. Develop text for brochures, fundraising pieces, and Web sites. Write op-ed pieces and letters to the editor. Direct, write, produce, and edit videos. Develop and implement strategic publicity plans.

New Jersey Corn Cooperative, New Brunswick, NJ
Communications Manager, June 2000–December 2003
Directed all aspects of corporate communications/public relations for 600-member cooperative. Managed production of monthly member newsletter, quarterly employee newsletter, and annual report. Served as spokesperson and liaison to local and national news media. Wrote news releases, pitched stories, created print ads/brochures, and assisted with speech writing. Directed public relations events at fairs, schools, and festivals. Performed all in-house photography.

Princeton Vineyards & Winery, Princeton, NJ
Sales Representative, Summers 1997 and 1998
Served as tasting room sales representative and tour guide for 30,000-gallon winery. Managed all tasting room operations and represented winery at festivals and other events.

EDUCATION

New York University, New York, NY
Bachelor of Science, Communication, May 2000

CHAPTER 11

Sample Resumes

If imitation is the sincerest form of flattery, it is also the best resume writing and job search strategy. Sample resumes give you a great place to start, whether you're writing your resume from scratch, or making your existing resume more effective.

Getting Started

In Chapter 8, you reviewed and analyzed several sample resumes. You are now ready to do the same for many more. The following samples represent varied career fields, yet they possess characteristics common to all great resumes. Don't limit your review to resumes that match your goals. Find one or two that do, and then investigate a few more that strike you as particularly appealing.

ALERT

Note that font sizes and word counts were reduced slightly to allow sample resumes to fit on the illustration pages. When creating your resume, use these as guides, but feel free to write as much as will fit, while maintaining a visually appealing document. Most resumes created on 8½" × 11" pages will contain more copy and lines than the samples.

Keep those pens, highlighters, and sticky notes handy! Buy more, if you must. You'll make the best progress, and get the most out of your reviews, if you take notes as you go. Circle elements that you think are particularly effective. Query the elements that don't work for you. Later, as you start writing your own first draft, you'll use these gut reactions to make your own resume as powerful as possible.

Also keep track of words, phrases, designs, and details that you find appealing. When looking at elements, consider how well these reflect who you are. If you pride yourself on being professional and slightly conservative, don't worry about adding lots of flash and style to your resume. Likewise, if you want to convey an attitude of being creative and edgy, don't structure your resume to look overwhelmingly professional and dry.

CHRIS SMITH

123 Main Street • Hometown, MT 00000 • (555) 555-5555 • csmith@company.com

ACCOUNTING EXPERIENCE AND ACHIEVEMENTS

ROSS PECOE, INC., Billings, MT
Senior Accountant, 2008–Present
Oversee all accounting and payroll functions for a $20 million publicly held company that develops, manufactures, and markets proprietary x-ray systems.

- Assist controller in preparing financial statements and SEC reports.
- Prepare budgets and projections and monthly budget-to-actual reports and distribute to managers.
- Review work of staff accountant and approve journal transactions for data entry.
- Manage accounting duties of a venture-capital-funded start-up spinoff organization, Beta Technologies, including financial reporting and coordinating annual audit with external auditors.
- Interact with systems and payroll services professionals regarding problems and solutions.
- Assisted with analyzing implications, making final decisions, and completion of consolidation of three European subsidiaries.

Accountant, 2006–2009
- Assisted with monthly closings and financial reporting.
- Worked directly with controller to prepare primary and secondary public stock offerings.
- Implemented Solomon general ledger accounting package.
- Installed and set up modules, developed procedures for new system, and trained staff.

STEADFAST CORPORATION, Cheny Creek, MT
Staff Accountant, 2004–2006
- Monitored cash and accounts receivable for venture-capital-funded software development firm.
- Assisted in general ledger close, including foreign currency translation of foreign subsidiaries.
- Trained new employees to administer the accounts payable and order entry functions.

GRADUATE AND UNDERGRADUATE ACCOUNTING STUDIES

BRONTE COLLEGE, Newcastle, MT
Master of Science in Accountancy, Expected Completion May 2013

CARROLL COLLEGE, Helena, MT
Bachelor of Arts, Business Management, Accounting/Finance emphasis, June 2004

TECHNICAL ACCOUNTING SKILLS AND COMPETENCIES

- Skills associated with progressively responsible internal auditing, managerial accounting, budgeting, and financial analysis roles.
- Capacities to use and teach Excel and QuickBooks.
- Experience interacting with external auditors, internal financial colleagues, as well as financial managers and senior executives.
- Capacities to draft, edit, and finalize detailed financial reports.
- Specialized knowledge of due diligence and risk analysis associated with venture capital funding and initial private offerings.

CHRIS SMITH

123 Main Street • Hometown, VA 00000 • (555) 555-1234 • Cell (555) 555-5678

csmith@company.com

QUALIFICATIONS

- More than twelve years of progressive sales and sales management responsibilities leading to current position as National Account Manager
- Experience developing and implementing marketing strategies, overseeing sales professionals, and developing effective sales relationships with direct users and resellers of personal computers and mainframes, as well as peripheral equipment, customer service contacts, and computer consulting services
- Capacities to hire, train, and motivate sales colleagues and to create reports identifying key profit areas and potential markets

ACHIEVEMENTS

- Progressive achievements within management and direct sales roles, directly contributing to expanded profits and sales
- A career averaging consistent percentage increases year after year, contributing to millions of dollars in sales and profits
- Capacities to generate continued sales growth within an industry where competitors increased annually and market required sensitivities to pricing and service

SALES ACCOMPLISHMENTS

STARBUCK COMPUTERS INC., Richmond, VA

2007–Present

National Account Manager

Develop and implement national sales strategy for computer and peripheral manufacturer, consultant, and support-service provider. Initiated, built, and nurtured relationships with several Richmond-based *Fortune* 500 corporations including Ackler Industrial, the Carnulton Group, Hanlon and Associates, and Polamin Company. Oversee resale accounts as well as direct-user accounts. Involves identification and analysis of potential business applications within target accounts and cultivation of key business relationships with senior management to facilitate sales.

- Average performance over five-year period was 125%.
- Grew Starbuck profits 200% over five years to $15 million amidst decreasing unit pricing, increasing sales goals, and enhanced competition.
- Completed all five years in the top 12% of the National Account Channel as Golden Star Award winner.
- Created new revenue streams resulting in an estimated $30 million in Starbuck sales and $40 million in new services for the company.
- Regularly report sales results and status of strategies to senior marketing executives and CEO.

CHRIS SMITH
Page Two

STARBUCK COMPUTERS INC., Richmond, VA

2004–2007

Dealer Account Executive

As team leader and dealer liaison, oversaw completion of relationship building, bidding, delivery, and all sales efforts required to market Starbuck products and services through dealer locations.

- Initiated cooperative sales strategy with reseller business owners.
- Designed marketing promotions and directed reseller's sales efforts into business and education accounts.
- Average performance over six year period was 110% and recognized by Golden Star Club Awards.
- Grew sales by 400% to $20 million.
- Oversee training and completed performance reviews of 10–15 Sales Representatives.

2002–2004

Corporate Chain Account Sales Representative

Provided administrative and technical sales support to Richmond corporate chain account locations, including Power Electronics, Computer Corral, and Circonne Computer.

- Regularly called upon accounts to maximize knowledge of retail personnel, address concerns, and promote in-store visibility.
- Developed marketing promotions and trained store personnel.
- Tracked individual store sales and profit data to determine efficient coverage schedule and recognize particular achievements.

Summers and
Part-time
2000–2002

Customer Support Representative

- Resolved customer issues including invoicing discrepancies, shipping errors, and hardware upgrades.

EDUCATION

1998–2002

UNIVERSITY OF TEXAS AT DALLAS, Dallas, TX
B.A., Communications and Political Science, May 2002

DANA JOHNSON

123 Main Street • Hometown, NY 00000 • (555) 555-6509 • djohnson@company.com

Administrative Qualifications

- Skills and perspectives gained through progressively responsible administrative roles.
- Abilities to prioritize tasks and complete tasks accurately and on time in deadline-sensitive settings.
- Professionalism required to address concerns of patients and clients while maintaining office efficiency and following standardized procedures and policies.
- Flexibility required to transform instructions and feedback of diverse supervisors into projects completed independently and thoroughly.
- Capacities to use, support, and train others to use Word, Excel, Access, and PowerPoint.

Administrative and Office Management Experience and Achievements

LOYALTY INVESTMENTS, Albany, NY
Administrative Assistant, 2008–Present
- Provide administrative support for new business development group; assist CFO with special projects.
- Ensure smooth workflow; facilitate effectiveness of fourteen sales consultants.
- Direct incoming calls; initiate new client application process; maintain applicant record database.
- Aid in streamlining application process.
- Assist in design and implementation of computer automation system.

JENNINGS HOSPITAL, Washington, D.C.
Radiation Therapy Department Secretary, 2006–2008
- Answered phones, scheduled appointments, greeted patients and visitors, and prepared and filed charts.
- Typed and printed invoices and requisitions.
- Supervised inventory and general office organization.
- Served as liaison between physicians, staff, and patients.

Additional Business Experience

GROVER FINANCE, Buffalo, NY
Telemarketing Sales Representative, Summers and Part-time 2003–2006
- Secured new business using customer inquiries and mass-mailing responses; provided product line information to prospective clients. Initiated loan application and qualifying processes.
- Maintained daily call records and monthly sales breakdown.
- Acquired comprehensive product-line knowledge and ability to quickly assess customer needs and assemble appropriate financial packages.

Education

HOFSTRA UNIVERSITY, Hempstead, NY
Bachelor of Arts, English, Concentration: Business 2008
- Dean's List two of four eligible semesters and overall GPA 3.3

TRIBORO JUNIOR COLLEGE, Denver, CO
Associate of Arts, Business, 2004–2006

Advertising Account Executive

Jamie Brown

123 Main Street • Hometown, NY 00000 • (555) 555-1234 • jbrown@company.com
987 Centre Avenue • Apartment 13 • New York, NY 10001 • (555) 555-5678

ADVERTISING ACCOUNT MANAGEMENT QUALIFICATIONS

- Marketing research, strategic planning, promotions, customer service, and sales talents nurtured by in-depth and diverse advertising, promotions, and retail internships and employment.
- Skills gained via courses including: Principles of Marketing, Marketing Projects and Cases, Psychology of Human Motivation, Public Relations Writing, Advertising, and Consumer Behavior.
- Blend of research, analysis, writing, and presentation talents.
- German, French, Dutch, and Farsi fluency, and conversational Spanish capabilities.
- UNIX, HTML, Excel, PowerPoint, PhotoShop, Netscape.

ADVERTISING, MARKETING, AND FINANCE EXPERIENCE

DAYS ADVERTISING, INC., Pittsford, NY
Intern/Assistant to Account Manager: Assisted with design of television and radio ads and proposals for varied clients, including Wegmans and Bausch & Lomb. Developed customer database. Summer 2011

ADEFFECTS, Rochester, NY
Intern/Assistant to Account Manager: Researched and developed promotional materials for retail, manufacturing, and restaurant clients. Gained knowledge of small business marketing. Suggested changes in advertising materials, consumer outreach strategies, and marketing literature. May 2010–July 2011

THE FINANCIAL GROUP, INC. DISCOUNT BROKERAGE FIRM, Pittsford, NY
Intern/Assistant to Operations Manager, January–May 2011

PEARLE VISION CENTER, Pittsford, NY
Sales Representative: Assisted customers and ordered inventory targeting upscale market. Summer 2006

IT HAPPENS, Antwerp, Belgium
Marketing Intern: Determined target markets and developed advertisement budget for concert and entertainment agency. Collected and analyzed financial and marketing data. Conducted market surveys to determine market penetration. Assisted graphic artists with ads, posters, and brochures. Summer 2008

BUSINESS, ECONOMICS, AND LANGUAGE STUDIES

UNIVERSITY OF ROCHESTER, Rochester, NY
Bachelor of Arts, French, with a major GPA of 3.5, May 2012
Bachelor of Arts, Psychology, May 2012
Minor: **Economics**

WILLIAM E. SIMON GRADUATE SCHOOL OF BUSINESS ADMINISTRATION, Rochester, NY
Management Studies Certificate, Marketing and Finance/Accounting Tracks, May 2012.

HOBART AND WILLIAM SMITH COLLEGES, Geneva, NY
Completed varied Economics and Liberal Arts Courses prior to transferring, 2008–2009.

JAMIE BROWN

123 Main Street • Hometown, PA 00000 • (555) 555-1234 • jbrown@company.com

MEDIA PLANNING QUALIFICATIONS AND ACHIEVEMENTS

- Area of expertise is advertising media planning, with special knowledge of television and magazine options.
- Ability to project and elicit client enthusiasm and drive using a quantitative yet common sense approach.
- Adept at analyzing client needs, demographics, pricing and account team strategies, and then developing appropriate courses of action to yield desired results.
- Seven years advertising media planning experience; handling accounts with up to $7 million annual budgets.
- Strong service and interpersonal skills with clients, colleagues, and media sales professionals.
- Proven supervisory skills, effectively training staff in new concepts and procedures, monitoring performance, and maximizing output.
- Expertise in Word, Excel, Access, and PowerPoint for development of plans, proposals, budgets, financial analyses and projections, as well as presentations.

MEDIA PLANNING EXPERIENCE

THE MERCER MEDIA GROUP   Philadelphia, PA
Senior Media Planner   2002–Present
- Direct all phases of media planning services for national accounts, primarily based in eastern region.
- Plan media and placement for five of the firm's largest clients, with annual media budgets ranging from $1 million to $7 million, and total media budgets in excess of $15 million.
- Oversee efforts of two Media Coordinators, a Media Assistant, and two support professionals.
- Created Excel and Access systems to track media plans and purchases, client quarterly sales, and profits.
- Regularly interact with account services colleagues and with clients to address queries, determine commitment to existing plans, and redirect plans as needed.

Account Supervisor and Media Coordinator   2000–2002
- Trained, guided, and directed staff of five while monitoring ad placement system.
- Assisted in creation of advertising campaigns and acted as liaison between client, agency, and media vendors, including selection, budget, and advertisement placement.

MERTON KASS & HOWE   Philadelphia, PA
Advertising and Public Relations Internship   Summers and Part-time 1998–2000
- Conducted market research, wrote press releases, produced traffic reports, worked media events, and assisted with advertising production.

EDUCATION

RUTGERS UNIVERSITY AT CAMDEN   Camden, NJ
B.A. in Mass Communication, with a minor in English   2000

PROFESSIONAL AFFILIATION

The Advertising Club of Pennsylvania

Applications Programmer

Francis Williams

123 Main Street • Apartment 13 • Hometown, NY 00000 • (555) 555-1234
fwilliams@company.com

APPLICATIONS PROGRAMMING EXPERIENCE

BENTLEY LIFE INSURANCE, New York, NY

2008–Present — **Programmer Analyst/Senior Programmer**

Supervised junior programmers on varied System Projects.

- Actively participated in projects involving e-commerce, CRM, BI, or ERP functions.
- Developed, maintained, and supported Sales Illustration Systems in C.
- Wrote "Illustration Software Installation" routine in INSTALIT software.
- Designed file transfer process for Mainframe to PC using NDM software.
- Hands-on experience with PC hardware, Windows, IBM, Novell Software, Emulation Software (Rumba, Extra, etc.), Dial-in Software (SimPC, XTalk, etc.), and have understanding of LAN technologies.
- Developed an Executive Information System on the mainframe using COBOL 2.

MEDWARE CORPORATION, New York, NY

2005–2008 — **Senior Programmer—Patient Scheduling System**

Served as senior member of programming and testing team for software company specializing in health care industry.

- Designed and implemented system enhancements and new products.

2003–2005 — **Programmer/Analyst**

- Developed online message system for members of the programming group.
- Instituted utilities that aided detection and repairs of client bugs.

SHADOW ASSOCIATES, Hartford, CT

Summers 2001, 2002 — **Co-op Computer Programmer**

- Developed and maintained program that monitored product availability and inventory for branch sites, displaying new product releases, and accessing updated information daily.

GRADUATE AND UNDERGRADUATE ENGINEERING EDUCATION

NEW YORK UNIVERSITY, New York, NY
MS Electrical Engineering, Software and Networks emphases, 2005
BS Engineering, 2003

QUALIFICATIONS

- Knowledge of C, COBOL, SQL Server 2000/2005, Web Services, Visual Basic, JavaScript, Assembly, C++ Cajon, Pascal, LISP, IBM, PL/I, Prolog, AION Databases: SQL/DS, Oracle
- Effective design, resource allocation, and status evaluation skills associated with large projects that shaped production testing and data collection processes.
- Proficient at designing and implementing program enhancements, including an online message system, database repair/troubleshooting utilities, and release system to update clients.

Corey Davis

123 Main Street • Hometown, NJ 00000 • (555) 555-1234 • cdavis@company.com

PROFESSIONAL PROFILE

- Over seven years in architecture and facility management-related industries with emphasis in computer design base, education, and communication.
- Skilled in three-dimensional CADD modeling and rendering.
- Particular ability to visualize in three dimensions and utilize computer software for design, budgeting, estimating, and project management activities.

PROFESSIONAL ARCHITECTURE EXPERIENCE

Computer Design Software, Inc.   **East Brunswick, NJ**
2006–Present   *Architect*
Provide industry consultation and implementation expertise in architecture and facilities management for firm developing, distributing, and providing user support for specialized software used by architects, contractors, and property managers.
- Assisted with development and testing of Computer-Aided Design and Database software
- Provided demonstration and technical support for pre- and post-sales activity
- Acted as subject matter expert for future software enhancements and requirements
- Served in leadership roles for various joint studies teaming with IBM and other major corporations in the evaluation of CDB software for architecture

Hanna, Olin and Sherman Architecture   **Philadelphia, PA**
2000–2006   *Architect*
Participated in conceptual design, design development, and construction documentation of architecture and landscape design.
- Created exploration, analytical, and presentation models materially and on computers for residential and commercial projects
- Fabricated sculptural wood and bronze detail elements installed in varied projects
- Projects included private residences, multifamily units, and professional offices

City of Philadelphia   **Philadelphia, PA**
1998–2000   *Building Inspector*

PROFESSIONAL REGISTRATIONS

Licensed Architect, State of New Jersey Certificate 2344888

EDUCATION

University of Pennsylvania   **Philadelphia, PA**
Master of Architecture   1998

Massachusetts Institute of Technology   **Cambridge, MA**
Bachelor of Science, Architecture   1996

CHRIS SMITH

123 Main Street ■ Hometown, IN 00000 ■ (555) 555-1234 ■ csmith@company.com

AREAS OF INSTRUCTIONAL EXPERTISE

- Eclectic experience teaching studio art, art appreciation, and art history within elementary and secondary public schools.
- Experience teaching studio art, crafts, and mixed media as private instructor and as director of special recreation program.
- Confidence developing group curriculum and exercises for students of varied ability levels, from beginner to expert.
- Expertise associated with media including: oils, acrylics, watercolors, ceramics, and airbrush.
- Experience supervising student teachers, developing district-wide curricula, and advocating for funding.
- Capacities to translate passion into effective learning plans, utilizing varied modalities and instructional techniques.

SCHOOL-BASED INSTRUCTION

GARY REGIONAL SCHOOL DISTRICT   GARY, IN
Secondary Art Instructor   **2000–Present**
- Developed new and updated existing curriculum regularly for Studio Art, Art History, and Art Appreciation courses.
- Studio Art focused on composition, color, and conceptual problem solving, requiring completion of projects using varied media, including: charcoal, pen and ink, acrylics, and airbrush.
- Inventoried, ordered, and controlled budget of approximately $10,000 annually.
- Implemented curriculum with classes for gifted art students, including a district-wide art competition and scholarship in 1998.

Elementary Art Instructor   **1996–2000**
- Visited school sites on a regular basis, implementing a creativity-focused curriculum.
- Teamed with teachers to incorporate art projects and related lessons into existing units.

STUDIO AND RECREATION-BASED INSTRUCTION

ART DUDE STUDIOS   GARY, IN
Private Art Instruction   **2006–Present**
- Planned and implemented private instruction focusing on talented teens and adults.
- Addressed specific portfolio development needs of students seeking admissions and scholarships to art schools.

GARY PARKS AND RECREATIONAL ASSOCIATION   GARY, IN
Summer Art Institute Director   **Summers 1998–2008**
- Created and facilitated arts and crafts activity programs offered at six sites throughout the city.
- Media included sewing, weaving, knitting, sculpting, clay, jewelry, painting, and drawing.
- Successfully hired, trained, and directed fifteen Arts Aides to supervise each site.

EDUCATION AND CERTIFICATIONS

INDIANA UNIVERSITY   BLOOMINGTON, IN
State of Indiana Secondary Education Certification in Art   **1994**
Bachelor of Fine Arts in Studio Art, *cum laude*   **1996**
State of Indiana Elementary Education Certification   **1996**

Corey Davis

123 Main Street • Hometown, IL 00000 • 555-555-1234 • cdavis@company.com

OBJECTIVE

Banking loan officer, branch management, or training position.

QUALIFICATIONS

- Outstanding record of achieving sales goals as branch manager; successfully conducting residential and commercial mortgage acquisition and personal and commercial loan transactions and marketing programs.
- Extensive experience developing commercial lending packages for private clientele, including financial restructuring, REFI, equipment financing; coordinating activities with COMIDA, GCIDA, IBDC, and ESCDC, and attorneys, appraisers, title companies, and governments.
- Capacity to train, supervise, and motivate others to achieve maximum performance.
- Experience in branch management, business development, and as commercial lending officer and training officer.
- Comprehensive knowledge of Cook County consumer, industrial, and commercial clientele.
- Expertise to develop marketing strategies and collateral, internal management programs, and professional business plans through utilization of Word, Excel, and PowerPoint.
- Successfully developed and implemented marketing strategies and collateral material.

BRANCH, LOAN, AND TRAINING ACHIEVEMENTS

BIG BANK OF ILLINOIS, Chicago, IL
Branch Manager/Commercial Business Development Officer, 1999–2004

- Co-managed District Officer Call Program to retain, expand, and track commercial customer base.
- Instituted Branch Neighborhood Equity Call Program, which enhanced sales of Home Equity and first and second mortgage products 33% over a six-month period.
- Designed and managed District Product Development Program which included development of H.E.L.O.C., Home Equity Loans, residential mortgage products (2-Year Fixed ARM, 5-Year Fixed ARM), Business Installment Loan (BIL), and marketing collateral.
- Served as one of two Chicago Area Sales Trainers, supervising professional sales training program which included Train-the-Trainer, market identification and definition, needs analysis, program development, implementation, results assessment, and follow-up responsibilities for a twenty-three-branch network.

UNIVERSITY SAVINGS AND LOAN ASSOCIATION, Evanston, IL
Branch Manager/Mortgage Development Specialist, 1990–1999

- Developed Branch Neighborhood Equity Call Program to introduce and expand Home Equity Programs, resulting in a 16% increase in Lines and Loans in first month.
- Designed and managed Branch Product Development and Customer Information and Sales incentives.

SECOND CITY SAVINGS BANK, Chicago, IL
Branch Manager/IRA Specialist, 1980–1990

- Designed brochures for IRA marketing program and instituted model for customer focus groups.
- Co-designed and managed new IRA marketing strategies through Customer/Client Focus Groups.
- Managed overall loan operations of third-largest branch, with transactions averaging over $10 million per year.

Corey Davis
Page Two

FINANCIAL SERVICES ACHIEVEMENTS

ILLINI LOANS FINANCIAL ASSOCIATES, Chicago, IL
Owner, Part-time 2000–Present
- Integrated all management, marketing, and client services efforts, including: insurance, commercial mortgage/equipment financing, coordinating SBA programs, factoring, lines of credit, letters of credit, warehousing, floor plans, leasing.
- Successfully placed loans for businesses of varied sizes and individuals with diverse scenarios; ranging from $5,000 LOC to $25 million development of fruit processing factory.
- Utilized knowledge of cash flow, capital formation, marketing analysis, and lending procedures, marketing skills to successfully address client needs and resolve issues.
- Originated, processed, and coordinated all closing activities related to residential mortgage/home equity loans. Established working relationships with attorneys, appraisers, borrowers, and title companies.

CONSULTING ACHIEVEMENTS

UNITED WAY OF GREATER COOK COUNTY, Chicago, IL
Office Manager/United Way, January–September 2010
Area-Wide Interim Director/Cook and Area Counties, January–September 2005
- Served within Train-the-Trainer capacities, training selected individuals to perform United Way presentations, track results, and input payroll deduction data.
- Implemented IT Systems for input format and follow-up procedures.
- Scheduled and performed group presentations.
- Organized and facilitated board meetings and "Cabinet" meetings for both United Way, Cook, and neighboring counties.
- Established formal Three-Year Business Plan for each county to increase overall total annual contributions.
- Served as Business Development Officer.

PROFESSIONAL DEVELOPMENT AND EDUCATION

- Illinois Credit School; AIB/IFE courses in credit, insurance of accounts, mortgage, consumer and commercial lending principles, real estate law; Chicago Association of Agents and Brokers; Illinois State Certified Instructor/Sales; State of Illinois Notary Public
- University of Chicago, Bachelor of Science, 1980

JAMIE BROWN

123 Main Street • Hometown, MD 00000 • (555) 555-1234 • jbrown@company.com

BANKING QUALIFICATIONS

- Experience in customer service-focused teller roles, completing personal and commercial banking transactions.
- Confidence training and motivating teller colleagues.
- Specialized accounting courses supported by business curriculum.
- Knowledge of Excel, Word, PowerPoint, and CS Professional Suite, as well as tax and Internet applications.

BUSINESS, FINANCE, AND ACCOUNTING EDUCATION

UNIVERSITY OF MARYLAND, University Park, MD
Bachelor of Science in Business Administration, with Finance and Accounting emphases, anticipated May 2008
- Overall GPA: 3.7; Finance and Accounting GPA: 3.7 (out of 4.0); Dean's Honor Roll all semesters
- Beta Gamma Sigma Business Honor Society President and Member
- The Honor Society of Phi Kappa Phi Honor Society, and Delta Sigma Pi, Business Fraternity, Member

SELECTED FINANCE, ACCOUNTING, AND BUSINESS COURSES

Money, Credit and Banking, Introduction to Marketing, Tax Accounting, Advanced Accounting, Intermediate Accounting, Auditing, Strategic Management, Cost Accounting, Financial Management, and Operations Management

BANKING AND ACCOUNTING EXPERIENCE

BANK OF MARYLAND, College Park, MD
Teller, Part-time 2010–Present
Process account transactions, reconcile and deposit daily funds. Inform customers of bank products, refer public to designated personnel, provide account status data, and handle busy phone. Orient, train, supervise, and delegate tasks for new hires. Assisted with planning and implementing extended-hours customer service strategies.

GORDON, ODOM & DAVIS, INC., Baltimore, MD
Accounting Intern, Spring 2012 and Fall 2012
Completed compilations, reviews, audits, and tax returns for individual and corporate clients. Created financial schedules and reports using Excel.

TRADER PUBLICATIONS, San Diego, CA
Accounting Assistant, Summer 2012
Compiled daily reports for magazine and advertising revenues. Completed accounts receivable and payable efforts.

LEGAL AID SOCIETY, San Diego, CA
Bookkeeping Volunteer, Summer 2011

LAW RELATED EXPERIENCE

SULLIVAN, DELAFIELD, ET AL, San Diego, CA
Legal Assistant, Summer 2012–Present

DANA JOHNSON
123 Main Street • Hometown, MN 00000 • (555) 555-1234 • djohnson@company.com

BOOKKEEPING QUALIFICATIONS

- Over twelve years' bookkeeping experience within progressively responsible roles.
- Experience overseeing comprehensive bookkeeping, including supervision of clerks and support staff.
- Capacities to address organizational finance related issues as well as those of individuals.
- Skills to develop financial data and summary findings on monthly, quarterly, and annual basis.
- Expertise in QuickBooks, Excel, TurboTax, and other financial software.

BOOKKEEPING EXPERIENCE

ASSOCIATES, INC.   EDEN PRAIRIE, MN
Senior Bookkeeper   **2004–Present**
- Oversee bookkeeping for mortgage and home equity loan firm, specializing in addressing first home purchases, debt consolidation, educational payment needs of clients from diverse financial backgrounds.
- Generate and present general ledger and investors' monthly reports for firm that generates over $10 million in mortgage and loan portfolios annually.
- Oversee A/R and A/P staff to ensure accuracy of accounts.
- Monitor efforts of third-party payroll services, checking accuracy of scheduled payments.
- Personally manage multiple accounts for major investor/real estate developer with commercial and residential properties in several states.
- Effectively interact with all finance savvy senior managers, specifically reporting to CFO.
- Support annual auditing and tax efforts of CPA firm.

MORNINGSIDE CO.   HOPKINS, MN
Bookkeeper   **2000–2004**
- Supervised general ledger through trial balance, as well as A/P, payroll, and payroll tax returns for construction and home improvement firm with annual revenues in excess of $2 million.
- Converted bookkeeping procedures from written documents to in-house computer system.
- Coordinated department's work flow, supervising A/R and A/P Clerks.
Accounts Receivable Clerk   **1999–2000**

THE DARNELL BANK   EDEN PRAIRIE, MN
Teller   **1995–1999**

EXCELSIOR CORP.   MANKATO, MN
Administrative Assistant   **1992–1995**

EDUCATION

SOUTHWEST STATE UNIVERSITY   MARSHALL, MN
Accounting and General Business Courses   **1995–1999**

FRANCIS WILLIAMS

123 Main Street, Apartment 13 • Hometown, CA 00000 • (555) 555-1234 • fwilliams@company.com

BUDGET ANALYSIS AND FINANCE ACHIEVEMENTS

2006–Present	Golden Life Insurance Company	Los Angeles, CA

Budget Analyst

- Balance $1.3 billion budget using internally developed and regularly revised software
- Reconcile accounts on ISA/ABC system to other financial systems
- Assist management in budget preparation
- Conduct training classes on the financial system for upper-level management
- Prepare comparison of expense to budget reports for executives on demand and on weekly, monthly, and quarterly basis
- Submit accounts and IRS filing for the Political Action Committee
- Generate financial analysis and reporting projects using Focus Report Writing and Excel, including macro programming, and MS Word
- Contribute annually to budget development and strategic planning processes

1992–2006	The Pacific Group	Los Angeles, CA
1996–2006	*Auditing Analyst*	

- Prepared contract proposals and illustrative cost calculations
- Constructed actuarial valuation and analyzed actuarial gains and losses
- Independently generated regular reports for forty individual clients and oversaw development of reports for sixty corporate clients
- Determined the minimum and maximum contribution allowable by law for the IRS
- Assured accuracy of comprehensive financial information database

1992–1995   *Accounting Technician*

- Maintained and reported on financial records and created financial statements associated with money market mutual fund for 60 corporate clients
- Balanced trial balance and generated journal entries
- Maintained, compared, and reconciled the fund on three computer systems
- Assisted system analysts in preparation and implementation of new computer system

FINANCE AND BUSINESS EDUCATION

	University of Washington	Seattle, WA
1997	*Bachelor of Science Degree in Finance*	

QUALIFICATION SUMMARY

- Competencies required to track and balance a $1.3 billion budget
- Record of developing, utilizing, and training others to use proprietary software and internalized systems for budget monitoring purposes
- Capacities to support executive decision making on budgeting
- Experience as regular contributor to groups making strategic financial plans
- Creativity associated with generating and explaining financial reports

COREY DAVIS

123 Main Street • Hometown, CO 00000 • (555) 555-1234 • cdavis@company.com

CASE MANAGEMENT AND ADVOCACY EXPERIENCE

THE WOMEN'S SAFE PLACE   GOLDEN, CO
Director of Case Management Services and Legal Advocate   *2000–Present*
- Provide counseling and referral services for residents of shelter for abused women and their children.
- Train and regularly interact with 24-hour hotline volunteers, supporting telephone crisis counseling and authorizing admission of residents on an emergency basis and for long-term transition periods.
- Conduct individual and group orientations, take case histories, and facilitate counseling sessions.
- Assist women applying for Temporary Restraining Orders and serve as liaison with legal counsel.
- Provide expert testimony during domestic violence legal cases and report outcomes to staff.
- Assist with public relations and fundraising and regularly contribute to grant writing activities.

FAMILY SERVICES OF DENVER   DENVER, CO
Social Worker   *1990–1995*
- Provided services for clients and families with medical, psychological, housing, and financial needs.
- Supervised agency volunteers and graduate student interns.
- Worked collaboratively with various community agencies to provide needed services.
- Conducted in-service training offered to staff and those from other agencies.

GREATER GOLDEN SCHOOL DISTRICT   GOLDEN, CO
Case Manager   *1990–1995*
- Served within counseling and referral roles for at-risk students and their families.
- Coordinated outreach, intake, and referrals for those with financial, educational, and medical issues.
- Maintained detailed case records and statistics for reports distributed to district and state officials.

LIVINGSTON HIGH SCHOOL   GOLDEN, CO
School/Family Counselor   *1986–1990*
- Provided individual counseling related to scheduling, college applications, and behavioral issues.
- Coordinated parent-teacher conferences and conducted family conferences and counseling sessions.

SOCIAL WORK AND COUNSELOR TRAINING

COLORADO STATE UNIVERSITY   FORT COLLINS, CO
Master of Arts, Social Work   *1990*
Master of Arts, School Counseling   *1986*
Bachelor of Arts, Sociology, with a minor in Education   *1985*

COLORADO COMMUNITY COLLEGE   DENVER, CO
Associate of Arts, Sociology   *1983*

CREDENTIALS, LICENSURE, AND AFFILIATIONS

- State of Colorado Licensed Social Worker and State of Colorado Counseling Certification
- American Association of Social Workers and State of Colorado Association of Social Workers

CHRIS SMITH, CPA

123 Main Street • Hometown, TX 00000 • (555) 555-1234 • csmith@company.com

ACCOUNTING QUALIFICATIONS

- Comprehensive experience in public and private accounting roles.
- Background in varied industries and specialized knowledge of in areas of engineering, oil, and gas.
- Skills gained via audit, tax services, supervisory, and training accomplishments.
- Specialized accounting degree supported by general business curriculum and updated by ongoing professional development.
- Knowledge of Excel, Creative Solutions, Lacerte Tax Program, QuickBooks, Word, Access, and FileMaker Pro.

ACCOUNTING EXPERIENCE

MASTERMIND ENGINEERING, Houston, TX   2002–Present
Accounting Manager: Complete SEC Reporting and Disclosure forms. Manage general ledger closing and maintenance. Supervise and review all accounting and finance areas. Administrate 401(k) pension plan. Implement accounting, payroll, and manufacturing software. Report directly to CFO, providing financial data and analytical reports to maximize profits and support managerial decisions. Hire, train, evaluate, and supervise accounting, bookkeeping, and analyst professionals.

DUNPHY & REILLY, INC., Houston, TX   1998–2002
Senior Internal Auditor: Conducted operational and financial audits of manufacturing subsidiaries. Designed and implemented audit programs to test the efficiency of all aspects of accounting controls. Recommended changes and improvements to corporate and divisional management. Trained and supervised staff auditors in all aspects of the audit engagement. Involved with corporate management in areas of acquisition and corporate development.

CHURCHILL NORTH, Houston, TX   1992–1998
Supervising Senior Accountant: Supervised, planned, and budgeted audit engagements. Oversaw and completed checks of audit reports, financial statements, and tax filings. Recruited, trained, supervised, and evaluated staff accountants. Gained experience from client assignments, including those in oil and gas, manufacturing, real estate, and nonprofit arenas. Proficient training in use of spreadsheet programs. 1994 to 1998.
Senior Accountant: Served as liaison between supervisor, staff accountants, and clients. Assisted with preparation of financial statements, tax filings, and audit reports. 1992 to 1994.

GORDON, ODOM & DAVIS, INC., Austin, TX   1990–1992
Staff Accountant: Completed compilations, reviews, audits, and tax returns for individual and corporate clients. Created financial schedules and reports using Excel and SuperCalc spreadsheet programs. Passed Audit, Law, and Theory portions of CPA exam at first sitting.

ACCOUNTING EDUCATION

UNIVERSITY OF TEXAS, Austin, TX
Bachelor of Science, Accountancy, May 1990

Chef

Jamie Brown

123 Main Street • Hometown, OR 00000 • (555) 555-1234 • jbrown@company.com

Professional Profile

- Over a decade of positions as pastry chef, bakery manager, and related roles in varied venues.
- Thorough knowledge in the preparation of an extensive assortment of baked goods, including pastries, cookies, puddings, muffins, breads, and specialties.
- Creative talents to develop attractive thematic customer- and event-inspired presentations.
- Experience addressing needs and budgets of restaurant, catering, and retail bakery.
- Competencies to organize production and personnel to maximize use of space and finances.
- Recipient of numerous culinary awards for superior creations inspired by passion for excellence.

Pastry Chef Achievements

THE BEVENSHIRE HOTEL, Eugene, OR
Pastry Chef and Bakery Manager, 2009–Present
- Plan and prepare desserts on a daily basis for restaurant patrons.
- Oversee all operations of retail bakery, and prepare desserts and breads for catered functions.

DELTA PINES BAKERY & CAFE, Corvallis, OR
Pastry Chef, 2006–2009
- Prepared an extensive assortment of desserts, rotating on a weekly basis, including cakes, cookies, cobblers, puddings, tarts, special-order desserts, and wedding cakes.
- Created breakfast pastries and breads for lunch specials.

THE PLUMROSE RESTAURANT, Corvallis, OR
Pastry Chef, 2004–2006
- Planned and executed monthly menu that included six desserts, two sorbets, two ice cream dishes, and two fresh breads daily for lunch and dinner.
- Ordered all bakery and dairy supplies and prepared desserts for retail store and special orders.

THE WILLARD HOTEL, Boston, MA
Assistant Pastry Chef, 2000–2004
- Worked with executive pastry chef, monitoring baking, mixing, and finishing of cakes, pastries, and a full range of bakery products on an as-needed basis.
- Completed special orders for banquets, catered functions, and hotel restaurant.

LE HOTEL DE VIVRE, Bangor, ME
Pastry Cook, 1998–2000

Culinary and Pastry Training

AMERICAN PASTRY ARTS CENTER, Medford, MA
Course in Chocolates and Candy, 1998–2000

GOURMET INSTITUTE OF AMERICA, Boston, MA
Associate of Culinary Arts, with Certificates in Food Services and Catering Management, 1998

Chris Smith

123 Main Street • Hometown, NY 00000 • (555) 555-1234 • csmith@company.com

EDUCATION, COCURRICULARS, AND HONORS

ALLENDALE COLUMBIA SCHOOL, Rochester, NY
Senior Year, 2010–2011
- Yearbook Editor-in-Chief
- Upper School Chorus
- Pittsford Crew Club, Varsity Crew Team Member
- Varsity Swimming Team Member and Captain

Junior Year, 2009–2010
- Yearbook Sports/Special Events Editor
- Explorers Post Program in Psychology
- Upper School Chorus
- Cum laude Society and High Honor Roll
- Varsity Swimming Team Member and Captain and Varsity Crew Team Member
- Della Simpson Book Award for Excellence in English and History
- Student Life Committee Class Representative

Sophomore Year, 2008–2009
- Co-chair Holiday Bazaar—raised $1,500 for Strong Children's Hospital
- Pittsford Crew and Varsity Swimming Team Member
- High Honor Roll
- Upper School Chorus
- Sophomore Class Forum Speaker

THE SANTA CATALINA SCHOOL, Monterey, CA
Freshman Year, 2007–2008
- Gold Cord Honor Roll and top 10 percent of class
- Varsity Swimming Team Member
- Amnesty International
- Lower School Volunteer Aide
- Co-chair St. Patrick's Day Dance

EMPLOYMENT

HARLEY SCHOOL, Pittsford, NY
Day Camp Counselor, Summers 2010 and 2008
- Planned and led activities and games for 5- and 6-year-old campers

Youth Swim Instructor, Part-time 2008–Present
- Prepared lessons, taught basic breathing and strokes, and motivated 6- to 9-year-old students

EDDIE BAUER, Victor, New York
Sales Associate, Summer 2009

HARRO EAST ATHLETIC CLUB, Rochester, New York
Lifeguard, Summer 2008

Chris Smith

Page Two

ATHLETICS ACHIEVEMENTS

ALLENDALE COLUMBIA SCHOOL, Pittsford, NY

Pittsford Crew, 2010–Present

- Pittsford Crew, Founded Fall 2008, William C. Warren Boathouse, constructed 2009 by donations, team fundraisers, and community support
- Compete in Western New York area regattas, Tail of the Fish, Cascadilla Invitational, New York State Scholastic Rowing Championships
- Port Side, Stroke, Club 4 New York State Scholastic Rowing Championship Gold Medal Winner
- Northeast Rowing Camp, Raymond, ME, summer 2010; worked with Yale University and University of Miami coaches focused on rowing posture, connection, and slide control
- 8:19, 2k erg score
- 21.15.77 5k erg score

Varsity Swimming Team Member, 2008–Present

- Section Five Athletic League, Male Season
- 500, 200, freestyle; 100 breaststroke
- School record, 400 freestyle relay, 200 medley relay, 200 freestyle relay

Captain, 2009–2010, 2011–2012

- Organized team activities dinners, served as liaison between team and coach, helped organize fundraisers for Florida training trip

THE SANTA CATALINA SCHOOL, Monterey, California

Varsity Swimming, 2007–2008

- 500, 200, freestyle; 100 breaststroke
- 3rd place, 100 breaststroke, league championships

TIGER AQUATICS, Stockton, California

USS Swim Club Team Member, 2000–2007

- Age group, year-round swim club
- Traveled throughout California for competitions

PERSONAL PROFILE

Resident of Hanover, NH. Lived in Washington, D.C.; Princeton, NJ; Stockton, CA; and Rochester, NY. Traveled to Spain, France, and Italy. Enjoy reading, politics, sports, and music.

FRANCIS WILLIAMS

123 Main Street • Hometown, PA 00000 • (555) 555-1234 • fwilliams@company.com

PROFESSIONAL PROFILE

- Instructional expertise at law school and undergraduate levels.
- Instruction and research interests: Business Administration, Legal Studies, Criminal Law and Procedures, Supreme Court Rulings, Legal Trends and History.
- Research, writing, and presentation skills nurtured as author, lecturer, teacher, clerk debater, and mediator.

TEACHING AND LEGAL EXPERIENCE

DREXEL UNIVERSITY, Philadelphia, PA

Professor, 2008–Present

- Teach undergraduates Criminal Law, Criminal Procedures, Crime in America, and Business Law.
- Stimulate class involvement through use of case studies, mock trials, and law-school simulation.
- Annually serve as Freshman Advisor to diverse students and Faculty Advisor to Pre-Law Majors.

UNIVERSITY OF PENNSYLVANIA SCHOOL OF LAW, Philadelphia, PA

Adjunct Professor, 2008–Present

- Teach Criminal Procedures to first-year students enrolled in the Evening Studies Program.

DICKINSON COLLEGE AND DICKINSON SCHOOL OF LAW, Carlisle, PA

Assistant Professor, 2005–2008

- Taught undergraduate courses in Business Administration and Law, including: Criminal Law, Crime in America; Courts and Criminal Law; Criminal Procedures; Crime in America; and The Courts.
- Taught first-year law students Criminal Procedures and Juvenile Procedures.

JOHN CARROLL UNIVERSITY, University Heights, OH

Adjunct Professor, 2002–2005

- Taught Legal Writing, Criminal Procedures, and Legal Reasoning to first-year students.

SUPREME COURT OF THE STATE OF OHIO, Columbus, OH

Clerk to the Honorable Justice Stanford Harvard, 2000–2002

SELECTED WRITINGS

- *Many Mondays in October: Supreme Court Trends in Criminal Rulings,* Law Texts Publishers, 2010
- *Undergraduate Studies of Criminal Procedures,* Law Texts Publishers, 2008

PROFESSIONAL, GRADUATE, AND UNDERGRADUATE STUDIES

JOHN CARROLL UNIVERSITY, University Heights, OH

Juris Doctor Degree 5th in a Class of 300, with Highest Honors, 2003

- Editor Law Review, 2002–2003; Law Review Staff, 2001–2002; and T.A. for Criminal Procedures, 2001–2002

CASE WESTERN RESERVE UNIVERSITY, Cleveland, OH

Master of Arts in Business Administration, with Honors, 1997

Bachelor of Science in Criminal Justice, *summa cum laude,* 1995

JAMIE BROWN

123 Main Street · Hometown, AR 00000 · (555) 555-4432 · jbrown@company.com

OBJECTIVE

Computer Programmer

PROFESSIONAL EXPERIENCE

2009–Present   PUBLIC AUTHORITY FOR CIVIL INFORMATION, Little Rock, AR
Technical Manager
- Performed and directed software coding, testing, and debugging for online and batch processes.
- Maintained over 300 assembler modules and developed 75.
- Formulated screen manager program, using Assembler and Natural languages, to trace input and output to the VTAM buffer.
- Developed program to monitor complete security control blocks, using Assembler and Natural.

2001–2004   STATE OF ARKANSAS, Fayetteville, AR
Systems Programmer
- Initiated start-up and implemented operations.
- Designed and managed implementation of a network providing the legal community with a direct line to supreme court cases.
- Developed a system that catalogued entire library's inventory.
- Used C++ to create a registration system for a university registrar.

EDUCATION AND PROFESSIONAL DEVELOPMENT

ARKANSAS TECH UNIVERSITY, Russellville City, AR
Completed varied programming courses, 2007–Present

UNIVERSITY OF ARKANSAS AT PINE BLUFF, Pine Bluff, AR
Bachelor of Science, Mathematics and Computer Science, 2007

CODING AND COMPUTER SCIENCE COURSES

Advanced IBM 370 Assembler, SNA Fundamentals, MVS/ESA Architecture, Natural 2 Programming Language, MVS/XA Concepts and Facilities, MVS/XA Job Control Language, MVS/XA Using Utility Programs, MVS/XA Using and Creating Procedures

OPERATING SYSTEMS, LANGUAGES, AND SOFTWARE

Windows 2000, UNIX, C++, Java, Visual Basic, Assembler, Oracle, SQL Server 2005

Dana Johnson, PsyD

123 Main Street • Hometown, FL 00000 • (555) 555-1212 • djohnson@company.com

PROFESSIONAL PROFILE

Bilingual English-Spanish psychologist who has served youth and adult populations within agency, clinical, and school settings. Experienced individual and group therapist within community programs offering services to clients from diverse socioeconomic and psychosocial backgrounds. Assessment, training, and referral professional; school counselor; and teacher of English as a Second Language.

QUALIFICATIONS, CLIENTELE, AND THERAPEUTIC STRATEGIES

Eclectic graduate and undergraduate studies focusing on family dynamics, rationale, emotive, and behavioral strategies. Background in family therapy, general psychotherapy, and assessment and treatment of behavioral and deficit disorders. Skilled developing and implementing treatment plans in social service and educational arenas. Experience coordinating service networks and collaborating with health-service professionals. Completed case management training with the Department of Social Services.

DOCTORAL, MASTERS, AND UNDERGRADUATE STUDIES

Nova University, Fort Lauderdale, FL
PsyD, Counseling Psychology, 2000
MA, Counseling Psychology, with Community Clinical Concentration, 2002

Barry University, Miami Shores, FL
BA, with Developmental Psychology and Human Development dual majors, cum laude, 1993

CLINICAL EXPERIENCE

2006–Present   **Mental Health Services of Ft. Lauderdale,** Ft. Lauderdale, FL
Counseling Psychologist: Facilitate individual and group counseling for clients diagnosed with varied neurotic, psychotic, developmental, and behavioral disorders. Collaborate with health-service professionals to develop treatment plans for emotionally disturbed adolescents. Assist clients in developing survival skills to aid transition from residential to independent living. Coordinate service networks for academic, psychological, and social assistance.

2004–2006   **Tyler Adoption Agency,** Miami Beach, FL
Counselor: Served as assessment, recruitment, and referral specialist. Traveled to community sites and executed presentations to recruit prospective parents for minority children. Conducted testing and home studies of prospective parents to determine eligibility. Followed up for evaluation purposes 3 months, 6 months, 1 year, and 2 years post-adoption. Served as referral source to private and public mental health services as needed.

2000–2004   **Dade County, Department of Social Services,** Miami Beach, FL
Bilingual Case worker: Assessed client needs, developed treatment plans, and managed cases. Communicated with court officials. Served as child advocate for court proceedings.

Dana Johnson, PsyD
Page Two

MULTICULTURAL SCHOOL COUNSELING AND TEACHING EXPERIENCE

1997–2000   **American School of Barcelona, Spain**
International Primary School Counselor: Administered psychological and educational testing for students ranging from Pre-kindergarten to 5th grades. Counseled students, families, and teachers. Designed remedial and therapeutic plans. Led group activities for self-image enhancement and behavior modification. Worked with teachers on preventive strategies for social and disciplinary problems.

1994–1997   **Institute of America,** Madrid, Spain
Guidance Counselor and English as a Second Language Instructor: Counseled students and families for clientele ranging from Pre-kindergarten to 12th grade. Administered psychological and educational testing. Designed complete record-keeping system for all students. Implemented behavior modification programs. Administered achievement, vocational, and college prep tests. Made policy on admissions and discipline. Worked with teachers on individual educational and behavioral programs. Taught English as a Second Language to students in grades 3–6.

Corcy Davis
123 Main Street • Hometown, OH 00000 • (555) 555-1234 • cdavis@company.com

CREDIT ANALYSIS AND FINANCE QUALIFICATIONS

- More than ten years experience in retail banking and commercial lending.
- Specialized expertise associated with credit and financial analysis and use of modeling and regression analysis to assess risk and project rates.
- Proficient analyzing financial statements, assessing risk, and evaluating credit worthiness.
- Experience using Excel, Lotus Notes, and internal systems for analyses and creating supporting illustrations for credit reports and presentations to colleagues and board.
- Experience using Dutch fluency and German conversational skills in business contexts.
- Naturalized U.S. Citizen.

FINANCE, ACCOUNTING, AND BUSINESS DEGREES

THE OHIO STATE UNIVERSITY GRADUATE SCHOOL OF MANAGEMENT, Columbus, OH
Master of Business Administration, with Finance Concentration, May 2008
- Completed Executive MBA Program for Finance with Honors, and overall GPAs of 4.0.
- Courses included: International Finance, Money and Capital Markets, Investment, Corporate Finance, Corporate Financial Reporting, and Global Macroeconomics.

THE OHIO STATE UNIVERSITY, Columbus, OH
Bachelor of Science, Business Administration, with Accounting Concentration, 2000

BANKING AND CREDIT ANALYSIS ACCOMPLISHMENTS

WISTERIA BANK, Grace City, OH
Senior Credit Analyst, 2008–Present
- Oversee efforts of eight Analysts working on commercial and personal lending teams.
- Review all documentation and recommendations before final determinations are rendered.
- Calculate and track positive and negative yield statistics, reporting findings to management.

Commercial Loan Credit Analyst, 2005–2008
- As member of lending team, analyzed and evaluated financial statements.
- Developed pro forma statements and cash flow projections.
- Documented findings; prepared independent recommendations on advisability of granting credits to corporate lenders.

Senior Personal Banker, 2002–2005
- Monitored overdraft reports, reviewed and executed consumer loans, supervised vault area, audited tellers, and provided customer service.

Personal Banker, 2000–2002
- Established and serviced professional clientele accounts. Expedited investments in treasury bills, repurchase agreements, CDs, retirement accounts, and discount brokerage for bank clients. Assisted branch corporate lender weekly on a revolving commercial loan.

Day Care Worker

Chris Smith

123 Main Street • Hometown, CO 00000 • (555) 555-5555 • Cell (555) 555-9999

DAY CARE QUALIFICATIONS AND COMPETENCIES

- Over nine years of experience within home and school settings, teaching and caring for children aged two months to seven years.
- Commitment to needs of infants, preschoolers, and kindergarteners, with record reflecting learning and loving.
- Background including courses in Childhood Development, Early Childhood Education, and Educational Psychology.
- CPR/first aid certified and valid driver's license, with perfect driving record.

DAY CARE, TEACHING, AND CHILD CARE EXPERIENCE

2009–Present   PRIVATE RESIDENCE, Livermore, CO
Nanny: Care for twin boys from the age of two months through two years. Provide environmental enrichment, personal care, and play supervision.
- Accompanied family on numerous trips and cared for children during illnesses.

2007–2009   BABY BEAR PRESCHOOL, Keystone, CO
Teacher: Taught infant, preschool, and after-school programs. Planned curriculum, organized activities, communicated with parents and staff regarding children's growth and development.
- Positively adjusted annual increase in students and move to new facility.
- Worked with owner on goals and assisted with annual licensing documentation and visitation.

2005–2007   THIS LITTLE PIGGY DAYCARE CENTER, Dove Creek, CO
Teacher: Planned and implemented infant program, blending developmental with custodial needs. Communicated with parents and colleagues regarding daily progress of children.
- Enhanced skills development through interactive play and song.

2003–2005   THE KID CORRAL, Wild Horse, CO
Teacher: Planned and implemented curriculum for toddler program. Enriched children's experiences through play, music, and art.

SPECIAL CARE EXPERIENCE

2005–Present   COALITION FOR RETARDED CITIZENS, Ivywild, CO
Volunteer

EDUCATION

2000–2003   METROPOLITAN STATE COLLEGE, Denver, CO
- Completed 30 credits in Education, with an emphasis on the day care setting.

Francis Williams

123 Main Street • Hometown, NJ 00000 • (555) 555-1234

DENTAL HYGIENIST QUALIFICATIONS

- Progressively responsible experience as a Hygienist, Assistant, and Office Administrator.
- Sound knowledge of medical terminology and clinical procedures.
- Certified in first aid, cardiopulmonary resuscitation, and electrocardiography.
- Additional experience as receptionist/secretary with an executive search/management consulting firm, financial management company, and realty firms.

LICENSURE

- New Jersey Dental Hygiene License National Board Dental Hygiene Exam (Written: 90)
- NERB Dental Hygiene Exam (Clinical: 93; Written: 90)

DENTAL HYGIENE AND OFFICE MANAGEMENT EXPERIENCE

HERBERT DICKEY, DDS   Brooklyn, NY

Dental Hygienist, Surgical Dental Assistant, and Assistant Office Manager   2009–Present
- Provide state-of-the-art individualized prophylaxis treatment to adult and adolescent patients.
- Administer teeth cleaning, gum massage, oral hygiene education, and periodontal scaling procedures, and supervise interns undertaking similar procedures.
- Schedule patients for appointments for surgical procedures and provide presurgical preparation.
- Record temperature and blood pressure, insert intravenous units, and administer sedatives.
- Provide postoperative care in person and via telephone follow-up.
- Record vital signs every ten minutes until patient is conscious; establish patient comfort; provide necessary information to patients regarding new medications and possible side effects.
- Handle accounts payable and receivable and health insurance transactions.

DR. RETTMAN, DMD   Upper Montclair, NJ

Dental Hygienist   2006–2009
- Provided prophylaxis treatment, teeth cleaning, oral-hygiene education, and periodontal scaling.
- Administer Novocain prior to painful procedures.

Dental Assistant   2004–2006
- Assisted dentist in prophylactic procedures: provided necessary tools, sterilized equipment, comforted patients.
- Provided secretarial assistance, including transcription database management, and scheduling.

Dental Trainee/Extern   2001–2004
- Initially, served in rudimentary observation and support roles, then advanced to Dental Assistant.
- Sterilized instruments, processed x-rays, scheduled appointments, maintained patient relations.

PROFESSIONAL TRAINING

KELLY SCHOOL OF DENTAL HYGIENE, New York, NY

AS in Dental Hygiene   June, 2006

Coursework included Radiology, Periodontology, Pathology, Dental Equipment, Oral Biology, and Pharmacology.

Chris Smith, DDS

123 Main Street • Hometown, WA 00000 • (555) 555-1234 • csmith@company.com

PROFESSIONAL DENTISTRY EXPERIENCE

2000–Present   PAYNE DENTAL ASSOCIATES, Bellingham, WA
Owner—General Practice
- Purchased large dental practice through a leveraged buyout.
- Determined and successfully implemented long-term growth strategies.
- Supervised a staff consisting of two other dentists and six support personnel.
- Provided comprehensive care for 2,000+ patients.
- Lead the office in steadily increasing production and revenues.
- Updated practice and computerized equipment.
- Presently facilitating transition of practice to new owner.

1998–2006   SEATTLE UNIVERSITY DENTAL SCHOOL, Seattle, WA
Clinical Instructor and Assistant Dental Clinic Director
- Supervised clinic with rotating groups of dental students and support personnel.
- Evaluated student performance via videotape voice-overs and written reports.
- Annually analyzed financial viability of clinic, instituted regularly revised plans to increase profitability, and managed business-related activities.

1996–1998   UNIFIED DENTAL CENTERS, Moses Lake, WA
Dentist
- Provided comprehensive dental care and trained staff members.
- Developed marketing plan, established and allocated marketing budget, and oversaw business operations of practice composed of one dentist, one hygienist, and one support professional.

1991–1996   UNIVERSITY OF WASHINGTON, Seattle, WA
Instructor of Clinical Periodontics
- Supervised small groups of students during their first contact with patients.
- Developed lessons, demonstrated periodontal procedures, and evaluated students.

PROFESSIONAL AND UNDERGRADUATE EDUCATION

UNIVERSITY OF WASHINGTON SCHOOL OF DENTISTRY, Seattle, WA
Doctor of Dental Surgery, 1991
- Completed comprehensive studies, including 2000 hours of clinical experience.
- Graduated 10th in a class of 400.
- Served as mentor for 1st- and 2nd-year students.

SEATTLE INSTITUTE OF TECHNOLOGY, Seattle, WA
Bachelor of Science Degree, Biology, 1987

Editor

Corey Davis

123 Main Street • Hometown, CA 00000 • (555) 555-5340 • cdavis@company.com

Editing, Writing, and Reporting Qualifications

- Research, writing, and editorial talents for interviewing, fact checking, script writing, and proofreading.
- Book, magazine, newspaper, and broadcast writing and editing experience.
- Confidence drafting, editing, and finalizing news, features, and sports stories.
- Production experience within varied print and broadcast media.
- Abilities gained through graduate studies and positions within magazine, newspaper, and television.
- Bilingual Spanish-English skills, Mac and Windows platforms and Internet.

Editorial, Writing, and Reporting Experience

BOOKS R COOL, INC., Long Beach, CA
Senior Editor, 2012–Present
- Evaluate general trade reference titles and assess profit potential, acquire titles, and negotiate contracts.
- Oversee publication, from development and editing to production, publicity, and marketing.
- Serve as in-house editor for internal and external newsletters and web documentation.

BOP and *BB* MAGAZINES, Studio City, CA
Staff Writer, 2010–2012
- Wrote and researched music- and celebrity-related stories.
- Interviewed various celebrities and wrote and maintained a monthly column.

TEEN MAGAZINE, Los Angeles, CA
Editorial Assistant, 2009–2010

THE BEACON HILL TIMES, Boston, MA
Reporting Intern, 2008

WHDH CHANNEL 7 NEWS, Boston, MA
Reporting and Production Intern, 2007

Professional Development

- New York University Graduate Publishing Program, 2007–Present.
- American Society of Magazine Editors Junior Editorial Seminar Series, Summer 2009.
- American Society of Newspaper Editors Training Seminars, 2007–Present.

Graduate and Undergraduate English and Communication Degrees

SIMMONS COLLEGE, Boston, MA
Master of Arts, English, January 2008

UNIVERSITY OF THE PACIFIC, Stockton, CA
Bachelor of Arts, Communication, with English minor, May 2006

Jamie Brown

123 Main Street • Hometown, TX 00000 • (555) 555-9873 • jbrown@company.com

ELECTRICAL ENGINEERING QUALIFICATIONS

- Success leading product development efforts for commercial, OEM, and government markets.
- Experience administering research and development activities, managing vendor and partner technology relationships, and satisfying customer expectations.
- A decade of project management, design, testing, and troubleshooting experience.
- Specialized knowledge of microprocessor development, marketing, and implementation.

ELECTRICAL ENGINEERING ACCOMPLISHMENTS

AEROSPACE SYSTEMS, Dallas, TX
Systems Engineering OEM Section Manager, 2004–Present
- Managed development of customized versions of personal computer products, meeting requirements of OEM customers, Japanese customers, and United States government agencies.
- Supplied personal computer products with customized security and networking functionality.
- Provided OEM customers with problem-solving support and systems integration engineering.
- Managed development of laptop PC in support of U.S. Navy Lightweight Computer Unit.

Design Evaluation Manager, 2000–2004
- Managed development support engineering group established to complete personal computer competitive analysis and design verification testing.
- Developed competitive analysis process resulting in more compact computer designs.
- Initiated test processes including electrostatic discharge; conducted susceptibility, emissions, and related problem solving to meet regulatory requirements.
- Developed test plans and processes to verify functionality of computer products.

BELL SYSTEMS, Arlington, TX
Senior Principal Design Engineer, 1996–2000
- Developed bus architecture enhancements to a Goldstone 10000-based in-store processor to meet customer performance requirements.
- Developed Goldstone 15000-based cluster terminal controller, emulating an IBM 3050.
- Developed a PCL 2/6 Channel interface in partnership with Expectations, Inc.

MITASHA CORPORATION, Galveston, TX
Microcontroller Operations Product Engineer, 1994–1996
- Designed wafer-sort production test hardware for the 6235 microcontrollers, incorporated as a plug-in card to a test system.
- Developed test process improvements, resulting in 85% gross margin and less returns.

AIR DESIGN CORPORATION, Houston, TX
Electrical Engineer Coop Student, Summer 1993

ENGINEERING EDUCATION

MASSACHUSETTS INSTITUTE OF TECHNOLOGY, Cambridge, MA
Bachelor of Science, Electrical Engineering, *cum laude,* June 1994

Chris Smith

123 Main Street • Hometown, MA 00000 • (555) 555-9873

Teaching Qualifications and Achievements

- Certification in Elementary Education, Music, and Secondary English.
- Experience teaching Elementary, Junior High, and High School Students.
- Competencies teaching choral and instrumental classes and directed choirs and bands.
- Success developing youth music programs by creating musicals tailored to student abilities.
- Musicals involved students composing, acting, choreographing, playing instruments, and singing.
- As classroom and private teacher, used audiovisual and electric piano computer systems.
- Formed **Music & More,** a civic musical theater company composed of multicultural youth.
- Accomplished pianist, singer, accompanist, conductor, composer, and writer.

Music Teaching Experience

1987–Present   E.M. VOICE AND PIANO, Boston, MA
Voice and Piano Teacher

- Instruct approximately seventy voice, piano, and composition students.
- Present six recitals annually, working with students to select and prepare performance pieces.
- Regularly use video and electronic piano computer system to provide audio and visual feedback.
- Students applied for admissions, auditioned for, and attended selective music programs; then progressed to professional performance and composition.

1995–1999   MASSACHUSETTS METHODIST CHURCH, Boston, MA
Director of Youth Choirs

- Prepared and conducted weekly rehearsals and performances for students grades K–12.
- Composed and directed eight Christmas pageants televised on local station.

1994–1997   "MUSIC AND MORE," Boston, MA
Musical Director

- Founded after-school musical theater company for students grades 2–12.
- Composed, directed, and accompanied original scores and scripts for various productions.

1982–1992   CHESTNUT HILL SCHOOLS, Chestnut Hill, MA
Primary Schools Choral Director/Show Choir Director

- Directed choral groups associated with six elementary schools.
- Introduced students kindergarten–2nd grades to music appreciation and vocal performance.
- Nurtured vocal performance skills within students 3rd grades–6th grades.
- Oversaw extracurricular Show Choir composed of approximately 175 students grades 9–12.
- Coached students in composing, choreographing, and performing original musicals.

Education and Credentials

Berklee College of Music, Boston, MA
Master of Music, 1988, and Bachelor of Music, 1980
Massachusetts Elementary and Secondary Teaching Credentials with certification in Music and English

Dana Johnson

123 Main Street • Hometown, CA 00000 • (555) 555-5543 • djohnson@company.com

EMERGENCY MEDICAL QUALIFICATIONS

- Knowledge of and experience implementing state-of-the-art Emergency Medical procedures.
- Proven capabilities assisting in emergency childbirth and heart attacks.
- Familiar with procedures for critical burns, shock, gunshot wounds, physical manifestations of child abuse, and spousal battering.
- Provided emergency treatment for rape victims while staying within the guidelines of the law.
- Certified to teach and administer CPR.

EMERGENCY MEDICAL EXPERIENCE

DOLAN AMBULANCE SERVICES, Visalia, CA
Head Emergency Medical Technician, 2008–Present

RUSSELL AMBULANCE SERVICES, Modesto, CA
Emergency Medical Technician, 2006–2008

MEDICAL LICENSES, CERTIFICATIONS, AND EDUCATION

- Certified, EMT License Visalia Hospital, 2006
- License # 4490223 State of California, 2006

MODESTO JUNIOR COLLEGE, Modesto, CA
Emergency Medical Technician Certification Program, 2005–2006

ATHLETIC TRAINING EXPERIENCE

UNIVERSITY OF THE PACIFIC ATHLETIC TRAINING INTERNSHIP, Stockton, CA
Sports Medicine Clinic, 2002–2005
Men's and Women's Tennis, Spring 2004 and 2005
Men's Basketball, Fall 2004 and 2005
- California Interscholastic Federation Wrestling Tournament, Spring 2003, 2004, and 2005
- Northern California Sectional High School Basketball Tournament, Spring 2003, 2004, and 2005
- Nike Volleyball Festival, Spring 2003, 2004, and 2005

ATHLETIC TRAINING EDUCATION

UNIVERSITY OF THE PACIFIC, Stockton, CA
Bachelor of Arts, Sport Sciences, with Biology minor, June 2005

Chris Smith

123 Main Street • Hometown, PA 00000 • (555) 555-1234 • csmith@company.com

OBJECTIVE

Executive Assistant Position

QUALIFICATIONS AND CAPABILITIES

- Extensive knowledge of bank administrative policies and procedures through six years of experience.
- Able to supervise employees and work with all levels of management in a professional, diplomatic, and tactful manner. Rapidly analyze/recognize department problems and solutions.
- Work on multiple projects under pressure and meet strict deadlines and budget requirements.
- Literate in MS Office Suite: Word, Excel, PowerPoint, Outlook, Access.
- Confidence drafting and proofreading correspondence.
- Proficient using shorthand, dictation machines, and multifunction calculators.

ADMINISTRATIVE SUPPORT EXPERIENCE

ERIE SAVINGS BANK, Erie, PA

Administrative Assistant to the Chief Executive Officer, 2008–Present

Coordinated and prioritized daily activities of board chairman. Performed administrative functions in support of CEO. Required an in-depth knowledge of the bank, financial community, investors, and customers. Assisted with preparation for board of directors and shareholder meetings. Recorded and distributed minutes of board, shareholder, and executive committee meetings. Maintained CEO's travel and appointment schedule, using computerized scheduling system.

Executive Secretary to the Senior Vice President Commercial Division, 2004–2008

Set up commercial loans on system. Prepared monthly reports for board of directors. Updated financial statements. Maintained appraisal files. Coordinated loan renewals.

SPARTAN TRUST COMPANY, Erie, PA

Administrative Assistant to the President and Chief Executive Officer, 2000–2004

Prioritized daily activities of CEO. Set up and maintained "tickler system." Composed, and edited correspondence for president. Assisted CEO with sensitive customer and employee relationships. Recorded and distributed management committee minutes. Maintained and distributed monthly department reports.

Executive Secretary to Executive Vice President and Senior Loan Officer, 1996–2000

Managed secretarial staff supporting commercial loan officers. Coordinated staff meetings and presentations to board of directors. Prepared monthly departmental and divisional reports for distribution. Updated and maintained Policy and Procedure Manual on a timely basis.

Commercial Finance Assistant, 1993–1996

Prepared daily client loan advances and payment activity. Maintained client loan/collateral statements. Assisted with preparation of departmental reports and loan agreements.

EDUCATION

PENNSYLVANIA STATE UNIVERSITY PITTSBURGH CAMPUS, Pittsburgh, PA

Continuing Education Program Participant, 1991–1996

ERIE INSTITUTE OF BUSINESS STUDIES, Pittsburgh, PA

Associate of Arts, Administrative Studies, 1991

Francis Williams

123 Main Street • Hometown, NJ 00000
(555) 555-0987 • fwilliams@company.com

Financial Planning Qualifications and Credentials

- Over a decade of progressively significant roles and achievements within planning, portfolio management, and client services.
- Personal responsibilities for more than $210 million in client assets.
- Recognized for outstanding asset-based performance and customer service.
- After completion of ABC Financial Consultant Sales Training and Advanced Training, served as trainer and curriculum developer.
- Licensed Series 6, 7, 63, and health and life insurance.

Financial Planning Accomplishments

ABC FINANCIAL CONSULTANTS, Princeton, NJ

2000–Present   **Financial Consultant/Financial Planner**
Serve in comprehensive financial planning role. Oversee individual and group portfolios. Serve as manager, supervisor, and trainer within corporate headquarters of firm responsible for over $800 million in client assets.
- Developed $210 million client asset base through aggressive prospecting and targeting campaign.
- Successfully built portfolio that includes stock, bonds, options, and insurance products for more than 450 clients.
- Gained expertise associated with estate planning, asset allocation, and wealth succession.

1998–2000   **Sales Associate**
- Worked directly with firm's top producer, profiling high net worth individuals for future business.
- Generated $90,000 for top producer through new account openings.
- Analyzed existing portfolios, assisting in development of accounts.

1997–1998   **Account Executive Trainee/Intern**
- Completed more than 35,000 account transactions annually.
- Completed comprehensive training related to trade settlement, NASD regulations, and customer service.
- Acted as liaison between sales force and New York operations.

Summers 1996 and 1997   MAPLEWOOD INVESTMENTS, Maplewood, NJ
Prospecting Intern

Education   IONA COLLEGE, Iona, New York
Bachelor of Arts in Economics, with Concentration in Management, 1998

CHRIS SMITH

123 Main Street • Hometown, TN 00000 • (555) 555-1234 • csmith@company.com

HUMAN RESOURCES EXPERIENCE

TENNESSEE MUTUAL INSURANCE   MEMPHIS, TN
Director of Human Resources and Staff Development   **2007–Present**
Develop and implement overall human resources policies. Provide leadership in the areas of personnel, payroll, labor relations, training, and affirmative action for operations with over 2,000 employees. Administer personnel and payroll procedures, policies, and systems to meet management and employee needs. Consult with chairman, executive board, managerial staff, and supervisors to ensure policy compliance with applicable statutes, rules, and regulations. Advance agency Affirmative Action Plan. Determine appropriate grievance procedures required to resolve labor disputes. Act as liaison for regulatory agencies: EOHS, OER, DPA, State Office of AA, and PERA. Maintain staff training program. Interface with legal staff when addressing discipline and grievances.

WILMONT INSURANCE CO.   NASHVILLE, TN
Director of Human Resources   **1997–2007**
Oversaw hiring, training, and all personnel responsibilities for insurance broker with 400 employees. Determined technology and procedures related to maintaining and updating personnel files, ensuring compliance with federal and state regulations pertaining to benefits and wages. Supervised grievance adjudication. Performed claim payment internal audits. Coordinated activity with reinsurance carriers.
Central Personnel Administrator   **1995–1997**
Coordinated statewide reclassification study. Organized questionnaires and individual interviews. Evaluated, analyzed, and rewrote job descriptions; prepared study package for senior management approval. Established related managerial files. Dealt with diverse personnel-related projects.

DEPARTMENT OF EMPLOYMENT AND TRAINING   NASHVILLE, TN
Supervisor   **1992–1995**
Claims Adjudicator   **1990–1992**

HUMAN RESOURCES AND BUSINESS EDUCATION

MILLIGAN COLLEGE   MILLIGAN, TN
Course work in Personnel Management and Human Resources   **2000–Present**

TENNESSEE WESLEYAN COLLEGE   NASHVILLE, TN
B.A. Management, with Personnel Track   **1990**

PROFESSIONAL PROFILE

- Over fifteen years of human resource experience; five as a director of comprehensive programs.
- Expertise recruiting, training, performance reviews, compensation, and affirmative action.
- Capacities to work with senior management to develop, implement, and monitor HR strategies including recruitment outsourcing, vendor management, and Web technology for contingent workforce management.
- Specialized knowledge of issues, policies, and procedures associated with the insurance industry.
- Commitment to ongoing professional development through continued courses and seminars.

Human Services Counselor

Jamie Brown
123 Main Street • Hometown, IL 00000 • (555) 555-1234 • jbrown@company.com

OBJECTIVE
Human Services Counselor/Administrator Position

QUALIFICATIONS
- Comprehensive case management experience for juveniles and families.
- Expertise assessing cases, developing treatment plans, facilitating crisis intervention procedures, and family therapy.
- Diverse counseling skills applicable to developmental and physical disabilities, and substance abuse.
- Experience with child abuse and neglect cases, as well as the needs of developmentally disabled youth.

EXPERIENCE

1998–Present SOCIETY FOR PREVENTION OF CRUELTY TO CHILDREN, Chicago, IL
Investigator/Case Manager
- Conduct assessments and develop treatment plans for family caseload.
- Maintain documentation of contracts and provide crisis intervention and family therapy.
- Serve as advocate for clients in court and with community agencies.

1996–1997 FARMINGTON JUVENILE COURT, Farmington, IL
Intern
- Tracked abuse/neglect cases to ensure that status reports and petitions were filed accurately and on time.
- Observed court hearings and trials and established court expectations.

1995–1996 PEORIA JUVENILE COURT, Peoria, IL
Intern
- Provided individual and group counseling for juvenile offenders in detention.
- Reviewed, updated, and cited findings of case files and incident reports.

2007–Present TEMPORARY RESOURCES, Peoria, IL
Human Service Worker
- As a temporary associate, served clients in hospitals, day programs, and private residences.
- Counseled and supervised adolescents in group homes and serve as substitute teacher at institutions such as the Stafford School for the Deaf.

2005–2007 ALLIED GROUP HOMES, Columbus, IN
Residential Manager
- Worked in several residential programs for all levels of developmentally delayed clients.
- Counseled and taught daily living, hygiene, and community awareness skills.

Summers 2003 to 2005 DEPARTMENT OF MENTAL HEALTH, Gardena, IL
Intern
- Assisted developmentally delayed adults, encouraging development of self-sufficiency.

EDUCATION BRADLEY UNIVERSITY, Peoria, IL
Bachelor of Science, Human Services, 2005

Corey Davis

123 Main Street · Hometown, AZ 00000 · (555) 555-8767 · cdavis@company.com

Underwriting Qualifications

- Underwriting and analytical skills, sales and marketing knowledge, and technical skills exhibited throughout past twenty years.
- Record of productivity and profitability in progressively responsible positions.
- Efficient supervisor, planner, organizer, and manager of time, projects, and professional peers.

Underwriting and Marketing Experience and Achievements

SCRIMSHAW INSURANCE CO., Tempe, AZ

2008–Present **Personal Lines Insurance Underwriter**
- Analyzed all personal lines of business to determine acceptability and to control, restrict, or decline, according to company guidelines.
- Supervised all personal lines of business for Arizona and New Mexico.
- Kept current with changing policies, rates, and procedures, explaining coverage, rules, forms, and decisions to agents, staff, and insured.

2003–2008 **Manual Rating and Policy Writing Supervisor**
- Delegated responsibilities, set objectives, and monitored work.
- Evaluated performance, established supervisory controls, and conducted audits.
- Implemented staff briefings, ongoing training, and updating materials.

CALIFORNIA INDEMNITY INSURANCE COMPANY, Sacramento, CA

2001–2003 **Senior Marketing Representative**
- Managed assigned territory including prospecting new distribution sources, rehabilitating nonperforming agencies, and terminating relationships.
- Served in lead role for all insured sales presentations by conducting strategy negotiations, making presentations, and facilitating actual presentation.

1999–2001 **Underwriting Manager—Commercial and Special Accounts**
1997–1999 **Senior Underwriter**
- Developed book of $25,000 to $1 million SIR deductible contracts.
- Served as Property/Inland Marine Specialist for division by handling all referrals, audits, and facultative reinsurance negotiations.

FIREMAN'S FUND INSURANCE COMPANY, Sacramento, CA

1994–1997 **Commercial Underwriter/Inland Marine Specialist**
1989–1994 **Personal Lines Underwriter/Client Customer Service Representative**

Professional Development, Seminars, and Education

- Insurance 21, 22, and 23 Courses, Underwriting School (six-week program), Senior Underwriting Seminar, Listening Seminar, Supervisory Seminar.
- Bachelor of Arts, University of Phoenix, 1998

Chris Smith

123 Main Street • Hometown, OH 00000 • (555) 555-6654 • csmith@company.com

Laboratory and Technical Expertise

- Proven ability in analysis, scientific theories, and procedures.
- Experience collecting and studying data from various biological sources.
- Proficient at producing and processing blood components.
- Skilled at performing tissue experiments using electron microscopy.
- Quickly and accurately learn and perform complicated tasks.
- Understanding of the differences between research within biotechnology and academic research.
- Experience organizing, writing, and editing detailed reports and research papers.
- Trainer for biochemists in routine blood-banking procedures.
- Experience within web design, graphic arts, layout, and related roles.
- Proficient in: Excel, Word, PowerPoint, PhotoShop, InDesign, Flash, Dreamweaver, and Internet research.

Laboratory and Technical Experience

American Red Cross, Cleveland, OH
Laboratory Technician: produce and process blood components. Label and release for transfusion and manufacture. Perform viral immunology testing and irradiation of blood products. 2011–Present

Biogen Inc., Cambridge, MA
Analytical Development Department Intern: qualified an SEC-HPLC method with subtraction of a twin peak in an Avonex formulation for use in the Quality Control Department. Edited images using Photo-Shop to illustrate a PowerPoint presentation delivered to corporate colleagues and internship peers. Summer 2011

Case Western Reserve University Hospital, Cleveland, OH
Department of Biochemistry and Molecular Biology Intern: Expressed proteins in E. Coli for use in protein translocation projects. Performed SDS-Page gels and Western blots to test protein expression. Summer 2010

Teaching and Computer Experience

Case Western Reserve University, Cleveland, OH
Biochemistry Laboratory Teaching Assistant: Assisted students in biochemistry laboratory. Worked with professors to prepare materials for use in the laboratory and graded quizzes and laboratory reports. Created webpage allowing students access to test results. 2010–2011
Educational Technology Consultant: Assisted faculty and students with computer-related problems with scanning and photographic manipulations. 2010–2012

Biological Sciences Education

Case Western Reserve University, Cleveland, OH
Bachelor of Science, Biology/Chemistry, with a major GPA of 3.3, May 2011
Courses include: Organic Chemistry I and II, Molecular Cell Biology, Biochemistry, Molecular Biology, Anatomy, Physiology, Biochemistry Laboratory, Immunology, and Topics of Biological Macromolecules.

DANA JOHNSON

123 Main Street • Hometown, NM 00000 • (555) 555-1234 • djohnson@company.com

LOCAL AREA NETWORK AND TECHNICAL COMPETENCIES

- Expertise in configuring, installing, and administering network infrastructure and telecommunications systems that support staff of up to 300 personnel.
- Skilled in planning and implementing network security, including building firewalls.
- Knowledge of Windows 2000, 2003, and NT4 network operating systems; Active Directory, NT4 domain administration, and primary network services.

TECHNICAL EXPERIENCE AND ACHIEVEMENTS

JEFFERSON MANUFACTURING CORP., Albuquerque, NM
LAN Coordinator, 2008–Present
- Analyze, develop, and maintain application software for multi-site engineering LAN.
- Provide training and user support for all applications to LAN users.
- Maintain departmental PC workstations including software installation and upgrades.
- Reduced data entry errors and process time by developing an online program allowing program manager to submit model number information.
- Replaced time-consuming daily review board meetings by developing a program allowing engineers to review and approve model and component changes online.
- Developed an online program that reduced process time, standardized part usage, and allowingengineers to build part lists for new products and components.

Computer Systems Analyst, 2004–2008
- Completed database management, systems analysis and design, workstation maintenance and repair, and LAN management tasks.
- Reduced process time and purchasing errors by developing an online program which allowed the purchasing department to track the status of all purchasing invoices.
- Developed purchase order program that improved data entry speed and reduced data entry errors.

LAFAYETTE, INC., Albuquerque, NM
Engineering Technician, 1999–2004
- Prototyped and tested new PC products, drawing schematics and expediting parts for these new PC products. Designed and coded multiuser database management software for engineering use.
- Expedited parts for twenty-five or more telecommunications terminal prototypes. Built, troubleshot, and transferred prototypes to various departments for testing.

ELECTRONICS AND TECHNICAL EDUCATION

UNIVERSITY OF NEW MEXICO, Albuquerque, NM
Bachelor of Science, Electronics, 2004

SAN THOMAS COMMUNITY COLLEGE, Albuquerque, NM
Associate of Arts, Information Technology, 2000

Francis Williams

123 Main Street • Hometown, VT 00000 • (555) 555-1234 • fwilliams@company.com

PROFESSIONAL PROFILE

- Library professional with community, secondary school, and university experience.
- Capacities to translate services, policies, and procedures into patron focused and educational outcomes.
- Specialized focus on community outreach, patron education, program planning, and public speaking roles.
- Experience using and instructing peers and patrons to use NLM Classification System, ALA filing rules, as well as various indexes and Internet resources.

LIBRARY EXPERIENCE AND ACHIEVEMENTS

KATHRYN F. BELL LIBRARY, Burlington, VT
Librarian, 2006 to Present
- Provide excellent patron services when covering circulation and reference desks.
- Give instructional guidance to patrons, including use of computerized and manual index tools and catalogs.
- Focus interactions on empowering and instructing patrons while creating positive relationships.
- Address reference questions by demonstrating proper Internet and printed resources.
- Plan and present regular community education programs.
- Record incoming periodicals and journals on computerized system and strip resources for security.
- Compile statistics on door count, circulation, photocopies, and reference activities.
- Serve on Acquisition Committee and provide quarterly and annual recommendations to Budget Committee.

Evening Librarian, 2004 to 2006
- Performed overall patron services and library operations, and supervised the evening clerk.
- Compiled and circulated specialized reference packet for series of community health seminars.

EAST CATHOLIC HIGH SCHOOL, Rutland, VT
Librarian/Audiovisual Coordinator, 2000 to 2004
- Supervised comprehensive secondary school library, overseeing volunteer, professional, and student staffs.
- Established annual educational plans and regularly supported instructional efforts of teachers.
- Completed daily patron services and operations efforts and supervised student study periods.
- Interacted with Budget Committee to establish and monitor annual budgets.
- Ordered publications as well as software, and maintained audiovisual equipment.

SIMMONS COLLEGE, Boston, MA
Library Graduate Intern, 1999 to 2000
- Via supervised rotations, learned about reference, periodical, acquisition, and special collection areas.
- Researched, wrote, and presented four special reports to library professionals and graduate student peers.

EDUCATION

SIMMONS COLLEGE, Boston, MA
Master of Library Science, 2000

UNIVERSITY OF VERMONT, Burlington, VT
Bachelor of Arts in English, 1998

Management Consultant

Jamie Brown

123 Main Street NW • Apartment 12 • Hometown, VA 00000 • (555) 555-6777 • jbrown@company.com

Consulting *Experience*	**American Management Systems** *Senior Consultant Government Practice*	**Washington, DC** *2010–Present*

- Ensured operational readiness of a division of the Internal Revenue System by preparing a staffing gap analysis and developing a database to record staffing demand of new organization; prepared package to submit new organizational design charts and functional statements to commissioner.
- Developed operational policies, procedures, and responsibilities handbook for IRS management.
- Developed survey tool to baseline office characteristics.

Consultant   *2002–2010*

- Evaluated underutilization of grant funds for Housing and Urban Development program. Analyzed grant expenditure data, developed hypotheses, led interviews, and wrote sections of final report.
- Provided analytical and technical support to Department of Energy, Office of Environmental Management. Tracked appropriations legislation, managed the research, maintenance, and production of a portion of EM's FY 2005 Budget Request that was submitted to Congress.

Research Analyst   *2007–2008*

- Developed organizational redesign and change management initiatives for the District of Columbia Metropolitan Police Department. Facilitated client team working groups, conducted best practices research, developed data collection and analysis tools, and developed new process diagrams.

Computer *Experience*	**University of Rochester Press** *Web Developer*	**Rochester, NY** *Fall 2006*

- Developed webpage; provided general public access to UR Press publication profiles and order forms, and enabled authors and editors to submit work.

Government *Experience*	**Labour Party Headquarters** *Intern*	**London, England** *Spring 2006*
	Democratic Congressional Campaign Committee *Intern*	**Washington, D.C.** *Spring 2005*

Education	**University of Rochester** *Bachelor of Arts in Political Science, with Concentration in Journalism, cum laude*	**Rochester, NY** *2007*
	European Programs Abroad *Overseas Studies Program Participant*	**London, England** *2006*

Qualifications

- Ability to manage cases from evaluation and data collection to analysis, presentation, and implementation.
- Significant knowledge of government systems, structures, funding, and organizational oversights.
- Ability to use Excel and Access to create financial models and related databases and Word, PowerPoint, LexisNexis for research, presentation development, and report writing.

Dana Johnson

123 Main Street · Hometown, NC 00000 · (555) 555-3456 · djohnson@company.com

Management Information Systems Profile

- Extensive and diverse computer hardware and software knowledge related to personal computer usage within business and educational settings.
- Expertise assessing hardware and software needs, estimating costs, purchasing, and installing.
- Capacities to hire, train, and monitor performance of Information Systems professionals.
- Experience working with outside consultants, service and product vendors, and third-party temporary and permanent placement agencies.
- Ability to use, teach, and support programming languages, operating systems, network configurations, as well as word processing, Internet, database, and spreadsheet applications.

Technical Qualifications

- Programming Languages: Borland C, C++, XML, JavaScript, HTML, Visual Basic.
- Operating Systems: Windows, Windows NT Server, UNIX, Linux, and Novell Netware.
- Network Technologies: LAN, WAN, VPN, Wireless Networks, Satellite Networks.
- Database: Access.
- Spreadsheet: Lotus 123 and Excel.
- Word Processing: Word for Windows and Word for Mac.
- Presentation and Publishing: Quark Xpress, PowerPoint, FrontPage.
- Webpage Development: PageMill and Fireworks.

Summary of Achievements

- Researched, wrote, and edited proposal used to identify needs and fund networks and desktop configurations composed of eight personal computers and two printers.
- Supervise three technology and systems consultants for office with thirty full-time employees.
- Planned and oversaw completion of special project teams related to existing and future technology needs and potential purchases.
- Regularly conduct software- and hardware-related troubleshooting and audit activities.
- Interact with product vendors and customer service and technology support professionals.
- Designed 24/7 backup and retrieval system for accounting databases and word-processing data.

Management Information Systems Experience

Maximum Data Systems, Charlotte, NC
Information Systems Manager, 2006–Present

Touchestone Systems, Inc., Charlotte, NC
Computer Consultant, 2004–2006

Gilford College, Greensboro, NC
Introduction to Computer Science Instructor, Part-time and Summers 2003–2005
Information Technology Consultant, Part-time 2002–2004

Education

Duke University, Durham, NC
Bachelor of Science, Computer Science, June 2004

COREY DAVIS

123 Main Street • Hometown, OR 00000 • (555) 555-1234

Brand Management Accomplishments

- Accountabilities include P&L for $500 million covering 100+ film products and 80+ cameras.
- Developed and implemented comprehensive annual marketing and strategic plans covering 150 products.
- Delivered and executed 5 national marketing plans and 25 new product launches.
- Created 4 new imaging categories and negotiated $40 million in first-year sales with a projected 20% increase in high-tech market sales in newly established distribution.
- Fully profiled and conducted outreach to 30 multi-location customers and won them back to Cressidine, securing $20 million in sales.
- As Product Manager of the International Division, traveled for 5 years between 5 South American countries and 10 European subsidiaries building product launch plans and developing relationships and knowledge of foreign customs and business protocols.
- Provide leadership for national sales force of 500+.
- Mentored and promoted numerous managers into key positions.

Brand Management and Marketing Experience

CRESSIDINE CORPORATION — Corvallis, OR
Brand Manager and Director of Marketing Operations for Technical Imaging — 2002–Present
- Spearhead implementation of corporate objectives within the Technical Imaging Division.
- Conceive and energize all marketing strategies and provide feedback on program performance and recommendations to corporate senior managers.
- Direct and supervise staff of 10 with responsibilities for generating $250 million in sales with a $150 million margin for core products.
- Prepare and effectively control a $7 million marketing expense and a $4 million advertising budget.
- Created first end-user direct mail strategy, generating a 30% response rate and selling 400,000 units in first year.
- Mounted trade show exhibitions including designing booths, collateral materials, and advertisements. Secured $200,000 in prebooked sales within a month of tradeshow presentations for 4 new products.

Group Marketing Manager for Technical Imaging — 1998–2002
- Responsible for developing relationships with major imaging companies and securing long term contracts for core products within a vertical market framework.
- Directed and monitored new product launch programs; developed pricing and selling strategies.
- Fostered and maintained key account relations.

Business, Marketing, and Management Studies

UNIVERSITY OF OREGON — Eugene, OR
Masters of Business Administration — 2000
Bachelor of Science in Business Administration — 1998

CHRIS SMITH

123 Main Street • Hometown, NH 00000 • (555) 555-1234 • csmith@company.com

PROFESSIONAL PROFILE

- Expertise conducting research required to develop strategically sound business plans and used plans to generate capital.
- Confidence addressing consumer product, health care, government agencies, and nonprofit issues.
- Capacities to develop state-of-the-art statistically viable projects and cite findings in comprehensive reports.

MARKET RESEARCH ACHIEVEMENTS

SEARCHER ASSOCIATES, Ossipee, NH

2011–Present **Market Research Consultant:** Established firm, conducted client outreach, recruited three associates, and oversee all operations activities. Build consumer behavior models using multivariate techniques, including regression and discriminate analysis, and cluster analysis. Analyze data from national survey to identify purchase intents and patterns for business-to-consumer direct marketers. Present information to senior management of client organizations. Specialized in entrepreneurial start-up activities, business plan development, and venture capital solicitation.

STEVEN ICE, INC., Derry, NH

2008–2011 **Vice President of Marketing:** Identified target markets, constructed complex questionnaires, conducted telephone interviews, compiled and analyzed data for research activities associated with entrepreneurial start-up. Conducted focus groups to identify market segments and penetration. Wrote and presented report to management including strategic recommendations. Addressed all marketing research needs. Gathered data to develop comprehensive business plan and marketing reports.

HAWTHORNE MANAGEMENT, Washington, DC

2000–2008 **Market and Strategic Management Research Consultant:** Conducted large-scale quantitative research projects based in customer satisfaction measurement and total quality implementation, including design, coordination, statistical analysis, and report generation. Specialized in business-to-business services, e-commerce, and health care.

1996–2000 **Research Associate:** Managed behaviorally based research projects including proposal writing; methodology, instrument and sample development; field coordination; data coding, analysis; and report writing. Included customer and employee studies, communication audits, market analysis, name/logo testing, constituency relations, positioning, and consumer studies.

INTERNATIONAL RESEARCH GROUP, Miami, FL

1993–1996 **Management Consultant:** Provided marketing, behavior, and research counsel for advertising, public relations, and marketing consulting firm. Participated in internal and external strategic planning for *Fortune* 500 firms, government agencies, nonprofits, and health-care providers.

WEBBER AND SONS, INC., Washington, DC

1988–1993 **Research Assistant:** Completed projects for insurance providers, hospitals, and private practices.

EDUCATION

GEORGETOWN UNIVERSITY, Washington, DC
Master of Arts, Applied Psychology, with concentration in Health Care Research, 1990
Bachelor of Arts, Psychology, *cum laude,* 1988

Jamie Brown

123 Main Street • Hometown, CA 00000 • (555) 555-1234 • jbrown@company.com

BUSINESS QUALIFICATIONS

- Knowledge gained from comprehensive business courses, including accounting and economics.
- Capacities to conduct topic-specific or problem-focused research and analysis.
- Confidence presenting research results verbally and via detailed reports and illustrated presentations.
- Experience prioritizing tasks and completing assignments accurately and on time.
- Comfortable within reporting hierarchies and motivating peers.
- Strong task management and personnel motivation capabilities gained through military training.
- Cross cultural skills enhanced through travel in Iraq, Africa, and Asia.
- Technical and mechanical aptitude applicable to manufacturing, troubleshooting, and technical settings and projects.
- Basic Russian language abilities.

EDUCATION

SACRAMENTO STATE UNIVERSITY, Sacramento, CA
Bachelor of Arts, Liberal Studies, anticipated June 2013.

AMERICAN RIVER COLLEGE, Sacramento, CA
Completed general education courses, 1998–2001.

BUSINESS-RELATED COURSES

Macro- and Microeconomics
Managerial Accounting
Public Speaking

Financial Accounting
Contemporary World Issues
Social Research Methods

MILITARY EXPERIENCE AND TRAINING

2008–Present   EXPLOSIVES DISPOSAL UNIT, Mare Island, CA
US Navy EOD Diver
- As Bomb Disposal Unit team member, give and receive briefings to task-related personnel, maintain and update classified publications, procure operations-related equipment, and process after-action documentation such as dive logs and equipment usage reports.

2005–2008   USS *BERGALL* (SSN-667) SUBMARINE SQUADRON
Submariner, Machinist Mate 2nd Class and Operations-Diver
- Operated and maintained submarine's atmosphere control equipment, such as breathing air/gas mixture levels, and potable water.
- Ordered and kept accounting of repair parts and supplies for both Auxiliary Division and Dive locker.
- Nuclear Weapons Armed Security Guard. Security Swimmer.

Dana Johnson
123 Main Street • Hometown, CA 00000
(555) 555-1234 • djohnson@company.com

Education

2010–2012   **University of California Los Angeles (UCLA),** Los Angeles, CA
Master of Music, with a major in Conducting, June 2007

2008–2010   **University of the Pacific (UOP),** Stockton, CA
Bachelor of Music, with a major in Music Education, May 2005

2006–2008   **California State University, Northridge (CSUN),** Northridge, CA
Completed Music and General Education Courses

Music Performance Experience

University of California Los Angeles, Los Angeles, CA
2011–2012   Conductor, Pianist, Composer, Studio Vocalist
2010–2011   Gospel Choir Accompanist and Vocalist

University of South Carolina, Columbia, SC
Summer 2010   Conductors Institute Participant

University of the Pacific, Stockton, CA
2008–2010   Trumpeter, Pianist, and Vocalist

California State University, Northridge, Northridge, CA
2006–2008   Trumpeter, Pianist, and Vocalist

Morris Chapel and St. Mary's Church, Stockton, CA
2004–2006   Conductor, Pianist, Organist, and Vocalist

Conducting and Music Teaching Experience

Marymount High School, Los Angeles, CA
2010–Present   Conductor and Teacher of Music Theory

UCLA Music Department, Los Angeles, CA
2010–2012   Choral Ensembles Student Conductor

Presentation Elementary School, Stockton, CA
2008–2010   Instrumental Music Teacher

Central Valley Youth Orchestra, Stockton, CA
2008–2010   Assistant Conductor

UOP Morris Chapel, Stockton, CA
2008–2010   Choir Director for Catholic Mass

Dana Johnson   Page Two

Employment History

Marymount High School, Los Angeles, CA
2010–Present   Director of Music

Audiences Unlimited, Inc., Los Angeles, CA
2010–Present   Studio Audience Coordinator

Honors and Affiliations

2010–Present   Conductor's Guild

2006–Present   California Music Educators Association, Southern California School Band
                      and Orchestra Association, International Association of Jazz Educators,
                      California Music Educators Conference, and International Trumpet Guild

Works Conducted

Beethoven's Symphony no. 8, first movement
Mayer's Andante for Strings
Hindemith's Five Pieces for String Orchestra
Haydn's Symphony no. 49, "La Passione"
Elgar's Serenade for Strings
Grieg's Holberg Suite
Mozart's Symphony no. 29
Sibelius's Andante Festivo for Strings
Bizet's Carmen Suite

Conducting Instructors

Steven Smithers, Stockton, CA
Dr. Mitchell Pearson, Los Angeles, CA

Trumpet Instructors

Peter Smith, Northridge, CA
Robert Horn, Los Angeles, CA

Jazz and Classical Piano Instructors

Stephanie Best, Los Angeles, CA
Patricia Peterson, Pasadena, CA

Nanny

Jamie Brown

123 Main Street • Hometown, CA 00000 • USA
Phone (409) 555-1234 • Cell (409) 555-5678 • jbrown@company.com

---

Objective Live-In Nanny/Au pair Position.

Qualifications

- Ability to develop trusting relationships with children and parents.
- Certified teacher with strong classroom and private tutoring experience.
- Skills to plan educational and recreational activities.
- Command of teaching conversational English.
- Cross cultural and European travel experiences, with passport, international driver's license, and working papers, and conversational abilities in Italian.
- Experience supporting children with special needs.

Childcare Experience

ROBERT AND THERESA SANTANA, Santa Clara, CA

2010 to Present *Nanny:* Provide live-in childcare for two boys, currently ages two and four. Supervise play, transport children to preschool and other activities, and assist with meals. Reinforce parental rules and values. Accompany family on short and long trips and vacations.

Teaching Credential and Training

NATIONAL UNIVERSITY, San Jose, CA
California Multiple Subject Credential, June 2009
Curriculum included: whole language instruction, curriculum, and instruction, and literature based integrated language arts.
Courses included: Foundations of Education, Curriculum and Instruction, Literature Based Integrated Language Arts, and Exceptional Children in the Classroom.

Teaching and Tutoring Experience

CATHOLIC DIOCESE OF SANTA CLARA, Santa Clara, CA

Summer 2009 *Summer School English Teacher:* Planned and implemented lessons focusing on literature, grammar, writing, and research. Addressed remedial needs of students.

PRESENTATION SCHOOL, Cupertino, CA

Spring 2009 *3rd Grade Student Teacher:* Independently established and presented lesson and unit plans. Created specific interdisciplinary Reading and Work unit, focusing on reading skills for varied jobs, including visiting career field representatives.

2006 to 2008 1st, 2nd, and kindergarten *Teacher's Aide*

Education UNIVERSITY OF SANTA CLARA, Santa Clara, CA
Bachelor of Arts, English, May 1999

FRANCIS WILLIAMS, RN, NP

123 Main Street • Hometown, MI 00000 • (555) 555-2322 • fwilliams@company.com

OBJECTIVE

Nurse Practitioner in a clinical, educational, research, or administrative setting

QUALIFICATION SUMMARY

- Eighteen years as an Adult Nurse Practitioner in primary care and women's health care
- Skilled in medical histories, physical exams, microscopy, laboratory testing, and medical prescription
- Expertise evaluating and managing wide scope of acute, chronic, and complex problems, and preventive and routine medical care
- Strong interpersonal/communication skills with patients and colleagues
- Skilled with elderly, adults, teens, those with mental disabilities, and the hearing impaired (using medical sign language)
- Provide counseling for mood problems and other health issues
- Abilities to develop health education materials; teach in-service lessons; and act as preceptor
- Experienced in committee leadership and participation

CLINICAL NURSING EXPERIENCE AND ACHIEVEMENTS

Ann Arbor Gynecologic & Obstetric Associates, P. C., Ann Arbor, MI
Nurse Practitioner, 2001–Present
- Provide gynecologic, obstetric, and primary care in collaboration with physicians in private practice
- Evaluate and manage acute and chronic gynecologic and obstetric problems, including: abdominopelvic pain, genitourinary problems, infections, breast concerns, endocrine-related problems, osteoporosis, and postoperative and pregnancy complications
- Evaluate and manage wide array of primary-care problems including EENT, allergic conditions, dermatological problems, infectious diseases, chest pain, and respiratory, gastrointestinal, and musculoskeletal problems
- Perform annual and employment exams and prenatal and postpartum care
- Counsel and prescribe for cholesterol and weight management, contraception, menopause, osteoporosis, and mood disorders
- Developed health education handouts and presented staff in-service training
- Performed periodic quality assurance review for on-site laboratory
- Acted as preceptor for nurse practitioner and physician assistant students

University of Michigan University Health Service, Ann Arbor, MI
Senior Nurse Practitioner, 1997–2000
- Evaluated and managed health problems including: infectious diseases; allergic conditions; dermatological problems; respiratory, gastrointestinal, genitourinary, endocrine, and musculoskeletal problems; traumatic injuries; and occupational health issues
- Provided routine and preventive care and employment and sports physical exams
- Initiated gynecologic services for Eastman School of Music
- Made health education presentations, acted as preceptor, and served on Training and HIV Task Force
- Coordinated University Health Services Library used by nurses, nursing students, and patients

FRANCIS WILLIAMS
Page Two

University of Michigan University Health Service, Ann Arbor, MI
Nurse Practitioner, 1994–1997
- Evaluated and managed wide variety of health problems for students
- Performed routine and preventive care and sports physical exams
- Became proficient in sign language used in medical context
- Made health education presentations to staff and students, acted as preceptor for students, and served on various committees

NURSING EDUCATION AND LIBERAL ARTS STUDIES

University of Michigan School of Nursing, Ann Arbor, MI
MS, Family Health Nurse Clinician, 2000, and BS, *magna cum laude*, Nursing, 1993

Ann Arbor County Community College, Ann Arbor, MI
Completed prerequisite science and pre-nursing courses, 1990–1991

Albion College, Albion, MI
BA, Religion, 1990

CREDENTIALS AND AFFILIATIONS

- American Nurses' Association Certification, Adult Nurse Practitioner
- Michigan State Certification, Family Health Nurse Practitioner with Prescription Privilege
- Michigan State License, Registered Professional Nurse
- Certified in CPR, most recent update 2011

COREY DAVIS

123 Main Street • Hometown, NM 00000 • (555) 555-5555 • cdavis@company.com
345 Mission Boulevard • Hometown, CA 00000 • (555) 555-0987

PARALEGAL QUALIFICATIONS AND ACHIEVEMENTS

- Outstanding case research, client relations, document management, and writing skills gained in progressively responsible positions over a thirteen-year period.
- Expertise gained as law office manager, compiling a training manual and supervising administrative support personnel, revamping accounting, debit, and credit systems.
- Trained and accomplished interviewer, negotiator, and mediator.
- LexisNexis, Westlaw, Word, FileMaker Pro, Excel, QuickBooks, and Internet skills.

PARALEGAL AND MANAGEMENT EXPERIENCE

LAW OFFICES OF BRENDAN ELLIS   Santa Fe, NM
Civil Litigation Specialist/Office Manager   2000–Present
- Manage office and staff of three secretaries, ensuring smooth operation of firm with three attorneys; billings in excess of $1.5 million; awards of over $10 million annually.
- Interview clients; prepare files and discovery; handle multiple cases.
- Request and review medical documentation; ascertaining evidence from appropriate parties.
- Negotiate and settle cases with defense attorney and insurance companies.
- Attend mediations and conciliations.
- Prepare clients for depositions and trials.
- Control and maintain law office accounts, utilizing accounting and billing software.
- Regularly attended seminars on personal injury law.

SANTA FE DISTRICT ATTORNEY'S OFFICE DOMESTIC VIOLENCE UNIT   Santa Fe, NM
Witness Advocate   Spring–Summer 2000
- Interviewed victims and witnesses, prepared documents, and organized information for court appearances.
- Assisted attorneys during trials, taking notes and facilitating access to evidentiary documents.

NEW MEXICO PUBLIC DEFENDER'S OFFICE   Santa Fe, NM
Legal Intern   Summers 1998 and 1999
- Researched and drafted motions on criminal law and procedural issues. Interviewed clients at New Mexico correctional institutions.
- Argued bail motions in several state district courts.
- Negotiated plea and bail agreements for defendants accused of misdemeanors. Attended criminal trials and depositions.

ATTORNEY DANIEL GALL   Santa Fe, NM
Legal Secretary/Legal Assistant   1996–2000
- Greeted clients, maintained files, and completed administrative tasks.
- Prepared documents for legal proceedings involving real estate transactions.
- Entered client information into Excel- and Access-driven computer system.

EDUCATION

SAINT JOHN'S COLLEGE   Santa Fe, NM
B.S., Human Resources Management, with Honors   2000
- Completed degree while employed and served as peer advisor to nontraditional students.

Pharmacist

Dana Johnson

123 Main Street • Hometown, CA 00000 • (555) 555-1234 • djohnson@company.com

OBJECTIVE   Pharmacist Position

EDUCATION   UNIVERSITY OF THE PACIFIC SCHOOL OF PHARMACY, Stockton, CA
PharmD, May 2005
Pre-Pharmacy Studies, 1999–2001

PHARMACY ACCOMPLISHMENTS

2005–Present   DAVID GRANT MEDICAL CENTER, Travis Air Force Base, Fairfield, CA
Pharmacist: Provide comprehensive pharmaceutical services for patients, assist physicians with identification of appropriate drug regimens, and support educational efforts targeting health care professionals and patients.

Spring 2005   *Internal Medicine Rotation:* Attended rounds with physicians; assisted physicians selecting proper drug regimens; monitored drug-to-drug interactions and patient lab results.

Fall 2004   *Clinical Psychiatric Rotation:* Monitored patient charts for drug-to-drug interactions; enhanced patient medication compliance; instructed patients regarding medication; and consulted with patients regarding discharge medications.

Winter 2005   VETERANS ADMINISTRATION OUTPATIENT CLINIC, Martinez, CA
Ambulatory Care Rotation: Monitored PT/INR in anticoagulation clinic; monitored patient status in cardiovascular and hypertension clinic; evaluated proper medication renewal in pharmacy refill clinic.

Winter 2004   LONGS DRUGS CORPORATE OFFICE, Walnut Creek, CA
Community Pharmacy Management Rotation: Undertook inventory control efforts and RXD orders; updated prices; completed key tagging for billing purposes; and developed positive customer service approaches and attitudes.

Summer 2004   WALGREENS PHARMACY, Cupertino, CA
Community Pharmacy Rotation: Processed new prescriptions and refills; took new prescriptions from physicians; processed third-party claims to Aetna, Blue Shield, and Foundation; labeled and organized inventory; assisted customers with OTC purchases and prescriptions.

June 2003-
June 2004   SMART FOOD PHARMACY, Stockton, CA
Pharmacy Intern

PROFESSIONAL AFFILIATIONS

California Pharmacists Association
American Pharmacists Association
Kappa Psi Pharmaceutical Fraternity

Chris Smith

123 Main Street • Hometown, IN 00000 • (555) 555-5094 • csmith@company.com

Physical Therapy, Sports Medicine, and Massage Therapy Qualifications

- Background in physical therapy and sports medicine, and clinical experience with adults, student athletes, and pediatric patients.
- More than 2,000 hours as Physical Therapist; 1,000 hours as Athletic Trainer; 4,000 hours as Physical Therapy Aid; 200 hours as Nurse; and 350 hours as Certified Massage Therapist.

Physical Therapy, Massage Therapy Experience

MIDWEST MEMORIAL HOSPITAL, Indianapolis, IN
Orthopedic In- and Outpatient Clinic Therapist, 2009–Present
- Develop treatment plans for chronic-pain and cardiac patients.
- Present regular in-service training on hip and knee prostheses.

DEARBORN COUNTY HOSPITAL, Richmond, IN
Cardiac Rehabilitation Therapist, 2008–2009
- Acted as program coordinator for exercise regimen and provided treatments using ultrasound, electric stimulation, massage therapy, and stretching/strengthening exercises.
- Coordinated aquadynamics program for chronic-pain patients.

CINNAMON MOUNTAIN, Mishawaka, WI
Pediatric Rehabilitation, Summers 2006–2008
- Coordinated treatment of amputee children and children with congenital birth defects.
- Created "Alive with Pride" program now functional at thirty national hospitals.
- Developed child-oriented play program and trained teachers via elementary school seminars.

XCEL ORTHOPAEDIC PHYSICAL THERAPY, Bloomington, IN
Physical Therapy Aid, Spring 2007–Spring 2008
- Assisted with ultrasound, muscle stimulation, massage, and interferential treatments.
- Served as translator, using Spanish-language skills with selected patients.

INDIANA UNIVERSITY, Bloomington, IN
Student Trainer, Spring 2004
Massage Therapy Intern, Fall 2004

Physical Therapy, Sports Medicine, and Nursing Training

INDIANA UNIVERSITY, Bloomington, IN
Bachelor of Science in Physical Therapy, May 2008
Performed independent research evaluating back and shoulder strength of musicians suffering from tendonitis. Presented findings to department and published in *Indiana Journal of Medicine*.

BLOOMINGTON COMMUNITY COLLEGE, Bloomington, IN
General Education Nursing, and Science Courses, 2004–2006
Massage Therapy Certificate, Summer 2006

FRANCIS WILLIAMS

123 Main Street • Hometown, MD 00000 • (555) 555-1234 • fwilliams@company.com

PROFESSIONAL PROFILE

- Over a decade of progressively responsible roles in private and municipal law enforcement.
- Specialized skills associated with community relations and maintenance of positive and professional attitudes among colleagues.
- Proven abilities to hire, train, evaluate, and motivate officers and support staff.
- Trained and certified law enforcement professional in frontline and management roles.
- License to carry firearms. Emergency Medical Technician. Certification in Radar Usage, Breathalyzer, and Identi-Kit software.

LAW ENFORCEMENT AND SECURITY EXPERIENCE

JOHNS HOPKINS UNIVERSITY POLICE DEPARTMENT   Baltimore, MD
Assistant Chief of Campus Police   2008–Present
- Assist with personnel, budget, and procedural oversights associated with a department of twenty full-time and twenty part-time security professionals.
- Recruit, train, and review performance of professional and administrative personnel.
- Protect life and property on and about the campus of Johns Hopkins University.
- Patrol on foot and via automobile, using strong observational and interaction skills.
- Uphold laws and codes of the State of Maryland and Johns Hopkins University.
- Cooperate with law enforcement agencies, regularly interacting with Deputy Sheriff.
- Conduct community outreach and educational efforts, focusing on alcohol use and abuse, safe dating, and property protection.
- Serve on Student Life Committees and assist with judicial investigations.

BUCKMAN ASSOCIATES   Bethesda, MD
Head of Security
2005–2008
- Managed all aspects of security for hotels and adjoining properties.
- Hired, scheduled, supervised, and evaluated personnel.
- Provided all policing functions, with emphasis on defusing potentially violent situations.
- Cooperated extensively with Baltimore and Bethesda Police Departments.

TOWN OF ROCKVILLE POLICE DEPARTMENT   Rockville, MD
Patrolman   2000–2005
- Performed all standard policing functions, earning excellent ratings annually.
- Interacted and communicated with town officials regarding proactive and reactive efforts.

LAW ENFORCEMENT TRAINING

BALTIMORE POLICE ACADEMY   Baltimore, MD
Graduate   2005

ROCKVILLE POLICE ACADEMY   Rockville, MD
Graduate   2000

COREY DAVIS

123 Main Street • Hometown, WA 00000 • (555) 555-1234 • cdavis@company.com

PROFESSIONAL PROFILE

- Experience as publicist, media consultant, publicity professional, and television booker.
- Extensive contacts within broadcast and print media, yielding successful placements of stories as well as interviews.
- Talents to establish and implement strategic media and promotional campaigns to generate multimedia coverage.
- Capacities to work with clients to attain marketing, attendance, and general publicity goals.

PRESS RELATIONS AND PROMOTIONS ACHIEVEMENTS

COVERAGE CONCEPTS CONSULTING, Pullman, WA
Personal Publicist and Consultant: Personally support media relations, campaign development, and implementation efforts associated with professional athletes, education, and not-for-profit clients. Interact with clients regularly to address needs and fine-tune annually updated strategic media plans. Draft, edit, and finalize news releases, speeches, and press packets. Develop and maintain relationships with regional and national print and broadcast media, supporting efforts to maximize desired coverage. Serve as client spokesperson and as press conference coordinator. *2008–Present*

CNBS TELEVISION, Pullman, WA
Production Assistant for "Confrontations": Booked main guests and panelists for weekly topical talk show. Generated and researched story ideas. Conducted video research. Edited teasers for show. Organized production details for studio tapings. Coordinated publicity ads in local newspapers. *2005–2008*

BARSTOW PUBLISHING COMPANY, Seattle, WA
Publicity Assistant: Publicized new books and authors. Assisted with television, radio, and print media tours and individual appearances. Created and implemented author questionnaire to maximize publicity generated through professional contacts. Wrote press releases and designed press packets. Responded to review copy requests. *2003–2005*

WNBN-TV, Tacoma, WA
Production Intern for "Sports Talk": Assisted producers of live daily sports interview and call-in show. Researched and generated story ideas. Preinterviewed guests. Covered shoots and wrote promos. Produced 5 segments. *2005–2006*

UNIVERSITY OF WASHINGTON, Seattle, WA
Sports Information Promotional Assistant: Implemented promotional campaigns, wrote copy, and designed advertisements. Enhanced attendance via creative competitions and corporate sponsored give-aways. *2004–2005*

THE CHERRY HAIKU, INC., Seattle, WA
Art Assistant: Produced paste-ups and mechanicals for full-service advertising agency. Operated Photostat and coordinated logistics for photo shoots. Brainstormed with creative team. Summers and Part-time *2002–2004*

EDUCATION

UNIVERSITY OF WASHINGTON, Seattle, WA
B.A. in Communications, cum laude, with a Minor in English, 2005

Public Relations Account Executive

JAMIE BROWN

123 Main Street • Hometown, NY 00000 • (555) 555-5555 • jbrown@company.com

PUBLIC RELATIONS EXPERIENCE

SYRACUSE HEART ASSOCIATION, Syracuse, NY
Public Relations Manager, 2010–Present
- Serve as consultant to seven state chapters regarding campaign problems and activities.
- Organize regional campaign meetings; speak at several campaign conferences.
- Review legislation and bring specific bills to the attention of the proper committee or individual.
- Staff the Legislative Advisory Committee and follow through on specific bills.
- Develop fundraising programs.
- Conducted the previous two annual campaigns for the newly merged Central Chapter.

Campaign Assistant for Greater Syracuse Chapter, 2005–2007
- Supervised chapter campaign duties and assisted the Executive Director with administrative responsibilities, such as personnel and budget.

BIG APPLE NATURAL FOODS, Syracuse, NY
Special Events Coordinator, 2008–2010
- Created and coordinated special events and promotions, within $425,000 marketing budget.
- Selected and wrote event advertising, promotional materials, and publicity copy.
- Handled charity fundraising, corporate image positioning, and community outreach efforts.

Assistant to the Director of Public Relations, 2007–2010
- Assisted in promotion and publicity of special events.
- Developed press kits and releases to initiate, maintain, and maximize media relations.
- Compiled easy to access and updated computerized publicity files using FileMaker Pro.
- Researched prospective consumer markets using Internet and direct contact techniques.
- Created direct-mail lists, updated media lists, and maintained task priority lists.

SYRACUSE UNIVERSITY, Syracuse, NY
Teacher's Assistant, Fall and Spring 2008

COMMUNICATION AND PUBLIC RELATIONS EDUCATION

SYRACUSE UNIVERSITY, Syracuse, NY
Bachelor of Arts in Public Relations, *magna cum laude*, June 2008

QUALIFICATIONS

- Ability to plan and direct successful fundraising, public relations, and promotions programs.
- Campaign development and implementation experience with major health agency.
- Extensive volunteer recruitment experience and success motivating diverse teams.
- Supervisory experience with both professional and nonprofessional staffs.
- Capacity to use Word, Excel, PowerPoint, and FileMaker Pro for drafting and editing, promotional materials, budgeting tasks, and graphics projects.

Dana Johnson

123 Main Street • Hometown, CA 00000 • (555) 555-2311 • djohnson@company.com

REAL ESTATE LENDING EXPERIENCE AND ACHIEVEMENTS

SAN JOSE AND SANTA CLARA HOME LOANS, San Jose, CA
Real Estate Loan Officer, 2011–Present
- Originate real estate loans, develop plan to expand business in Santa Clara County.
- Conduct cold calls, create individualized mortgage broker packets, complete individual and group presentations designed to generate Conventional, FHA/VA, PERS, JUMBO, and CHAFA loan business.

BAY AREA BANK, Santa Clara, CA
Real Estate Loan Officer, 2008–2011
- Originated real estate loans, developed marketing plan to expand business in Santa Clara County.
- Conducted cold calls, created individualized mortgage broker packets, completed individual and group presentations designed to generate loan business, and implemented first-ever real estate expo promotional event.

HOUSING LENDING, Fresno, CA
Wholesale Account Executive, 2006–2009
- Marketed loan and financing programs to financial institutions and mortgage brokers in San Joaquin, Merced, Fresno, and Stanislaus counties.

CALIFORNIA MORTGAGE SPECIALISTS, INC., San Mateo, CA
Professional Real Estate Loan Auditor, 2002–2006

SANTA CLARA SAVINGS, Santa Clara, CA
Loan Officer in Residential Lending Department, 1996–2002
Loan Underwriter/Processor in Residential and Government Loan Departments, 1992–1996
Loan Underwriter in Secondary Market Department, 1990–1992
Loan Packager in Loan Processing Department, 1988–1990

BUSINESS AND FINANCE DEGREE

SANTA CLARA UNIVERSITY, Santa Clara, CA
Bachelor of Science in Business Administration, 1990

PROFESSIONAL PROFILE

- More than 20 years of experience in mortgage banking and finance, with emphasis on customer service loan qualifications and accurate risk analysis.
- Experience as loan consultant enhancing qualification potential and prospective customers.
- Expertise with Conventional, FHA/VA, PERS, JUMBO, Community Home Buyer, and CHAFA loan programs for homes in Santa Clara, San Joaquin, Merced, and Stanislaus counties.

JAMIE BROWN

123 Main Street • Hometown, CT 00000 • (555) 555-1234 • jbrown@company.com

Recruiting Qualifications

- Experience developing and implementing comprehensive college recruiting program.
- Capacities to source, screen, and select candidates based upon strategic qualification criteria.
- Abilities to conduct interviews, train interviewers, and facilitate decision making regarding offers.
- Developed recruiting, selection, and training associated with internship program.
- Broad-based human resources knowledge to effectively interact with senior management.
- Extensive knowledge of recruitment Web sites for candidate mining, job postings, and resume review.

Recruiting, Human Resources, and Management Achievements

NORMAN'S DEPARTMENT STORES   NEW LONDON, CT
Manager of Executive Recruitment   *2010–Present*

Oversee all logistical and financial aspects of program recruiting twenty Management Development Program participants annually for regional chain of fifteen stores. Involves on-campus interviews, career fairs, and information sessions held at seven target schools and participation in three multi-school consortium events.

- With VPs of Human Resources, Merchandising, and Operations, review and revise annual college recruiting strategies and yield targets.
- Develop, propose, and monitor annual college recruiting budgets of approximately $75,000.
- Regularly review and establish target school listings, contacts, and recruiting dates.
- Train college team liaisons and leaders to make effective campus recruitment presentations.
- Organized senior executive involvement in Career Days second interview processes.
- Facilitate College Recruiting Team discussions regarding Management Development Program offers.
- Recruit for, hire, and oversee fifteen Summer Interns and ten academic year interns annually.
- Assist training staff with planning educational and social activities associated with initial portions of a ten-week program that blends classroom instruction with career networking and skills training.

Assistant Store Personnel Manager   *2006–2010*

- Hired, reviewed, and supported the needs of full-time and part-time sales professionals.
- Tracked daily, weekly, and monthly coverage data, to minimize costs and maximize coverage and service.
- Conducted various training sessions including: customer service, register operations, and security.
- Received award for overall achievement and outstanding performance in human resources.

Children's Department Manager   *2004–2006*

- Merchandised children's clothing and accessories, analyzing and marketing a $2 million inventory.
- Trained and developed staff of fifteen sales associates in customer-service skills and selling techniques.
- Achieved 20% sales increase over one-year period and chosen manager of the year in 2005.

Education

CONNECTICUT COLLEGE   NEW LONDON, CT
BA, Spanish Modified with Government Studies   *June 2005*

Francis Williams
123 Main Street • Hometown, CA 00000 • (555) 555-8876 • fwilliams@company.com

Restaurant Management and Service Experience

NORDSTROM, San Francisco, CA
Champaign Exchange Café Manager, 2009–Present
- Oversee operations of 250-seat facility averaging over $10,000 daily sales, offering American cuisine luncheon and dinner service to store patrons.
- Schedule, motivate, and supervise staff of twenty-five full-time and part-time servers per shift.
- Monitor daily and monthly receipts and expenditures.
- Communicate with store and corporate management regarding sales targets and profit strategies.

SHAKESPEARE'S TAVERN, London, ENGLAND
Assistant Manager, 2007–2009
- Oversaw operations of 175-seat facility averaging over £2,000 daily food sales and £2,000 wine and alcohol sales, offering luncheon, dinner, and after-dinner service.
- Supervised staff of thirty employees per shift.
- Monitored food costs, effectively communicated with chef and prep staff regarding costs.
- Prepared and submitted weekly, monthly, and quarterly reports to owners.
- With chef, planned weekly menus.

CLUB METROPOLIS, Montreal, CANADA
Assistant Manager, 2005–2007
- Scheduled and supervised staff, controlled inventory, deposited cash, maintained physical plant, and completed daily and weekly reports for after-hours club catering to elite patrons.
- Supervised up to twenty employees per shift.
- Completed management training program.

Bartender and Bar Manager, 2004–2005
- Served patrons, purchased wine, alcohol, beer, and mixes.

Food Services Training and Experience

CALIFORNIA SCHOOL OF CULINARY ARTS, San Francisco, CA
Restaurant Management Certificate, 2009

PROFESSIONAL BARTENDING SCHOOL OF MONTREAL, Montreal, CANADA
Certificate, 2004

ROYAL CANADIAN AIR FORCE, Toronto and Montreal, CANADA
Completed Class A & C Cooking School, 2000–2004

Languages

Bilingual French-English

Retail Buyer

DANA JOHNSON

123 Main Street • Hometown, MD 00000 • (555) 555-1234 • djohnson@company.com

BUYING EXPERIENCE AND ACCOMPLISHMENTS

CALVIN CLOTHES COMPANY, Baltimore and Bethesda, MD and Washington, DC

2007–Present *Baltimore Junior Apparel Department Buyer*
- Developed sales volume from $5.5 million to $7.5 million.
- Consistently achieved net operating profit of 50%, highest in company.
- Implemented promotional strategies and developed key classifications directly responsible for volume increase.
- Developed electronic and direct communication networks supplying product knowledge to sales staff and impacting strategic planning of vendor programs.
- Instituted e-mail communication strategies and status-tracking efforts.
- Chosen as Merchant of the Year 2008, 2009, and 2010.

2005–2007 *Bethesda Divisional Sales Manager*
- Handled furniture, electronics, and basement store, with 2005 volume of $5.6 million.
- During mall expansion, held store sales volume within plan by achieving 12% increase.
- Priorities included constant evaluation of stock levels and content, goal setting, development of key personnel, and achieving a high motivational level.

2003–2005 *Washington Assistant Buyer*
- Acted as liaison with vendors and warehouse to assure timely merchandise delivery of men's coordinates, coats, swimwear, and activewear.
- Interpreted, analyzed, and responded to OTB, selling reports, and seasonal plans.

2001–2003 *Washington Assistant Store Manager*
- Promoted from trainee to Assistant Manager within twelve months.
- Conceptualized and implemented employee training and effectiveness program.

2000–2001 *Executive Trainee*

PROFESSIONAL DEVELOPMENT AND EDUCATION

CALVIN CLOTHES COMPANY EXECUTIVE TRAINING SEMINARS, Baltimore, MD
Computerized Buying Techniques, Loss Prevention, Sales Motivation, Buyer-Store Communication Skills, Retail Mathematics and Quantitative Techniques, Buying Segmentation and Consumer Behavior, Merchandising, Personnel Management, and Profits

UNIVERSITY OF DELAWARE, Newark, DE
Bachelor of Science in Marketing, 2000

QUALIFICATION SUMMARY

- Capacities to translate strategic plans into profitable purchases and merchandising plans.
- Experience using communication programs and talents to maximize sales at store level.
- Quantitative skills required to establish market segmentations, maximize profits, and analyze sales figures.
- Commitment to understanding consumer attitudes, developing relationships with suppliers, and reinforcing positive achievements of sales professionals and operations personnel.

Corey Davis

123 Main Street • Hometown, CA 00000 • (555) 555-1234 • cdavis@company.com

Objective Qualifications Summary

Retail sales position using:

- Experiences within retail sales in diverse department and specialty store settings.
- Curiosity regarding consumer attitudes and behaviors and desire to sell based upon product qualities.
- Marketing and consumer behavior skills gained via business and psychology courses and projects.
- Outgoing personality, persuasion skills, and excitement about meeting sales goals.
- Time and task management and leadership skills nurtured as campus office holder.
- Knowledge of computerized registers and inventory control, and abilities to use Word, Power-Point, and Excel to create sales materials and reports.

Sales, Marketing, and Customer Service Experience

NORDSTROM, San Mateo, CA
Salesperson, Seasonally 2007–Present and Summers 2010 and 2011

NATIONAL SHOPPING SERVICE, Los Angeles, CA
Mystery Shopper, Part-time 2008–Present

THE LIMITED, San Mateo, CA
Salesperson, Part-time and Summers 2006–2008

CRYSTAL MOON JEWELRY, San Mateo, CA
Stockperson and Administrative Support Person, Part-time 2005–2008

WEINSTOCKS, Sacramento, CA
Sales Associate, Part-time 2001–2006

Education

SAINT MARY'S COLLEGE, Miraga, CA
Bachelor of Arts, anticipated May 2013
Major in Psychology and minors in Business and Studio Art
Delta Gamma Sorority Treasurer, 2012–2013; Activities Committee, 2011–2012

CALIFORNIA STATE UNIVERSITY HAYWARD, Hayward, CA
Completed psychology and business courses, Summer 2004

Marketing and General Business Courses and Projects

Marketing Management, Management and Organizational Behavior, Financial Accounting, Consumer Behavior, and Designing Effective Organizations
- Created hypothetical business to assess and create overall marketing plan.
- Developed, administered, and interpreted survey distributed at St. Mary's athletic events to determine target market profiling.
- Examined organizational structure of QVC Shopping Network.

Francis Williams

123 Main Street • Apartment 13 • Hometown, CA 00000 (555) 555-1234 • fwilliams@company.com

RETAIL MANAGEMENT AND SALES ACHIEVEMENTS

SPINNER RECORDS CORPORATION   LOS ANGELES, CA
Manager   **2009–Present**
- Manage Spinner's largest-volume store, with approximate sales of $30,000/week.
- Handle all merchandising, inventory control, ordering, cash control, and maintenance.
- Oversee store opening and closing procedures.
- Direct sales floor activities, assist customers, and address customer concerns.
- Input data to prepare daily sales reports and regularly use weekly and monthly data to develop sales and promotional strategies.
- Hire, train, and coordinate a staff of twenty-six.
- Work with Spinner corporate colleagues as well as record company professionals to develop local marketing and advertising strategies, supplementing national campaigns.
- Inspire sales staff to develop and implement special promotions and events.
- Won two merchandising display contests.
- Received the "Super Spinner" Sales Award for exceeding sales goals.

Assistant Manager   **2007–2009**
- Fulfilled all management responsibilities in absence of manager.
- Opened and closed store, handled customer service issues, and oversaw cash control.
- Supervised and motivated employees.
- Assisted with merchandising and promotions efforts.

SANTA ANA MEN'S SHOPPE   SANTA ANA, CA
Assistant Manager   **2002–2007**
- Hired, trained, and supervised staff of six serving customers of specialty men's clothing store.
- Provided exceptional customer service to high-end consumers, regularly including direct e-mail and phone contact, and relationship building.
- Tallied daily receipts and made bank deposits.
- Maintained inventory levels, monitored merchandise, provided feedback to owner/buyer regarding trends and need for reorders.

LENNY'S TOYS   SANTA ANA, CA
Assistant Manager   **Summers and Part-time 1998–2002**
- Hired, trained, and supervised three shifts of four sales associates daily.
- Tallied daily receipts and made bank deposits.
- Maintained inventory levels, ordered merchandise, and independently tracked all special orders.

BUSINESS AND RETAIL EDUCATION

COMMUNITY COLLEGE OF LOS ANGELES   LOS ANGELES, CA
AA, Business Administration, with Retail Management Certificate   **2007**
SANTA ANA COMMUNITY COLLEGE   SANTA ANA, CA
Completed General Education and Business Courses Part-time   **2000–2004**

School Psychologist

Chris Smith

123 Main Street • Hometown, NY 00000 • 555-555-1234 • csmith@company.com

Graduate and Undergraduate Counseling and Psychology Education

LOYOLA MARYMOUNT UNIVERSITY, Los Angeles, CA
PhD, Counseling and Human Development, Dissertation to be defended July 2013
- Dissertation: "Ethnic Identity Development of Multi-ethnic College Students"
- As Rotary Scholarship Recipient received Full Tuition Award and Counseling Assistantship Stipend
MA, School Counseling, May 2008
TOWSON UNIVERSITY, Towson, MD
B.S., Psychology, August 2004

College Counseling and Teaching Experience

LOYOLA MARYMOUNT UNIVERSITY, Los Angeles, CA
Counseling and Mental Health Services Intern, September 2010–July 2011, January 2012–May 2012
- Counseled undergraduate and graduate students with personal, academic, and career issues.
- Addressed psychological and developmental needs of multicultural and diverse 3,600 undergraduate and 1,000 graduate students.
- Assessed and diagnosed clients on the basis of presenting problem, history, and rating on Personality Assessment Inventory (PAI).
- Participated in two hours of individual supervision and one hour of group supervision per week.
- Served as a liaison between Counseling Center and University Health Services through involvement in the development of "Feel Fit in February" speakers series and outreach program designed to meet the health needs of student populations.

Graduate Assistant, September 2009–May 2012
- Facilitated the CACREP accreditation process by designing program curriculum to meet standards by researching programs, developing and presenting graphs and charts, and attending faculty meetings.
- Designed the Counseling Student's Handbook for the master's and doctoral programs.
- Researched trends in Client-Centered Therapy, examining the influence of Carl Rogers on the field of professional counseling.
- Contributed to the enhancement of the Counseling and Human Development program by attending faculty meetings related to the development of the program, and by investigating new ideas to strengthen the curriculum and overall structure of the program.

Instructor/Supervised Intern in School and Community Counseling Course, September 2011–May 2012
- Planned and presented lectures, hosted guest speakers, and facilitated weekly discussions based on topics relevant to students' internship experiences in either a school setting or a community agency setting. Topics included diversity, confidentiality and ethics, eating disorders, and crisis intervention.
- Supervised students individually and in a group via taped sessions and experiences at internship sites.

Counselor Supervisor for Practicum Course, January 2011–May 2011 and January 2012–May 2012
- Supervised four masters students individually who were counseling students within a K–12 school setting.

Counselor Supervisor for Professional Orientation and Practice, January 2011–May 2011
- Supervised masters students learning counseling techniques through the use of role playing.

Chris Smith
Page Two

School Counseling and Teaching Experience

TORRANCE UNIFIED SCHOOL DISTRICT, Torrance, CA
School Counselor, September 2008–June 2009
- Counseled students individually and in groups; designed specific counseling programs to meet needs.
- Responded effectively to various on-campus crises via crisis intervention strategies.
- Coordinated and oversaw IEP meetings and specific meetings designed to help high-risk students become more successful in school.
- Consulted daily with teachers and parents regarding student performance.
- Teamed with psychologist presenting information for special education students to parents and teachers.
- Facilitator of workshops, presentations, and programs for students, teachers, and staff.

WISEBURN SCHOOL DISTRICT, Hawthorne, CA
School Counselor Intern, December 2007–June 2008
- Developed and implemented guidance services in a multicultural setting; included social skills groups, divorce groups, and disability awareness program.
- Conducted individual and group counseling for students in grades K–5.

CULVER CITY HIGH SCHOOL, Culver City, CA
School Counselor Intern, January 2008–June 2008
- Counseled students on personal, educational, and career issues.
- Worked with the "Latinos Unidos" club to improve cultural awareness.
- Developed and implemented preschool curriculum to enhance language skills of developmentally delayed students.
- Coordinated with parents on designing an educational plan to facilitate the development of their children.

REDONDO BEACH UNIFIED SCHOOL DISTRICT, Redondo Beach, California
Substitute Teacher, September 2006–January 2009
- Instructed academic lessons to K–12 population; lesson development and classroom management.
- Worked with developmentally challenged students.

Professional Affiliations

Member, American Counseling Association
Member, Association for Counselor Education and Supervision
Member, Association for Multicultural Counseling and Development
Member, American College Counseling Association

Language Development

Spanish Grammar Course, University of Rochester, January 2012–Present
Spanish Language Course, University of Navarra, Spain, August 2011–September 2011
Spanish Language Course, Eurocenters Salamanca, Spain, July 2010–August 2010

COREY DAVIS
123 Main Street • Hometown, WA 00000 • (555) 555-1234 • cdavis@company.com

TEACHING ACCOMPLISHMENTS

Tacoma High School, Tacoma, WA
Chairperson, Mathematics Department, 2008–Present
- Serve as math instructor and Director of the Math Evaluation Committee.
- Develop report for submission to the National Association of Schools and Colleges.
- Develop and monitor budgets, assess goals, programs, plans, and professional performance.
- Select and approve departmental texts, and write and upgrade course descriptions as necessary.
- Evaluate instructional staff, advise on contract renewal, and evaluate candidates for new hires.
Mathematics Instructor, 2004–Present
- Instruct grades 9–12 in Trigonometry, Algebra I & II, Geometry, Pre-Calculus, and Business Math.
- Develop curricula and lesson plans, select texts, and design tests.
- Initiated remedial math program and afterschool tutorial sessions for students needing extra assistance in math.
- Conduct summer school sessions in remedial math and SAT preparation.

Stagg High School, Stockton, CA
9th–12th Grade Mathematics Student Teacher, Fall 2004
- Implemented lessons for and assessed students in Honors Algebra, and Honors Trigonometry.
9th–10th Grade Algebra and Geometry Mathematics Field Work Teacher's Assistant, Spring 1998

TUTORIAL EXPERIENCE

Private Tutoring, Stockton, CA and Tacoma, WA
Tutor for Middle and High School Mathematics Students, 2002–Present
- Helped students with homework assignments and enhanced general understanding of concepts and approaches associated with Algebra, Trigonometry, Calculus, and General Math classes.

University of the Pacific, Stockton, CA
Mathematics Department Grader for Inferential Statistics, 2003–2004
Mathematics Resources Center Proctor for Algebra and Trigonometry, 2003–2004
Mathematics Department Grader for Finite Mathematics, Statistics, and Calculus, 2002–2003

Parklane Elementary School, Stockton, CA
Teacher's Aide for Summer Youth Employment Training Program, Summers 1999 and 2000

EDUCATION AND MATH DEGREES

University of Washington, Seattle, WA
MS in Secondary Education and Curriculum and Instruction, with Mathematics Specialization, 2006

University of the Pacific, Stockton, CA
BS in Mathematics, with Mathematics Education major, Single Subject Credential, Fall 2004

San Joaquin Delta Community College, Stockton, CA
Associate of Arts in Mathematics, June 2002

Jamie Brown

123 Main St. • Apt. 13 • Hometown, MD 00000 • (555) 555-9821 • jb@company.com

Social Work Experience

Baltimore Central School District, Baltimore, MD
District Social Worker, 2010–Present
- Provide direct social work services to elementary, middle, and high school students and their families.
- As member of interdisciplinary team, establish, implement, and monitor effectiveness of Independent Educational Programs.
- Regularly communicate with parents, teachers, and special education professionals regarding individual students.
- Conduct group discussions with students and parents pertaining to developmental, behavioral, and medical issues.

Johns Hopkins University Children and Teen Clinic, Baltimore, MD
Clinical Social Worker, 2008–2010
- Diagnosed, evaluated, and treated children, adolescents, adults, and families living within the guidelines of Care and Protection Petitions.
- Interacted with legal, medical, and psychological professionals.
- Provided individualized social-work services for children and adolescents, including pregnant teens, foster home residents, and those meeting court mandated criteria.
- Maintained accurate and thorough documentation via case records.

Baltimore County Juvenile Court Clinic, Baltimore, MD
Field Placement Intern, 2007–2008
- Diagnosed, evaluated, and treated children, adolescents, adults, and families.
- Conducted evaluations and supported department.

Johns Hopkins University Hospital, Baltimore, MD
Pediatric Social Work Intern, 2006–2008
- Provided clinical services, family counseling, and referrals for patients and families.
- Conducted home visits and completed follow-up evaluations.
- Participated in classroom-based education program for potential kidney transplant patients.

Education

Social Work and Psychology Studies
Johns Hopkins University, Baltimore, MD
Master of Social Work, May 2008

Colby College, Waterville, ME
Bachelor of Arts, Psychology and Bachelor of Arts, Sociology, cum laude, June 2006

Qualification and Capabilities

- Capabilities to serve within comprehensive social work capacities in school or health care settings.
- Experience creating and implementing treatment plans for clients with psychosocial, behavioral, and health-related disorders.
- Capacity to manage cases, maintain accurate case records, and create detailed reports.

CHRIS SMITH

123 Main Street, Apartment 13 • Hometown, UT 00000 • (555) 555-1234 • csmith@company.com

OBJECTIVE   Speech and Language Pathology Position with Clinical Fellowship Year.

QUALIFICATIONS

- Experience diagnosing and treating children displaying apraxia, language delay, hearing impairment, and articulation disorders and adult-exhibiting motor speech disorders and aphasia.
- Ability to accurately administer hearing screenings and tympanometry readings.
- Perspectives and skills required to effectively work on diagnostic evaluation team.
- Skills to document cases, communicate with colleagues, and correspond with clients and families.
- Fluency using Visual Phonics and American Sign Language.

GRADUATE AND UNDERGRADUATE PROFESSIONAL DEGREES

Brigham Young University, Salt Lake City, UT
Master of Arts in Communicative Disorders, December 2007
Bachelor of Arts in Communicative Disorders, *magna cum laude*, May 2005

- Graduate overall GPA 3.98 and undergraduate major GPA 3.91 (out of 4.0)
- Outstanding Senior Award in Communicative Disorders Department, May 2005
- The Honor Society of Phi Kappa Phi member and Utah Speech and Hearing Association member

CLINICAL AND RESEARCH EXPERIENCE

Elmwood Elementary School, Salt Lake City, UT
Language, Speech, and Hearing Intern, February–May 2012

- Administered group therapy to Preschool–6th grade students with articulation and language disorders.
- Worked with students in classroom and independently outside of the classroom.
- Involved in Individualized Education Plan (IEP) assessments and meetings.

Brigham Young University Speech and Hearing Center, Salt Lake City, UT
Student Clinician, September 2010–Present

- Diagnosed, then planned and administered therapy to children with apraxia, language delay, hearing impairment, and articulation disorders.
- Used Visual Phonics and American Sign Language with hearing impaired child client.
- Diagnosed, then administered therapy to adult displaying motor speech disorders and aphasia.
- Established home programs to effectively train and motivate parents, spouses, and others.
- Wrote case summaries documenting clinical goals, approaches, and achievements.

Clinical Diagnostic Team Member, 2008–2010

- Interviewed, assessed, and wrote reports on stuttering, articulation, and language delay disorder cases.

Brigham Young University Language Disorders Department, Salt Lake City, UT
Visual Phonics and Down syndrome researcher, 2010–2012

Bret Harte High School, Salt Lake City, UT
Special Education Classroom Volunteer and ASL Tutor, Summers 2009 and 2010

Jamie Brown

123 Main Street • Hometown, NC 00000 • (555) 555-1234 • jbrown@company.com

Systems Engineering Profile

- Extensive and diversified hardware and software knowledge.
- Expertise in prototype computer testing.
- Comprehensive investigative and research skills.
- Knowledge of programming languages, operating systems, as well as word processing, database, and spreadsheet software applications including: Windows, Macintosh, UNIX, Assembler Natural, C++, Java, Pascal, COBOL, Visual Basic, Word, Excel, Access, and Oracle.

Systems Engineering and Programming Experience

Maximilian Data and Computer Systems   **Charlotte, NC**

Systems Engineer   *2007–Present*

Coauthored software test plan for computer prototypes. Researched, wrote, and edited test procedures. Developed computer engineering test tools. Wrote database application to track and generate reports on problems found during development. Organized preproduction testing of prototypes. Analyzed requirements for new processes to improve product testing. Created software that automated work-related processes, such as generating status- and engineering-change request reports.

Systems Programmer   *2004–2007*

Maintained over 300 assembler modules and developed 75. Formulated screen manager program to trace input and output to the VTAM buffer. Developed program to monitor complete security control blocks.

University of Georgia School of Law   **Atlanta, GA**

Systems Programmer   *Summers 2000–2002 and Full-time 2002–2004*

Initiated start-up network and implemented operations. Designed and managed implementation of a network providing the legal community with a direct line to supreme court cases. Developed a system that catalogued entire library's inventory. Used C++ to create a registration system for a university registrar.

Engineering and Technical Education

Georgia Tech University   **Atlanta, GA**

B.S. in Computer Science   *May 2002*

Georgia Tech University   **Atlanta, GA**

Post-baccalaureate coursework   *2002–Present*

Courses included: JavaScript, Visual Basic, Web Services, ASP/NET, CH/NET, VB/NET, Web Forms, Advanced IBM 370 Assembler, SNA Fundamentals, MVS/ESA Architecture, Natural 2 Programming Language, MVS/XA Concepts and Facilities, MVS/XA Job Control Language, MVS/XA Using and Creating Procedures.

Dana Johnson

123 Main Street • Hometown, FL 00000 • (555) 555-1234 • djohnson@company.com

TECHNICAL WRITING EXPERIENCE

2009–Present RIZZO ASSOCIATES, Melrose, FL
Technical Writer and Senior Project Administrator
- Research data and accurately describe the installation, removal, erection, and maintenance of all military hardware.
- Outline wiring diagrams, draw part breakdowns for illustrators, draft and finalize all descriptions associated with use of and training to use military hardware.
- Serve as overall program lead for specific projects in A-3, EA-3, and EP-3E programs.
- Work on IPB, MIM, and IFMM for all maintenance levels.
- Transform various source materials, including engineering drawings and wiring diagrams into user-targeted written and disc-driven documentation and illustrations.

2004–2009 CAPABIANCO PUBLISHING, Winter Park, FL
Technical Writer
- Supported efforts to develop and finalize illustrations and documentation associated with military hardware.
- Served as project lead, including editing, layout, and corrections.

2000–2004 DARK WILLOW ENGINEERING CORPORATION, Killarney, FL
Editor/Writer
- Edited and wrote large proposals for government contracts.
- Designed format and coordinated production.
- Organized and maintained up-to-date dummy book through several revision cycles.
- Interpreted client requirements and determined applicability of proposal responses.

EDUCATION

UNIVERSITY OF FLORIDA, Gainesville, FL
BS in Civil Engineering, 2004
Additional coursework in Computer Science, Mathematics, English Literature, and Journalism.

TECHNICAL WRITING AND PROJECT MANAGEMENT QUALIFICATIONS

- Proven abilities to structure technical writing projects and motivate others to complete components accurately and on time.
- Capacities to transform technical information into detailed illustrations and documentation.
- Sensitivities related to creation of classified training and support materials for military hardware.
- Security Clearance Level IA.
- Project and team management skills nurtured via observation and experience.
- Capacities to identify specific task components, set realistic deadlines, then monitor and motivate others.
- Expertise in Word, PowerPoint, Excel, and CAD.

Telemarketer

Francis Williams

123 Main Street • Hometown, FL 00000 • (555) 555-1234 • Cell (555) 555-5678 • fwilliams@company.com

TELEMARKETING QUALIFICATIONS

- Outstanding selling and closing capabilities illustrated by a proven track record of exceeding goals.
- Well versed in active listening techniques, nurturing conversations through appropriate questioning.
- Drive and focus required to meet contact and sales quotas, meeting established deadlines.
- Confidence in cold calling and direct sales roles, marketing services and products to businesses and clients.
- Pride associated with using earnings as telemarketer to pay for college tuition and expenses.
- Business Administration, Public Speaking, Persuasive Writing, and Marketing courses.

ACHIEVEMENT SUMMARY

- Induction into national club of Top Ten Percent 2010, 2011, and 2012.
- Awarded Golden Ring Award for meeting sales goals throughout Fiscal Years 2010 and 2011.
- Personally responsible for over $500,000 FY 2011–2012 annual sales as a result of accounts gained.
- Record of consistently reaching or exceeding established goals for more than four years.

TELEMARKETING EXPERIENCE

2010–Present   **ESP TELECOMMUNICATIONS**, Saint Petersburg, FL
Telemarketing Professional
- Cold-called residential and commercial consumers, assessing domestic and international calling needs, and then recommending and marketing long-distance programs.
- Consistently achieved at least 125% of sales goals.
- Landed largest commercial accounts during 2011–2012 and 2010–2011 Fiscal Years.

2008–2010   **TEST REVIEW EDUCATION GROUP**, Miami, FL
Marketing Assistant
- Cold-called high school and college students and parents, marketing college and graduate school entrance exam preparation courses.
- Yielded 35% attendance at seminars and simulations used to market services.

RETAIL SALES EXPERIENCE

2005–2008   **KAYBEE TOYS**, Miami, FL
Sales Associate
- Addressed inquiries of customers, maintained inventory levels, and trained salespeople.

EDUCATION

ROLLINS COLLEGE, Winter Park, FL
Bachelor of Arts, English, anticipated May 2013
MIAMI DADE JUNIOR COLLEGE, Miami, FL
Associate of Arts, Liberal Studies, August 2011

COREY DAVIS

123 Main Street • Hometown, MA 00000 • (555) 555-1234 • cdavis@company.com

SPORTS MEDICINE STUDIES

ITHACA COLLEGE, Ithaca, NY
BA Sports Medicine, May 2007

ATHLETIC TRAINING EXPERIENCE

ITHACA COLLEGE, Ithaca, NY
Senior Trainer, 2007–Present
Conduct hydrostatic weighing and skinfold body fat tests. Set up individual rehab and strengthening programs, and serve as nutrition and fitness consultant to all teams. Oversee all student trainers.
Rehabilitation Trainer, 2005–2007
Student Trainer, 2004–2007

WORLD WRESTLING FEDERATION, Syracuse, NY
Athletic Trainer for Syracuse and Rochester Appearances, 2006–Present

FITNESS EXPERIENCE

MIDTOWN RACQUETBALL CLUB, Milford, MA
Aerobic Instructor, Summers 2003–2006

TOTAL HEALTH AND FITNESS STOP, Hopedale, MA
Aerobic Instructor, Summer and Part-time 2002

FOCUS ON FITNESS, Ashland, MA
Aerobic Instructor, Summers and Part-time 2000–2002

WORLD GYM, Framingham, MA
Aerobic Instructor, Part-time 2000–2004

CERTIFICATIONS AND AFFILIATIONS

ACE (American Council on Exercise) Personal Trainer Certification and Fitness Instructor Certification; American Heart Association, Basic Life Support and Cardiac Care Certified. Standard First Aid Certified. Member NATA (National Athletic Trainers Association).

QUALIFICATIONS

- Experience implementing programs designed to prevent and treat injuries of athletes in a variety of sports including football, wrestling, volleyball, basketball, swimming, water polo, and tennis.
- Taught a variety of weekly classes including hi-lo, low impact, body sculpting, and step. Introduced funk aerobics to participants ages 15–65.
- Taught "FITKIDS" classes for ages 3–6 and ages 7–11.

Chris Smith

123 Main Street • Hometown, IL 00000 • (555) 555-1234 • csmith@company.com

Travel Industry Qualifications

- Four years of experience acquired via travel industry employment and training.
- Thorough knowledge of various reservation transactions, including booking, ticketing, sales, customer service, and dealing with contracted vendors to ensure customer reservation specifications.
- Expertise assisting individuals, groups, and corporate accounts with specialized knowledge of cruise industry and Disney packages.

Professional Experience and Achievements

SURGE AND SIEGE TRAVEL, INC.   Joliet, IL
Air and Sea Coordinator   2009–Present
- Coordinate air ticketing requests and tour departures using APOLLO and SABRE systems.
- Serve as agency representative specialized in cruise industry.
- Regularly attend sessions hosted by cruise and air carriers, educating self regarding options and plans.
- Track international and domestic fares, sharing data with colleagues daily.
- Issue tickets and final itineraries for air and cruise customers.
- Maintain and file pertinent materials and assist with updating of Web site (*www.surgetravel.com*).
- Assist with projects associated with marketing of Disney World, Disneyland, and Disney Cruises.
- Serve as group leader for numerous cruise and resort familiarization trips.
- Prepare detailed financial reports and assist senior management with development of strategic goals.

QUICK TRIP TRAVEL   Evanston, IL
Travel Consultant   2007–2009
- Arranged individual and group travel, regularly yielding monthly billings in excess of $10,000.
- Promoted agency via weekly visits to senior residences as well as college campuses.
- Regularly attended training sessions related to airline offerings and reservation systems updates.

GOTTA FLY TOURS   Wheaton, IL
Computer Operator/Intern   2005–2007
- Trained to use SABRE and other airline, cruise, and resort reservation systems.
- Administered ARC ticket stock and accountable documents.
- Rotated through specialty areas and assisted with accounting activities.

Professional Training and Education

MIDWEST TRAVEL SCHOOL, Chicago, IL
Certificate, 2007

DEPAUL UNIVERSITY, Chicago, IL
Bachelor of Arts, History, 2005

WINDY CITY COMMUNITY COLLEGE, Chicago, IL
Associate of Arts, Geography, 2003

Jamle Brown

123 Main Street • Hometown, MD 00000 • (555) 555-1234 • jbrown@company.com

Tutorial and Teaching Qualifications

- Capacities to teach and tutor various high school subjects, including English, Literature, Creative Writing, U.S. and World History, and self-paced SAT Preparation and GED curriculum.
- Tutored and taught English as a Second Language to university students in the U.S. and abroad.
- Experience as tutor, instructor, and teaching assistant addressing needs of college and high school students with varied backgrounds, abilities, and motivations.
- Multicultural sensitivities gained through overseas studies and successes within ESL roles.

Undergraduate and Overseas Studies

Loyola College, Baltimore, MD
Bachelor of Arts in English, emphasis in Professional Writing, May 2012
- Overall GPA, 3.6; English GPA, 3.8; and Dean's List 6 of 6 Eligible Semesters

Josef Eotvos Kollegium, Budapest, HUNGARY
Hungarian Language, Literature, and Politics courses, Fall 2011

University of Koln, Koln, GERMANY
German Language, History, Government, and Literature courses, Spring–Summer 2011

University of Edinburgh, Edinburgh, SCOTLAND
Took Scottish History course, Summer 2010

Tutorial and Teaching Experience

Loyola College, Baltimore, MD

Summer 2012 — Summer Enrichment Program Advisor and Tutor: Advised, tutored, and taught specialized courses to selected group of high school students. Planned and implemented 10-week Study Skills, SAT Preparation, and Writing Skills seminars, focusing on at-risk students with the potential to succeed in college. Created assignments-based "Reality Academy," an ideal high school.

2008–2012 — International Students Association Tutor: Taught and tutored English as a Second Language to Japanese, German, and Russian students.

2010–2012 — Writing Center Tutor and Persuasive Paper Writing Seminar Instructor

2003–2007 — Study Skills Center English and History Tutor

St. Luke's School, Baltimore, MD

2007–Present — Substitute Teacher and Tutor Grades 8–12

Baltimore County Women's Facility, Baltimore, MD

2011–Present — GED Student Teacher

Private English Tutoring, Budapest, HUNGARY and Koln, GERMANY

2011 — English as a Second Language Tutor

DANA JOHNSON

123 Main Street • Hometown, OR 00000 • (555) 555-1234 • djohnson@company.com

CERTIFICATIONS AND QUALIFICATIONS

- State of Oregon Licensed Animal Health Technician.
- Seven years of progressively responsible clinical, research, and supervisory experience.
- Generalist experience with all species and varied procedures in private practices and state-affiliated research and treatment facility.
- Specialist skills and competencies associated with surgery.

ANIMAL CARE EDUCATION

UNIVERSITY OF OREGON, Eugene, OR
BA in Animal Health Technology, 2009

UNIVERSITY OF PORTLAND, Portland, OR
AS in Animal Health Technology, 2005

VETERINARY AND ANIMAL CARE EXPERIENCE

UPPER VALLEY ANIMAL CARE CLINIC, Marylhurst, OR
Senior Surgical Assistant, 2009–Present
- Perform pre- and postoperative care and emergency care.
- Monitor ventilation and vital statistics of premature and critically ill animals.
- Collect and ship blood samples, perform intravenous and arterial catheterization, intubation of endotracheal and nasogastric tubes.
- Organize labs for and oversee veterinary students and clinical instruction sessions.
Surgical Assistant, 2007–2009
- Assisted clinicians and students treating patients, and provided pre- and post-operative care.

NEWMAN ANIMAL CARE CLINIC, Medford, OR
Surgery Intern, Part-time 2007–2009

CHRIS SMITH, D.V.M., Portland, OR
Veterinary Assistant, Part-time 2003–2005
- Assisted with daily diagnosis and treatment, and served as ICU specialist, completing oral, IV, IM, SQ, fluid therapy, radiology, hematology, immunology, and chemotherapy related tasks.
- Administered, assisted, and maintained anesthesia during surgery.

UNIVERSITY OF OREGON RESEARCH CENTER, Eugene, OR
Animal Technician/Research Assistant, Part-time 2003–2005
- Directed hygienic procedures on 300 animals, including surgery and necropsies.
- Conducted research on pet food products and analyzed studies on nutrition, zinc, urine, feces, fluid therapy, medication, breeding, and artificial insemination.
- Collaborated in testing new vaccine for feline leukemia, submitting reports for FDA approval.
- Supervised and scheduled twenty center and union employees in conducting research.

VOLUNTEER EXPERIENCE

HURRICANE KATRINA RELIEF
Served two weeks on rescue team with members of Oregon Humane Society to find missing pets, rescue animals, and assist with relief efforts in aftermath of Katrina.

Francis Williams

123 Main Street • Apartment 13 • Hometown, HI 00000
(555) 555-0988 • fwilliams@company.com

FOOD SERVICES EXPERIENCE

THE PALMS   Kaneohe, HI
Head Waiter   2010–Present

- Manage, open, and close high-volume four-star restaurant.
- Hire, train, schedule, and supervise wait staff.
- Lead weekly quality assurance and menu discussion sessions.
- Oversee special catering events held on-site and at residences of patrons.
- Address concerns and special requests.
- Reconcile gratuity intake in accordance with tax regulations.

PALUA SAILS RESTAURANT   Kaneohe, HI
Head Waiter   2008–2010

- Provided efficient service to full bar, serving area, and catered affairs.
- Trained new wait staff.

CANDLE IN THE WIND   Honolulu, HI
Barback   Part-time 2006–2009

- Handled customer service and cash intake.
- Assisted with liquor inventory.
- Performed security services.

BLUE HAWAII RESTAURANT   Honolulu, HI
Busboy   Part-time 2004–2006

- Set and cleared about twenty tables of large dining room per evening.
- Trained new bus people.

SPECIALIZED TRAINING AND RECOGNITION

- Completed Palms Patron Services Training offered to Head Waiters and tenured servers.
- Regularly rated "superior" in all weekly, monthly, and annual performance reviews.
- Certified in the SIPS program for responsibly serving alcohol
- Attended Restaurant Association training sessions: "Customer Satisfaction Is in Your Hands" and "Teaching Others to Service."

EDUCATION

HAWAII LOA COLLEGE   Kaneohe, HI
BA in Liberal Arts expected 2013

APPENDIX A

Before-and-After Resumes

In this section you'll find examples of before-and-after re-sumes. The before versions were reviewed by a resume coach. You'll see the coaches comments and an example of a revised resume based on these comments. Use these before-and-after resumes to rework your own resume using the coach's feedback.

Note: The following resume samples were created under very tight space requirements. On a normal sheet of paper you could fit more lines and have wider margins, thus allowing for more content. A good rule of thumb is to allow half-inch margins on the top, bottom, left, and right.

Advertising Account Executive (Before)

CHRIS SMITH

123 Main Street	csmith@company.com	987 Centre Avenue
Hometown, NY 00000		Hometown, NY 10001
(555) 555-1234		(555) 555-5678

EDUCATION

2009–2012 UNIVERSITY OF ROCHESTER, Rochester, NY
Bachelor of Arts, French, with a major GPA of 3.5, May 2012.
Bachelor of Arts, Psychology, with a major GPA of 3.3, May 2011.
Minor: **Economics,** with a minor GPA of 3.4.
- Management Studies Certificate, for completion of courses taught by faculty of college and the William E. Simon School of Business Administration.
- Economics Council, Activity Board, and *Campus Times* Staff Writer.

2008–2009 HOBART AND WILLIAM SMITH COLLEGES, Geneva, NY

EXPERIENCE

Spring 2011 NY THE FINANCIAL GROUP DISCOUNT BROKERAGE, Pittsford,
Intern/Assistant to Operations Manager: Used computerized financial transactions and market tracking systems. Updated customer databases using Excel. Interacted with and completed administrative projects for licensed representatives and addressed client inquiries from throughout the United States.

Summer 2011 DAYS ADVERTISING, INC., Pittsford, NY
Intern/Assistant to an Account Manager: Assisted with design of television and radio ads and proposals for varied products and clients, including Wegmans and Bausch & Lomb. Developed customer database.

2010–2011 ADEFFECTS, Rochester, NY
Intern/Assistant to an Account Manager: Researched and developed promotional materials for local retail, manufacturing, and restaurant clients. Gained knowledge of small business marketing. Recommended changes in client advertising materials, consumer outreach strategies, and marketing literature.

Summer 2011 PEARLE VISION CENTER, Pittsford, NY
Sales Representative: Implement strategy targeting upscale markets.

Summer 2009 IT HAPPENS, Antwerp, Belgium
Marketing Intern: Determined target markets and developed ad budget for concert, event planning, and entertainment agency. Conducted market penetration surveys. Assisted graphic artists producing ads, posters, brochures, and reports.

CHRIS SMITH

123 Main Street • Hometown, NY 00000 • (555) 555-1234 • csmith@company.com
987 Centre Avenue, Apartment 13 • Rochester, NY 00000 • (555) 555-5678

ADVERTISING ACCOUNT MANAGEMENT QUALIFICATIONS

- Marketing research, strategic planning, promotions, customer service, and sales talents nurtured by diverse advertising, promotions, and retail internships and employment.
- Skills gained via courses including: Marketing, Marketing Projects and Cases, Motivation, Public Relations Writing, Advertising, and Consumer Behavior.
- German, French, Dutch, and Farsi fluency, and conversational Spanish capabilities.
- UNIX, HTML, Word, Excel, PowerPoint, InDesign, PhotoShop, and Internet skills.

ADVERTISING AND MARKETING EXPERIENCE

DAYS ADVERTISING, INC., Pittsford, NY
Account Management Intern: Assisted with design of TV and radio ads and proposals for clients, including Wegmans and Bausch & Lomb. Developed client database. Summer 2011

ADEFFECTS, Rochester, NY
Account Management Intern: Researched and developed promotional materials for retail, manufacturing, and restaurant clients, using knowledge of small business marketing. Suggested client changes in outreach strategies, and marketing literature. 2010–2011

PEARLE VISION CENTER, Pittsford, NY
Sales Representative: Implemented strategy targeting upscale markets. Summer 2011

IT HAPPENS, Antwerp, Belgium
Marketing Intern: Determined target markets and developed advertisement budget for concert, event planning, and entertainment agency. Conducted surveys to determine market penetration. Assisted graphic artists with ads, posters, brochures, and reports. Summer 2008

BUSINESS, ECONOMICS, AND LANGUAGE STUDIES

UNIVERSITY OF ROCHESTER, Rochester, NY
Bachelor of Arts, French, with a major GPA of 3.5, May 2012.
Bachelor of Arts, Psychology, with a major GPA of 3.3, May 2012.
Minor: **Economics,** with a minor GPA of 3.4.

WILLIAM E. SIMON SCHOOL OF BUSINESS ADMINISTRATION, Rochester, NY
Management Studies Certificate, Marketing and Finance/Accounting Tracks, May 2012

FINANCE EXPERIENCE

THE FINANCIAL GROUP, INC. DISCOUNT BROKERAGE FIRM, Pittsford, NY

Intern/Assistant to Operations Manager, Spring 2011

- Identifying information uses only two lines.
- Left-justified block text format is e-friendly; can be uploaded to websites and copied and pasted into e-mail.
- Experience presented under targeted "headline."
- Education presented under targeted headline to highlight specialized studies.
- Courses presented in Qualification Summary to highlight significance.
- Chris is a focused, yet typical, soon to be graduate. His "before" resume is multipurpose. Chris's strategy of having a multipurpose and a targeted resume is sound.
- Both possess qualities worthy of modeling.
- Think about the "headlines" used in the after version and about changes in the order of presentation.
- How did the qualification summary change your reaction to this resume?

- Watch choice of font. Use a font that is easy to read and universal so that poor font substitutions or errors will not occur for your audience; i.e., Times, Bookman, Garamond, or Arial.

- Education presented first, without dates, under general "header" is confusing format.

- Experience under basic and generic header is presented in a confusing format.

- Difficult to see chronological or functional progress year-to-year or job-to-job.

Jamie Drown

123 Main Street
Home (555) 555-5555

Hometown, CO 00000
Cell (555) 555-9999

EDUCATION
30 Education credits, with day care emphasis, and English minor.
Metropolitan State College, Denver, CO

EXPERIENCE
2009-Present
NANNY
Care for twin boys from the age of two months through two years. Assist in selecting toys and equipment, provide environmental stimulation, personal care, and play.
Private residence, Livermore, CO

2007-2009
TEACHER
Taught infant, preschool, and afterschool programs. Planned curriculum, organized activities, communicated with parents and staff regarding growth and development. Suggested equipment to enrich children's experiences and helped create a stimulating environment.
Baby Bear Preschool, Keystone, CO

2005-2008
TEACHER
Planned and implemented curriculum for infants. Communicated with parents and other staff regarding daily progress of children.
This Little Piggy Daycare Center, Dove Creek, CO

2003-2005
TEACHER
Planned and implemented curriculum for toddler program. Enriched children's experiences through play, music, and art.
The Kid Corral, Wild Horse, CO

2001-2003
CAREGIVER
Provided care in clients' homes, administering physical therapy when necessary. Planned activities to stimulate and improve children's skills and environment.
Residences, Dove Creek, and Keystone, CO

2005-Present
VOLUNTEER
Ivywild Coalition for Retarded Citizens, Ivywild,

COSKILLS AND INTERESTS
Valid driver's license; perfect driving record. CPR/first aid certified.
Skiing, reading, music, arts and crafts.

Jamie Brown

123 Main Street • Hometown, CO 00000 • (555) 555-1234 • Cell (555) 555-9999

DAY CARE QUALIFICATIONS AND COMPETENCIES

- More than nine years of diverse experience within home and school settings, teaching and caring for children ranging in ages from two months to seven years.
- Commitment to the needs of infants, preschoolers, and kindergarteners.
- Academic background including courses in: Childhood Development, Early Childhood Education, Educational Psychology, and Assessments.

DAY CARE, TEACHING, AND CHILD CARE EXPERIENCE

2009–Present   PRIVATE RESIDENCE, Livermore, CO
Nanny: Care for twin boys from the age of two months through two years. Provide environmental enrichment, personal care, and play supervision.
- Accompanied family on trips and cared for children during illnesses.

2007–2009   BABY BEAR PRESCHOOL, Keystone, CO
Teacher: Taught infant, preschool, and after-school programs. Planned curriculum, organized activities, communicated with parents and staff regarding children's growth and development.
- Positively adjusted to annual increase in students and move to new facility.
- Worked collegially with owner on goal development.
- Assisted with annual licensing documentation and visitation.

2005–2007   THIS LITTLE PIGGY DAYCARE CENTER, Dove Creek, CO
Teacher: Planned and implemented infant program, blending developmental and custodial needs. Communicated with parents regarding student progress.
- Enhanced skills development through interactive play and song.

2003–2005   THE KID CORRAL, Wild Horse, CO
Teacher: Planned and implemented curriculum for toddler program. Enriched children's experiences through play, music, and art.

2003–2009   PRIVATE CAREGIVER, Wild Horse, Dove Creek, and Keystone, CO

2005–Present   COALITION FOR RETARDED CITIZENS VOLUNTEER, Ivywild, CO

EDUCATION

2000–2003   METROPOLITAN STATE COLLEGE, Denver, CO
- 30 credits in Education, with an emphasis on day care.

- Professional and e–friendly Garamond font.

- Qualifications and competencies appearing first serve as objective and preview of assets.

- Experience under targeted "headline" in easy to review format.

- Date timeline shows chronological and functional progress.

- Jamie is an experienced nanny and day care professional. Her current employer has informed her that she will no longer be needed full time. For the increasingly professional worlds of day care, private child care, and preschools, she has created a very appealing and marketable resume.

- Jamie has kept her audience in mind and has targeted her resume and job search at upscale day care facilities and parents.

Financial Planner (Before)

Dana Johnson

123 Main Street
Hometown, NJ 00000

(555) 555-1234
djohnson@company.com

Experience

ABC FINANCIAL CONSULTANTS, Princeton, NJ
July 2000–Present
Financial Consultant/Financial Planner
- Developed $210 million client base via prospecting.
- Built portfolio that includes stock, bonds, options, and insurance products for more than 450 clients.
- Implemented financial plans and operations through account development and growth.

October 1998–July 2000
Sales Associate
- Worked directly with firm's top producer, profiling high net worth individuals for future business.
- Generated $90,000 for top producer via new accounts.
- Analyzed portfolios to expand account performance.

September 1997–October 1998
Account Executive Trainee/Intern
- Supervised about 35,000 accounts in the area of trade settlement, NASD regulations, and customer inquiries.
- Reported recommendations to upper management.
- Acted as liaison with New York operations.

MAPLEWOOD INVESTMENTS, Maplewood, NJ
Summers 1996 and 1997
Prospecting Intern
- Planned, created documents for, and oversaw invitations and confirmations for three annual Summer Financial Seminars.
- Researched stock and updated transactions.

Related Training

Successfully completed ABC Financial Consultant Sales Training and Advanced Training program in Princeton, NJ, headquarters. Licensed in Series 6, 7, 63, and health and life insurance.

Education

IONA COLLEGE, Iona, New York
Bachelor of Arts degree in Economics, 1998

Dana Johnson

123 Main Street • Hometown, NJ 00000 • (555) 555-1234 • djohnson@company.com

Financial Planning Qualifications and Credentials

- Over a decade of progressively significant roles and achievements in planning, portfolio management, and client services.
- Personal responsibilities for more than $210 million client assets.
- Recognized for asset-based performance and customer service.
- Served as trainer and curriculum developer.

Financial Planning Accomplishments

ABC FINANCIAL CONSULTANTS, Princeton, NJ

2000–Present **Financial Consultant/Financial Planner**

Serve in comprehensive financial planning roles. Oversee individual and group portfolios. Serve as senior manager, supervisor, and trainer within corporate headquarters of firm responsible for over $800 million in client assets.

- Developed $210 million client asset base through aggressive prospecting and targeting campaign.
- Successfully built portfolio that includes stocks, bonds, options and insurance products for more than 450 clients.
- Implemented financial plans and operations through account development and growth.
- Gained expertise associated with estate planning, asset allocation, and wealth succession.
- Completed ABC Financial Consultant Sales Training and Advanced Training Program. Licensed in Series 6, 7, 63, and health and life insurance.

1998–2000 **Sales Associate**

- Worked directly with firm's top producer, profiling high net worth individuals for future business.
- Generated $90,000 through new account openings.
- Analyzed portfolios to expand account performance.

1997–1998 **Account Executive Trainee/Intern**

- Completed about 35,000 account transactions annually.
- Completed comprehensive training related to trade settlement, NASD regulations, and customer service.

Summers 1996 and 1997 MAPLEWOOD INVESTMENTS, Maplewood, NJ
Prospecting Intern

Education

IONA COLLEGE, Iona, New York
Bachelor of Arts degree in Economics, 1998

- Bookman Old Style is good font choice.

- Dana is an experienced financial services professional. She is not in active job search mode, but because of her status she is frequently called upon to serve as a spokesperson and seminar leader and she regularly updates her resume.

- The "before" version appears professional, but lacks focus. It doesn't highlight achievements. The "after" version, introduced via a qualifications and credential section, is achievement-oriented, and it highlights career growth.

- Bookman Old Style font is a well received typeface.

- Identifying information is four lines long and format is unappealing.

- Typical multipurpose resume for soon to be graduate is good, but can be better if candidate offers summary of qualifications to give resume greater focus.

- Experience and Education under generic headers.

- Education presented with minimal explanation.

- All experiences are detailed, even those irrelevant to current career goal.

- "Before" resume emphasizes administrative clerical skills rather than medical industry skills.

Francis Williams

123 Main Street
Hometown, NY 00000
(555) 555-1234

fwilliams@company.com

987 Centre Ave.
Homeville, NY 10001
(555) 555-5678

EDUCATION

UNIVERSITY OF ROCHESTER, Rochester, NY
Bachelor of Arts, Health and Society, Anticipated May 2013
Management Certificate in Public Sector Analysis, May 2014
Completed Language and Cultural Studies in Rome, Italy Spring 2011

ACTIVITIES AND LEADERSHIP

SIGMA DELTA FRATERNITY
President, 2012–2013, Secretary, 2010–2011, and Member, 2009–Present
STUDENT HEALTH ADVISORY COMMITTEE
Member, 2011–2012

EXPERIENCE

CHECK YOUR PULSE AMERICA RESEARCH STUDY, Rochester, NY
Research Assistant: Helped design aspects of nationwide research study dealing with stroke prevention. Responsibilities included distribution of questionnaire, data entry, and report writing and editing. Fall 2011

NYS VETERANS NURSING HOME, Wood Cliff, NY
Human Resources Assistant: Supported various recruiting, payroll, and benefits activities. Collected, reviewed, and rated resumes. Communicated with candidates by phone and e-mail. Summer 2012

THE CARDIOLOGY GROUP, Wood Cliff, NY
Administrative Assistant: Greeted and scheduled patients, maintained files, assisted with billing, communicated with insurance carriers and pharmacies, and completed special tasks as assigned. 2008–Present

YOUR INSURANCE GROUP, White Plains, NY
Office Assistant, Summer 2011

COMPUTER AND OFFICE SKILLS

Word, Excel, PowerPoint, Access, and Internet capabilities.
Abilities to serve in receptionist, billing, and human resources roles.

Medical Product Sales (After)

Francis Williams

123 Main St. • Hometown, NY 00000 • (555) 555-1234 • fwill@company.com
987 Centre Ave. • Homeville, NY 10001 • (555) 555-5678

MEDICAL PRODUCT SALES QUALIFICATIONS

- Knowledge of health care, business, and economics-related topics gained from courses including: Accounting, Microeconomics, Business Administration, Changing Concepts of Disease, Medical Sociology, Domestic Social Policy, Organizational Psychology, and Statistics.
- Confidence and experience communicating with physicians, health care practitioners, patients, and others associated with medical devices.
- Research, project management, time management, writing, and oral communication skills gained from employment, education, and activities.
- Capacities to conduct topic-specific research, identify trends or key issues, and document findings in reports as well as presentations.
- Persuasive communication style, required to educate regarding protocols and studies specific to medical products and treatment techniques.
- Word, Excel, PowerPoint, Access, and Internet capabilities.

HEALTH AND SOCIETY AND BUSINESS EDUCATION

UNIVERSITY OF ROCHESTER, Rochester, NY
Bachelor of Arts, Health and Society, anticipated May 2013
- Health and Society Major focused on study of Community and Preventive Medicine, as well as history and economics of health care delivery.
- Sigma Delta Fraternity President, Secretary, and Member.
- Student Health Advisory Committee, Member and Class of 2013 Senator.

WILLIAM E. SIMON SCHOOL OF BUSINESS ADMINISTRATION, Rochester, NY
Management Certificate in Public Sector Analysis, anticipated May 2014
- Certificate for completion of business, economics, and policy-focused courses taught by faculty of the college and of the Simon School.

TEMPLE UNIVERSITY ROME, Rome, Italy
Completed Language and Cultural Studies, Spring Semester 2011

HEALTH CARE, BUSINESS, AND RESEARCH EXPERIENCE

CHECK YOUR PULSE AMERICA RESEARCH STUDY, Rochester, NY
Research Assistant: Helped design aspects of nationwide research study dealing with stroke prevention. Fall 2011

NYS VETERANS NURSING HOME, Wood Cliff, NY
Human Resources Assistant: Supported recruiting, payroll, and benefits activities. Summer 2012

THE CARDIOLOGY GROUP, Wood Cliff, NY
Administrative Assistant, Summers and Part-time 2007–Present

YOUR INSURANCE GROUP, White Plains, NY
Office Assistant, Summer 2011

- Left-justified block text header format is visually appealing.
- Objective is presented via a qualifications summary.
- Marketing, business, and health care courses are presented first in qualifications section, highlighting significance.
- A goal targeted summary of qualifications is first, immediately followed by detailed education. This gives primary emphasis to the most important information.
- Summary of qualifications supplemented by a cover letter, shows commitment and the capabilities to succeed.

COREY DAVIS

123 Main Street • Santa Fe, NM 00000 • (555) 555-5555

EXPERIENCE

BRENDAN ELLIS CIVIL LITIGATION SPECIALIST/OFFICE MANAGER
Santa Fe, NM 2008–Present
- Manage office and staff of three secretaries, ensuring smooth operation of firm.
- Interview clients; prepare files and discovery.
- Request and review medical documentation; ascertain evidence information, and process all with the appropriate parties.
- Negotiate and settle cases with defense attorney and insurance companies.
- Attend mediations and conciliations.
- Prepare clients for depositions and trials.
- Control and maintain law office accounts.

BROWNINGTON, INC. ADMINISTRATIVE ASSISTANT
Albuquerque, NM 2003–2008
- Confirmed all manpower hours and prepared logs to bill various sites.
- Provided clerical support to twenty-four software engineers.
- Recognized for "Excellence in Customer Satisfaction Southwest Region."

WILD RAIN EXOTIC GIFTS MANAGER/SALESPERSON
Silver City, NM 2000–2003
- Sold art and memorabilia on consignment.
- Hired, trained, and supervised eight sales personnel.
- Handled accounts, managed orders, and created promotions.

SANTA FE DISTRICT ATTORNEY'S DOMESTIC VIOLENCE WITNESS ADVOCATE
Santa Fe, NM Spring–Summer 2000
- Interviewed victims and witnesses, prepared documents, and organized information for court appearances.
- Assisted attorneys during trials.

NEW MEXICO PUBLIC DEFENDER'S LEGAL INTERN
Santa Fe, NM Summers 1998 and 1999
- Researched and drafted motions on criminal law and procedural issues.
- Interviewed clients at New Mexico correctional institutions.
- Negotiated plea and bail agreements for defendants.

ATTORNEY DANIEL GALL LEGAL SECRETARY/LEGAL ASSISTANT
Santa Fe, NM 1995–2000

EDUCATION

SAINT JOHN'S COLLEGE BS, HUMAN RESOURCES MANAGEMENT
Santa Fe, NM 2000

COREY DAVIS

123 Main Street • Hometown, NM 00000 • (555) 555-5555 • cdavis@company.com
After May 2008: 987 Centre Avenue • Hometown, CA 00000 • (555) 555-1234

PARALEGAL QUALIFICATIONS AND ACHIEVEMENTS

- Case research, client relations, document management, and writing skills gained in progressively responsible positions over a twelve-year period.
- Expertise as law office manager, compiling training manual, supervising support personnel, revamping accounting, debit, and credit systems.
- Trained and accomplished interviewer, negotiator, and mediator.
- LexisNexis, WestLaw, Word, FileMaker, Excel, QuickBooks, and Internet skills.

PARALEGAL AND MANAGEMENT EXPERIENCE

LAW OFFICES OF BRENDAN ELLIS   Santa Fe, NM
Civil Litigation Specialist/Office Manager   2000–Present
- Manage office and staff of three secretaries, ensuring smooth operation of firm with three attorneys and billings of $1.5 million and awards over $10 million annually.
- Interview clients; prepare files and discovery; handle multiple cases.
- Request and review medical documentation; ascertain evidence information and process all with the appropriate parties.
- Negotiate and settle cases with defense attorney and insurance companies.
- Attend mediations and conciliations.
- Prepare clients for depositions and trials.
- Control and maintain office accounts, using accounting and billing software.

SANTE FE DISTRICT ATTORNEY'S DOMESTIC VIOLENCE UNIT   Santa Fe, NM
Witness Advocate   Spring–Summer 2000
- Interviewed victims and witnesses, prepared documents, and organized information for court appearances.
- Assisted attorneys during trials, taking notes, and facilitating access to evidentiary documents.

NEW MEXICO PUBLIC DEFENDER'S OFFICE   Santa Fe, NM
Legal Intern   Summers 1998 and 1999
- Researched and drafted motions on criminal law and procedural issues. Interviewed clients at New Mexico correctional institutions.
- Negotiated plea and bail agreements for defendants accused of misdemeanors. Attended criminal trials and depositions.

ATTORNEY DANIEL GALL   Santa Fe, NM
Legal Secretary/Legal Assistant   1996–2000

EDUCATION

SAINT JOHN'S COLLEGE   Santa Fe, NM
BS, Human Resources Management, with Honors   2000
- Completed degree part-time while employed.

- Qualifications and achievement summary support objective and showcase experience.

- Experience under specialized headline focuses on legal background.

- Capitalization, italics and bullets are used effectively.

- Education makes mention of receiving degree while working full time as a Legal Secretary. This fact should also be highlighted in a cover letter.

- Candidate calls attention to geographic move with new relocation address and date.

- Bullets showcase career progression and growth within field. Achievements are cited, as are job titles.

- Poor choice of font. Resume is visually unappealing.

- Lengthy objective contains unnecessary wording or "fluff."

- Experience and Education appear under basic and generic header.

- Titles use old-fashioned underlining technique (looks dated and is often unreadable to resume scanning technology.)

- Paragraph experience descriptions are difficult to read quickly.

- Internship information is poorly presented.

Chris Smith

123 Main St., Hometown, CA 00000 (555) 555-1234, cs@company.com

CAREER OBJECTIVE

Challenging pharmaceutical sales position with a progressive organization seeking dynamic and driven sales professional.

EXPERIENCE

Pearls and Gemstones Corporation, San Francisco, California
6/11–Present
Sales Associate: Sell and market polished gemstones for the San Francisco office of international gemstone and pearl distributor and jewelry manufacturer.

Bank of Hong Kong, Hong Kong   6/10–8/10
Trader: International Securities Dealing Room: Responded to customers' executing orders in the areas of American and foreign equities, bonds, and options. Received training in and gained working knowledge of Bloomberg and Reuters information systems.

Bank of Hong Kong, San Francisco, California   11/07–10/09
Credit Analyst: International Lending Department: Prepared proposals on prospective customers and renewals and reaffirmations of existing facilities for credit committee. Performed financial statement, cash flow, and projection analysis. Conducted research using Bloomberg, Moody's, and S&P analysts and publications.

Computer Associates International, San Jose, California   1/07–9/07
Quality Assurance Analyst: Implemented quality assurance for inter/intranet-enabled, multiplatform, enterprise management solution used worldwide.

EDUCATION

University of California, Berkeley, California
Bachelor of Arts   Class of 2007
Major: Political Science. Minor: Economics.
Dean's List Fall 2001 and Spring 2000 and Overall GPA: 3.34/4.0

University of New South Wales, Sydney, Australia   Spring 2006

HONORS

International Internships, London, England
Gordon McMaster, MP: British Parliament   9/05–12/05
Performed research, assisted in speech writing, aided constituents.
IPA Political Internships, Washington, DC
Senator Barbara Boxer: U.S. Senate   6/05–8/05
Wrote research briefs on pending legislation.

Pharmaceutical Sales (After)

Chris Smith

123 Main Street • Hometown, CA 00000 • (555) 555-1234 • csmith@company.com

OBJECTIVE

Pharmaceutical Sales Position using and expanding upon. . .

- Record of success within direct marketing and information-driven sales roles.
- Confidence nurturing relationships via direct calls using information dissemination strategies.
- Capacity to understand and share knowledge of pharmaceutical products and protocols.
- Abilities to set goals, document efforts and outcomes, and maximize achievements.
- Bilingual English-Mandarin abilities and cross-cultural sensitivities.

SALES AND SALES SUPPORT ACHIEVEMENTS

PEARLS AND GEMSTONES CORPORATION, San Francisco, CA   2011–Present

Sales Associate for Loose Diamond Division: Sell gemstones for international distributor and manufacturer. Sales methods include appointments onsite, telemarketing, trade show exhibiting, and Internet. Customers include manufacturers, retail and department stores, and catalogues.

- *Directly involved in sales to house accounts totaling $2.5 million in 2006.*
- *Indirectly involved in sales to salespersons accounts totaling $3 million in 2006.*

COMPUTER ASSOCIATES INTERNATIONAL, San Jose, CA   2007

Quality Assurance Analyst: Analyzed business applications for functionality and marketability. Reviewed RFPs (Request For Proposal) and identified key marketing leverage points. Implemented quality assurance for worldwide projects and software products.

- *Supported customer service and sales representatives in refining product to match customer needs.*

BUSINESS AND FINANCE EXPERIENCE

BANK OF HONG KONG, Hong Kong   Spring 2010

Securities Trader: Executed American and foreign equities, bonds, and option orders.

BANK OF HONG KONG, San Francisco, CA   2007–2010

Department Credit Analyst: Prepared proposals on prospective customers and renewals for credit committee. Researched using Bloomberg, Moody's, and S&P analysts and publications.

BUSINESS, ECONOMICS, AND LIBERAL ARTS EDUCATION

UNIVERSITY OF CALIFORNIA, BERKELEY, Berkeley, CA   2003–2007

Bachelor of Arts Political Science, with minor in Economics,

- Intern for Member of British Parliament, Fall 2000, and Senator Boxer, Summer 2000.

HAAS SCHOOL OF BUSINESS ADMINISTRATION, Berkeley, CA   2003–2005

- Management Certificate for completion of Marketing and Business courses.

- Garamond font is good choice for attractive layout.

- Objective and candidate's assets are effectively blended together.

- Experience is set off by specific achievements as noted in the header.

- Bilingual skills are cited.

- Sales experience gets greater emphasis with specific numeric achievements noted in italics.

JAMIE BROWN

123 Main Street, Hometown, NY 00000 (555) 555-1234

EXPERIENCE

SYRACUSE HEART ASSOCIATION, Syracuse, NY
Public Relations Manager, 2010–Present
Organizing: Serve as consultant to the seven state chapters. Organize statewide and regional campaign meetings; speak at campaign conferences. Lobbying: Review legislation regarding the Society and bring specific bills to attention of proper committee or individual. Staff the Legislative Advisory Committee and follow through on specific bills. Fundraising: Develop fundraising programs. Conducted two annual campaigns for newly merged Central Chapter. Serve as chair for New York Independent Health Agency Committee and secretary for Combined Federal Campaign. Training: Developed orientation courses held for new employees; acted as training coordinator.
Directorial Assistant for Greater Syracuse Chapter, 2005–2007
Assisted the Executive Director with administrative responsibilities, such as personnel and budget.

BIG APPLE NATURAL FOODS, Syracuse, NY
Special Events Coordinator, 2008–2010
Created and coordinated special events and promotions. Selected and wrote event advertising and promotional materials. Managed $425,000 marketing budget. Handled charity fundraising, corporate image positioning, and community outreach activities.
Assistant to the Director of Public Relations, 2007–2008
Assisted in promotion and publicity of special events. Drafted press releases. Developed press kits; maintained media relations. Compiled publicity files. Researched prospective consumer markets.

SYRACUSE UNIVERSITY, Syracuse, NY
Teacher's Assistant, Fall and Spring 2008
Assisted professor in editing book. Developed lesson plans. Graded midterm exams for class of eighteen.

ABC KID KAMP, Syracuse, NY
Coordinator, Summers 2007 and 2008
Organized daily activities program for forty-five children. Developed promotional strategies for potential markets.

COMPUTER SKILLS

Word, InDesign, PowerPoint

EDUCATION

SYRACUSE UNIVERSITY, Syracuse, NY
Bachelor of Arts in Public Relations, magna cum laude, June 2008

Public Relations Account Executive (After)

123 Main Street • Hometown, NY 00000 • (555) 555-1234 • jbrown@company.com

SYRACUSE HEART ASSOCIATION, Syracuse, NY
2010–Present
- Serve as consultant to seven state chapters regarding campaign problems and activities.
- Organize statewide and regional campaign meetings; and speak at several campaign conferences.
- Review related state legislation activities and bring specific bills to the attention of proper committee or individual.
- Staff the Legislative Advisory Committee and follow through on specific bills.
- Develop fundraising programs and conducted two annual campaigns for newly merged Central Chapter.
- Serve as chair for New York Independent Health Agency Committee and secretary for Federal Campaign.
- Assisted with developing and teaching new employee orientation courses.
2005–2007
- Supervised chapter campaigns and assisted Executive Director with campaign personnel and budget.

BIG APPLE NATURAL FOODS, Syracuse, NY
2008–2010
- Managed $425,000 budget to coordinate special events and create advertising and promotional materials.
- Handled charity fundraising, corporate image positioning, and community outreach efforts.
2007–2008
- Assisted in promotion and publicity of special events.
- Drafted, edited, finalized, and distributed press releases and kits to initiate and maximize media relations efforts.
- Researched prospective consumer markets using Internet and direct contact techniques.
- Created direct-mail lists, updated media lists, and maintained task priority lists.

SYRACUSE UNIVERSITY, Syracuse, NY
 Fall and
Spring 2008
SYRACUSE UNIVERSITY, Syracuse, NY
 June 2008
- Campaign development and implementation experience with major health agency.
- Supervisory experience with both professional and nonprofessional staffs.
- Ability to plan and direct successful programs for fundraising, public relations, and promotions-oriented clients.
- Extensive volunteer recruitment experience and success motivating diverse teams.
- Experience representing agency interests to legislators and lobbyists.
- Capacity to use Word, InDesign, and PowerPoint for drafting and editing promotional materials, budgeting and financial tasks, and graphics projects.

- Identifying information is presented on one line.
- Resume format has more visual appeal for a creative field.
- Headlines use descriptive phrases and are italicized and bolded for emphasis.
- Use of lines to set off content continues to give this resume a more creative edge.
- Bullets set off responsibilities and content and allow reader to peruse resume quickly.
- Qualifications offer good conclusion and "closure" for the reader.
- Bold use of job titles showcase upwardly mobile career progression.
- Summer college position omitted—dated and no longer necessary.

Real Estate Professional (Before)

Dana Johnson

123 Main Street
(555) 555-1234

Hometown, CA 00000
djohnson@company.com

EDUCATION

SANTA CLARA UNIVERSITY, Santa Clara, CA
Bachelor of Science in Business Administration, 1990

EXPERIENCE

SAN JOSE AND SANTA CLARA HOME LOANS, San Jose, CA
Real Estate Loan Officer, 2011–Present
- Originated real estate loans, developed marketing plan to expand business.
- Conducted cold calls, created individualized mortgage broker packets, completed individual and group presentations designed to generate Conventional, FHA/VA, PERS, JUMBO, Community Home Buyer, and CHAFA loan business.

BAY AREA BANK, Santa Clara, CA
Real Estate Loan Officer, 2008–2011
- Originated real estate loans, developed marketing plan to expand business.
- Conducted cold calls, created individualized mortgage broker packets, completed individual and group presentations designed to generate loan business.
- Planned and implemented first-ever real estate expo promotional event.

HOUSING LENDING, Fresno, CA
Wholesale Account Executive, 2006–2008
- Marketed loan and financing programs to financial institutions and mortgage brokers in San Joaquin, Merced, Fresno, and Stanislaus counties.
- Conducted cold calls, created customer specific material packets, completed individual and group presentations designed to generate loan business.
- Trained mortgage brokers, loan officers, and real estate agents in Conventional, Jumbo, FHA/VA, PERS, Community Home Buyer, and other niche programs.

CALIFORNIA MORTGAGE SPECIALISTS, INC., San Mateo, CA
Professional Real Estate Loan Auditor, 2002–2006
- Audited loans determining FHLMC/FNMA, FSLIC, or private investor marketability.
- Reviewed notes and deeds of trust to determine accuracy and legality.
- Interacted with Savings and Loan and Mortgage professionals in western U.S.

SANTA CLARA SAVINGS, Santa Clara, CA
Loan Officer in Residential Lending Department, 1996–2002
- Responsible for residential and commercial loans in California and throughout U.S.
- Managed loan processing and underwriting staff of ten.
- Evaluated residential loans for approval or denial and FHLMC/FNMA conformance.
- Coordinated loan closing with production, closing, and with legal staffs.
- Traveled to project sites to establish positive relations with builders and sales representatives and outline financing and efficient loan procedures.

Loan Underwriter/Processor of Residential and Government Loans, 1992–1996
Loan Underwriter in Secondary Market Department, 1990–1992
Loan Packager in Loan Processing Department, 1988–1990

Real Estate Professional (After)

Dana Johnson

123 Main Street • Hometown, CA 00000 • (555) 555-1234 • djohnson@company.com

REAL ESTATE LENDING ACHIEVEMENTS

SAN JOSE AND SANTA CLARA HOME LOANS, San Jose, CA
Real Estate Loan Officer, 2011–Present

- Originated real estate loans, developed marketing plan to expand business in Santa Clara County.
- Conducted cold calls, created broker packets, completed presentations to generate Conventional, FHA/VA, PERS, JUMBO, and CHAFA loans.

BAY AREA BANK, Santa Clara, CA
Real Estate Loan Officer, 2008–2011

- Conducted cold calls, created individualized mortgage broker packets, completed individual and group presentations designed to generate loan business.
- Planned and implemented first-ever real estate expo promotional event.

HOUSING LENDING, Fresno, CA
Wholesale Account Executive, 2006–2008

- Marketed loan and financing programs in San Joaquin, Merced, Fresno, and Stanislaus counties.
- Conducted cold calls, created customer-specific material packets, completed individual and group presentations designed to generate loan business.

CALIFORNIA MORTGAGE SPECIALISTS, INC., San Mateo, CA
Professional Real Estate Loan Auditor, 2002–2006

- Audited loans to determine marketability to FHLMC/FNMA, FSLIC, or private investors.
- Interacted with Savings and Loan and Mortgage professionals in western U.S.

SANTA CLARA SAVINGS, Santa Clara, CA
Loan Officer in Residential Lending Department, 1996–2002

- Evaluated residential loans for approval or denial and FHLMC/FNMA conformance.
- Traveled to project sites to establish positive relations with builders and sales representatives.

Loan Underwriter/Processor in Residential and Government Loan Departments, 1987–1991
Loan Underwriter in Secondary Market Department, 1990–1992
Loan Packager in Loan Processing Department, 1988–1990

PROFESSIONAL PROFILE

- More than 15 fifteen years in mortgage banking, customer service, finance, loan qualifications, and risk analysis.
- Expertise with Conventional, FHA/VA, PERS, JUMBO, and CHAFA loans.
- BS in Business, Santa Clara University, 1990 and continuing professional studies.

- Good mix of fonts between Arial for headlines and Century Schoolbook for content.

- Identifying information condensed to two lines.

- Headlines are clearly defined.

- Achievements presented first to showcase promotions and accomplishments.

- Profile offered last as a "closing" statement to the reader.

- The Before-and-After Resumes of this candidate are both good, with largely style and format preference up to individual taste.

- Times New Roman font is good choice, very traditional.

- This is a good multipurpose resume, but candidate may want to develop alternative with stronger career focus.

- Education and Work Experience use generic, nondescriptive headers.

- Good use of italics for highlighting.

- Bullets might help reader to peruse quickly and extract information more easily.

Francis Williams

123 Main Street	PO Box 987
Hometown, OH 00000-0000	Homeville, OH 00001-0000
555. 555.1234	fwilliams@college.edu

EDUCATION

The Ohio State University	Degree: BSBA
Columbus, OH 43210	Major: Business, Marketing
GPA: 3.30/4.0	Expected Graduation Date: 2013

WORK EXPERIENCE

February 2012–April 2012 — Intern, Birthright Israel
46 East Sixteenth Avenue — Columbus, OH 43201
Recruited and interviewed candidates for national Birthright Israel program. Recruitment included campus-wide telephone and marketing campaign.

July 2011–August 2011 — Intern, NetAds, Inc.
2880 San Thomas Expressway — Santa Clara, CA 95051
Designed database tracking sales leads and developments. Initiated and developed early stages of contact with potential clientele. Marketed product to more than 400 potential clients, including Visa, DreamWorks Animation, and Knight-Ridder Press.

October 2010–January 2012 — Server, World Cuisine Café
106 West Vine Street — Columbus, OH 43215
Used thorough knowledge of varied food menu and over 75 different fine wines and spirits to guide guests through fine-dining experience. Demonstrated prompt, accurate service.

October 2008–December 2008 — Intern, Abercrombie and Fitch Co.
4 Limited Parkway — Columbus, OH 43068
Analyzed sales and presented findings to supervisors. Photographed students at local college campuses for research and development. Designed men's garment for Spring line.

October 2006–September 2010 — Receptionist, Worthington Realtors
882 High Street — Worthington, OH 43085

INTERESTS, ACTIVITIES, AND HONORS

Alpha Phi Women's Fraternity Alumni Relations Director: January 2012–Present
American Business Women's Association Fundraising Chair: April 2012–Present
Ohio State University Community Commitment Volunteer: September 2009–Present
Project Open Hand Columbus, Volunteer: April 2010–Present
Susan G. Komen Breast Cancer Foundation, Fundraiser: 2007–Present
America Israel Public Affairs Committee Member: February 2012–Present
The Ohio State University Trustees Scholar: 2011

Student Seeking Internship (After)

FRANCIS WILLIAMS

PO Box 987 • Homeville, OH 00000 • Cell: 000.000.0000 • fwilliams@college.edu
123 Main Street • Hometown, OH 00000 • 555.555.1234

LOBBYING AND FUNDRAISING INTERNSHIP QUALIFICATIONS

- Experienced as fundraiser and program recruiter for campus organizations.
- Confidence in event planning, marketing strategy development, and outreach.
- Capacity to draft and finalize correspondence, promotional materials, and brochures.
- Research, analytical, and presentation skills associated with lobbying and topical reports.
- Business knowledge gained from courses including: Accounting, Finance, and Marketing.

BUSINESS AND MARKETING EDUCATION

THE OHIO STATE UNIVERSITY, Columbus, OH
Bachelor of Science, Business Administration, anticipated May 2013
- Major: *Business, Marketing* and Secondary Major: Business, Transportation Logistics
- Overall GPA: 3.30, Trustees Scholar, and National Dean's List Scholar
- University of Dreams Internship and Professional Development Program, 2012

FUNDRAISING, OUTREACH, AND LEADERSHIP ACHIEVEMENTS

- Susan G. Komen Breast Cancer Foundation, Fundraiser, 2007–Present
- America Israel Public Affairs Committee, Member, February 2012–Present
- Alpha Phi International Fraternity, Director, Alumni Relations, January 2012–Present
- American Business Women's Association, Chairperson, Fundraising, April 2012–Present
- The Ohio State University Community Commitment, Volunteer, September 2009–Present
- Project Open Hand Columbus, Volunteer, April 2010–Present

OUTREACH, MARKETING, AND ADMINISTRATIVE ACHIEVEMENTS

BIRTHRIGHT ISRAEL, Columbus, OH
Recruiting and Marketing Intern, Spring 2012
- Recruited and interviewed candidates for national program providing free travel to Israel.
- Recruitment included campus-wide telephone and marketing campaign.

NETADS, INC., Santa Clara, CA
Marketing Intern, Summer 2011
- Designed database tracking sales leads and initiated contact with potential clientele.
- Marketed to 400 potential clients, including Visa, DreamWorks Animation, and Knight-Ridder Press.

ABERCROMBIE AND FITCH CO., Columbus, OH 43068
Marketing Intern, Fall 2011
- Analyzed sales and presented findings to supervisors.

WORTHINGTON REALTORS, Worthington, OH
Receptionist, Summers and Part-time 2006–2008

- Book Antiqua font is good alternative type choice. Candidate may want to experiment with resume in different fonts to see if one generates more employer interest than the other.

- Qualifications summary gives focus to internship sought by candidate.

- Headlines highlight significant entries and make good use of keywords.

- Bullets give reader opportunity to peruse quickly for facts.

- Most important information appears first.

- This candidate chose to have one multipurpose resume and one targeted resume. Good strategy for an effective job (or internship) search.

Teacher (Before)

- Font looks plain and old-fashioned.

- Teaching Qualifications are last and lost to reader.

- Candidate has gathered appropriate information, but failed to give resume visual appeal for reader. Creates disadvantage for candidate's solid qualifications.

Corey Davis

123 Main Street • Hometown, NJ 00000 • (555) 555-1234 • cd@company.com

Experience

EDISON TECHNICAL AND VOCATIONAL HIGH SCHOOL, Edison, NJ
9th Grade General Science Teacher, September 2011–Present

EDISON TECHNICAL AND VOCATIONAL HIGH SCHOOL, Edison, NJ
Biology Teacher (Contract Substitute), January–June 2011

MAPLEWOOD-SOUTH ORANGE SCHOOL DISTRICT, Rochester, NY
Substitute Teacher K-12, October–December 2011

NEWARK ACADEMY, Rochester, NY
Substitute Teacher K-5, October–December 2011

Education

FAIRLEIGH DICKINSON UNIVERSITY, Madison, NJ
MS, Math/Science/Technology Education, expected August 2013
- Received Eisenhower Grant to study critical thinking in classrooms
- Researched and wrote thesis: Problem Based Learning to Increase Engagement in an Urban Science Classroom
- Created Interdisciplinary Biology, English, and Social Studies unit
- Developed and used problem-based learning projects as well as inquiry based learning units within classroom settings

DREW UNIVERSITY, Madison, NJ
BS, Ecology and Evolutionary Biology, May 2010

Selected Courses

Human Genetics & Evolution, Biochemistry, Ecology, Evolution, Cell Biology, Mammalian Anatomy, Evolution of the Earth (geology), Calculus I and II, Statistics for Biologists, Probability, History and Philosophy of Education, Foundations of Math/Science/Technology, Teaching Math/Science, Inquiry in the Classroom, Classroom Dynamics, Differentiating Instruction, Developing Literacy Skills, Literacy through Math/Science/Technology, Assessment, Problem-Based Learning

Teaching Certifications and Qualifications

NJ STATE CERTIFICATION IN BIOLOGY, 7TH–12TH GRADES, June 2012
NJ STATE CERTIFICATION IN GENERAL SCIENCE, June 2012

Corey Davis

123 Main Street · Hometown, NJ 00000 · (555) 555-1234 · cdavis@company.com

Teaching Certifications and Qualifications

- NJ State Certification in Biology, 7th–12th grades, June 2012
- NJ State Certification in General Science, June 2012
- Creativity and knowledge to create lessons for students at various readiness levels
- Interest in teaching science, mathematics, as well as Spanish
- Experience co-teaching in an inclusion classroom

Science, Mathematics, and Education Studies

FAIRLEIGH DICKINSON UNIVERSITY, Madison, NJ
Master of Science, Math/Science/Technology Education, anticipated August 2013

- Received Eisenhower Grant to study how to bring critical thinking into classrooms
- Thesis: Problem Based Learning to Increase Engagement in an Urban Science Classroom
- Created a unit incorporating literacy building strategies into science
- Developed and used problem-based and inquiry based learning units within classroom settings
- Developed unit differentiated for three different readiness levels

DREW UNIVERSITY, Madison, NJ
Bachelor of Science; Ecology and Evolutionary Biology; Psychology minor, May 2010

Science, Mathematics, and Education Coursework

- Human Genetics & Evolution, Genetics, Biochemistry, Ecology, Evolution, Cell Biology, Principles of Experimental Biology Lab, Animal Behavior, Mammalian Anatomy, Evolution of the Earth
- Calculus I and II, Statistics for the Sciences, Statistics for Biologists, Probability
- Foundations of Math/Science/Technology, Teaching Math/Science, Inquiry in the Classroom, Classroom Dynamics, Differentiating Instruction, Literacy through Math/Science/Technology, Assessment, Problem Based Learning

Teaching Experience

EDISON TECHNICAL AND VOCATIONAL HIGH SCHOOL, Edison, NJ
9th Grade General Science Teacher, September 2011–Present
Biology Teacher (Contract Substitute), January–June 2011

MAPLEWOOD-SOUTH ORANGE SCHOOL DISTRICT, Rochester, NY
Substitute Teacher K–12, October–December 2011

NEWARK ACADEMY, Rochester, NY
Substitute Teacher K–5, October–December 2011

- Century Schoolbook is a professional and appropriate font.
- Certifications and Qualifications presented as lead to reader. Sets tone for resume.
- Summary entries replace individual job descriptions.
- Headlines highlight significant education and courses, as well as the strengths of this candidate in specific subjects.
- Corey is about to complete Master's degree which is prompting this job search for improved career opportunity.
- After several interviews, Corey determined employers were very focused on most recent coursework, so candidate emphasized this content.

Resumes Before-and-After Review

Once you complete your draft, you must next complete your critique. Your silent or spoken answers to the following questions will reveal whether your resume is ready for distribution.

If answers to the following queries are all "yes, yes, yes," your resume has evolved from "before" to "after" status, and it is ready for distribution. If some answers are "no," keep working. You're on the right path.

IDENTIFYING INFORMATION

❑ Is your name in larger font and bolded?
❑ Is your address, phone, and e-mail presented as part of the header?
❑ If more than one address or phone appears, is there a logical reason why, and is this information presented using as few lines as possible?

OVERALL APPEARANCE AND FIRST IMPRESSION

❑ At first glance, is the resume neat, easy to visually scan from top to bottom, and presented in a logical format?
❑ Is the font type and size easy to read and professional in appearance?
❑ Can you scan down the page and identify a logical pattern of headline placement as well as highlighting techniques?
❑ Are capitalization, boldface, italics, indentation, and page placement used to highlight specific information in easily identifiable patterns?
❑ Can the resume be cut and pasted into an e-mail message and still retain logical formatting?

OBJECTIVE

❑ It's okay to include an objective but, if you do, make sure it's meaningful and reflective both of the position you're applying to and your background.
❑ Does this statement project knowledge of your desired field and use field-specific phrasing?
❑ Is it presented in as few words as possible?

QUALIFICATION OR ACHIEVEMENT SUMMARY

❏ Does this paragraph, or better—bullet point listing—support the stated objective?

❏ If no objective appears, does the headline used for this section clearly project your goal?

❏ Does this paragraph or bullet point listing reveal that you understand the qualification criteria, specialized terminology, and keywords associated with your target job?

❏ Does the headline used inform the reader quickly that you have a sense of focus?

❏ Does this section reveal a thorough projection to the future as well as reflection to the past?

❏ Does the statement reflect upon competence as well as confidence?

❏ Are most significant goal-related qualification statements presented first, and less important last?

❏ If viewed independently from the resume, or within a cover letter, does this section project focus and an impressive knowledge of target-specific field and functional roles?

EDUCATION AND PROFESSIONAL DEVELOPMENT

❏ Do special headlines reinforce objective-related focus?

❏ If a traditional header is used, does it downplay the importance of this section?

❏ Does the order of appearance accurately portray significance, with most important information presented first and least important later, if not last?

❏ Does this section present school(s), degree(s), area(s) of concentration, courses, or honors?

❏ Do courses, papers, and projects listings appear as subheadings or as independent headlines?

❏ For soon-to-be or recent grads, are complimentary (over 3.0) overall or subject-specific GPAs included?

❏ Is specialized, goal-focused training and development presented under a specific headline?

❏ If specifically related to job search target, are experiences referred to in a qualification summary?

EXPERIENCE

❏ Do special headlines reinforce objective-related focus and impact order of presentation?

❏ Do the headlines project knowledge of targeted fields and draw attention to related achievements?

❏ Do headlines catch the eye, revealing through quick review, the nature of entries that follow?

❏ If a traditional header is used, does it downplay the importance of this section?

❏ Are entries described using active and accomplishment-oriented phrasing, including facts and figures when possible?

❏ Are goal-specific experiences grouped under appropriate headlines and presented in order of significance?

❏ If specifically related to job search target, is a special headline used and are experiences referred to in a qualification summary?

❏ If entries are simply cited, with no descriptions, are they obviously of less importance than others?

❏ Are organizations, titles, and dates easy to see, revealing an obvious pattern and logic?

❏ Have you, for space as well as goal-directed strategies, presented only the most significant experiences, with most important appearing first, and least important later?

COMMUNITY SERVICE, CO-CURRICULAR ACTIVITIES, AND SPECIAL CATEGORIES

❏ For soon-to-be or recent college grad, are leadership roles and achievements cited?

❏ If specifically related to job search target, is a special headline used and are experiences referred to in a qualification summary?

❏ If listed by experienced candidates, do all entries seem relevant to your stated goal?

❏ Are activities presented in easy to read and easy to follow patterns, avoiding acronyms and an overly lengthy listing of detail?

❏ If specifically related to job search target, are experiences referred to in a qualification summary?

OVERALL PRESENTATION, LAST GLANCE, FINAL DETAILS

❑ Are most important headlines presented first, with most significant information appearing under each?

❑ If your resume is more than one page, is the most important information on the first page and does the second page have your name and a page number header?

❑ If you have more than one targeted resume, are the objectives clear, did you change order of presentation for each, and are summaries of qualifications target-specific?

❑ Does the resume present a professional image, with easy to recognize highlighting patterns, and with a top-to-bottom and in a last-glance logical format?

❑ If a qualification summary appears last, does it summarize goal-directed competencies and capabilities accurately and dynamically?

❑ Can you elaborate upon the resume in a cover letter?

❑ Would a prospective employer sense goal-oriented competence and confidence even without an accompanying letter?

❑ Can you elaborate upon the resume and use it as a clear guide during an interview?

❑ Are you ready to duplicate and distribute your resume?

Your answers must all be affirmative to all these questions, or you are not ready for the final steps. Don't be overly analytical or self-critical. Finish and use your resume. If needed, you can always update, and it will only take another day!

Helpful Websites

This section identifies some additional obvious and not-so-obvious research and job search support tools. Any job search in this technology-driven world will benefit from Internet resources that are available to advance your career. This means taking advantage of job boards (where openings are posted), employer websites (where internal opportunities are listed or you can apply online), and other sites such as business networking sites, career guidance sites, and blogs (where people make comments about an industry, company, type of job or other work-related matters). Use a mix of technological resources along with traditional print publications, industry associations, and, of course, your local library, to get the most information you can about a prospective employer or job openings that might be a good fit for your skills, experience, and career goals.

Remember, web-based resources are critical because job seekers and resume writers have a lot of "homework" to do. You must conduct pre-research (research before job search), set goals, enhance field-focused vocabulary used in resumes and during interviews, and develop a hit list of prospective employers. The following listing of websites is offered to facilitate your efforts for job search success. Identify those that address your needs, and use those that are appropriate to your strategies and goals. This is just a small representation of what is available on the web.

The Big Job Boards

www.careerbuilder.com

One of the most popular multiple industry, national posting, resume collection, and job search information sites, this site includes help wanted ads from more than 200 newspaper markets and metropolitan areas in electronic format. Beyond resume posting, participants are able to browse jobs and apply online, distribute resumes, take career tests, use the site's free salary calculator, look for local and regional career fairs, get career advice from experts and have their resumes critiqued. You can search jobs by a wide variety of variables including: company, industry, category, location, and more.

www.monster.com

This is literally and figuratively, one of the "monsters" of all posting, resume collection, and career advice sites. This creatively advertised and widely recognized job board offers employer research, search-agent capabilities, and job search advice. Like all the big boards, it is very user-friendly. This site promotes with great pride that it contains millions of resumes and millions of postings for job seekers of all stages and ages, including internship candidates, soon-to-be and recent college grads, and experienced professionals. Additional site amenities include: scholarship research, information about online degrees, and Monster en Español (*www.monster.es*).

Additional Excellent Job Board Sites

www.indeed.com

Indeed calls itself "a search engine for jobs." It collects job listings from many job boards, newspapers, company career pages, and other sites. At the time of this writing, it listed almost 600,000 jobs posted in the last seven days.

www.simplyhired.com

This is another job board search engine where you can browse by state, job title, company name, or industry. Post your resume on up to five major job boards at no cost. Conduct special searches by these unique categories: dog-friendly employers, mom-friendly companies, employers for the fifty-plus, and eco-friendly employers for those who want to go "green."

www.vault.com/wps/portal/usa

You can search jobs on Vault.com, but it also has one of the best libraries of career guides and employer profiles. Additionally, you can search information on more than 3,000 companies, and their message boards offer enormous insight as to what it might be like to work at one of your target employers.

More Web Resources by Specialty or Audience

www.aarp.org/work

AARP (formerly the American Association of Retired Persons) hosts an excellent resource for fifty-plus candidates that addresses occupational information, career transition, job loss, skills training, and general news for those who want to continue to work.

www.careertv.com

Like to watch videos? This interactive site is perfect for you. Their video menu includes employers, resumes, universities, job advice, and more. It's a favorite resource of the "YouTube" generation.

www.collegegrad.com

Often called the "number one entry level job site," this board is chock-full of advice for those ready to put their toe into the employment pool. Good info for newbies and those with limited work experience. Special features include their listing of the Top Entry Level Employers for the current year, including the number of anticipated hires at each. They also offer a video component where job seekers can create a video resume, view career videos, and watch the "Job Search Minute" video series.

www.craigslist.org

This site offers classified job listings for 450 cities worldwide. Choose your location and browse what's available. Search by date or criteria such as telecommute, contract, internship, part-time, nonprofit, or keyword.

www.dice.com

This is where those seeking computer/information technology careers go. A good resource with job tools for the high-tech professional.

www.diversityjobs.com

Provides hundreds of thousands of job openings for candidates seeking workplace diversity. They state their mission as one of work force empowerment for African Americans, Hispanics, the disabled, Asian Americans, veterans, members of the LGBT community, and other diversity groups.

www.efinancialcareers.com

Candidates seeking positions in accounting, finance, banking, investment banking, and the financial markets will find a wealth of information for all industries and all levels of experience.

www.governmentjobs.com

If you are looking for a job in the public sector, this site offers search capabilities by location, category, earnings, and keyword.

www.guru.com

Want to freelance? Find independent projects in categories such as Creative, IT, Business Consulting and Office Administration.

www.job-hunt.org

This is one of the web's most valuable and powerful resources for job seekers. This site brings the best Internet tools and sites to the job hunter's attention. It does not collect resumes or offer job postings, but it will direct visitors to other excellent Internet sites on virtually any area of employment.

www.jobster.com

With its useful job search tips and local directory, this is a good place to get your feet wet on business networking through the Internet. Read the featured profiles, do some searching, and start talking online to people who might be able to steer you toward your "dream job."

www.linkedin.com

A major online network of more than 14 million business professionals worldwide, this site will help you identify and contact colleagues, clients, partners, and individuals who can assist with your job search.

www.lloydstaffing.com

This is a nationwide staffing service specializing in a variety of industries including sales, IT, health care, and finance. Temporary opportunities, as well as direct hire and executive search positions are offered.

www.nacelink.com

This site brings together students, colleges, and employers. It is a not-for-profit job board and helps students tap into the valuable resources also offered by their campus career placement centers.

www.net-temps.com

This is a job board focused on temporary, temp-to-hire, and full-time employment found exclusively through the staffing industry. Job information includes date of posting, duration of assignment/contract, and full work descriptions.

www.quintcareers.com

Quintessential Careers offers comprehensive career development advice, news, and tools on all topics related to the job search. Visitors receive expert guidance at all levels of their career. Outstanding content.

www.retirementjobs.com

Those in the fifty-plus age bracket, can go to this smart niche site to search jobs, take an online class, find out about companies certified as "age friendly," and read real life success stories.

www.6figurejobs.com

An award-winning site aimed at senior level management, this site offers a mix of openings from employer and search firms. It offers free membership to all visitors with full access to their comprehensive resources and a feature for online networking.

www.theladders.com

This is a great resource for executive job seekers targeting positions above $100,000. Visitors may view some job opportunities at no charge, but there is also a fee to join for full access to the site.

www.weddles.com

No book could omit what is widely known as the definitive site for online job information! Founded by employment guru, Peter Weddle, this outstanding site offers tips for success and more importantly, Weddle's User's Choice Awards, which recognize job-oriented websites that provide the best level of service and value to visitors. Other excellent content includes an Association Directory, ideal for gathering leads for networking purposes.

Index

We Have

EVERYTHING
on Anything!

With more than 19 million copies sold, **the Everything® series** has become one of America's favorite resources for solving problems, learning new skills, and organizing lives. Our brand is not only recognizable—it's also welcomed.

The series is a hand-in-hand partner for people who are ready to tackle new subjects—like you!

For more information on the Everything® series, please visit *www.adamsmedia.com*

The Everything® list spans a wide range of subjects, with more than 500 titles covering 25 different categories:

Business	History	Reference
Careers	Home Improvement	Religion
Children's Storybooks	Everything Kids	Self-Help
Computers	Languages	Sports & Fitness
Cooking	Music	Travel
Crafts and Hobbies	New Age	Wedding
Education/Schools	Parenting	Writing
Games and Puzzles	Personal Finance	
Health	Pets	